Thinking Africa with V.Y. Mudimbe

Africae Studies

Series editors: Clélia Coret, Annael Le Poullennec,
Séverine Marchi and Barbara Morovich

Africae and Twaweza Communications, 2025
Africae Books online: https://books.openedition.org/africae
Twaweza Communications,: https://www.twawezacommunications.org/

Thinking Africa with V.Y. Mudimbe

Edited by Salim Abdelmadjid,
Marie-Aude Fouéré and Maëline Le Lay

Abdelmadjid, Salim, Marie-Aude Fouéré, and Maëline Le Lay. 2025. *Thinking Africa with V.Y. Mudimbe.* Africae Studies. Paris, Nairobi: Africae and Twaweza.

Archiving of web pages: The mention "[archive]" in notes and bibliographies indicates an archived version of the web document in the Wayback Machine (https://web.archive.org).

ISBN (print version): 978-9966-128-25-6
ISBN (digital version): 978-2-493207-17-3

Image cover: Details from Sammy Baloji, *A Blueprint for Toads and Snakes* (2018). https://framerframed.nl/en/exposities/solo-exhibition-sammy-baloji/. With the kind permission of the artist and the owner.

Africae is the book imprint of the French research institutes in Africa south of the Sahara (UAR 3336).

Africae	UAR 3336 Africa South of the Sahara – CNRS	Twaweza Communications
IFRA-Nairobi. Laikipia Road, Kileleshwa	3 rue Michel-Ange	Twaweza House Mpesi Lane, Westlands,
Nairobi, Kenya	75016 Paris, France	Nairobi, Kenya

Table of Contents

List of Contributors

Salim Abdelmadjid is a senior lecturer in philosophy at Université Toulouse Jean Jaurès. A former student at the École normale supérieure in Paris, he holds an agrégation and a doctorate in philosophy for a thesis entitled "Un concept d'Afrique" ("A Concept of Africa") at Université Paris-Sorbonne. He edited the issues "Europe" and "Europe (II). Le milieu du gué / Europa (II). In mezzo al guado" of the journal *Noesis in* 2018 and 2020. Author of the chapter "Éléments en vue de la thématisation de l'effectuation épistémologique de la négativité africaine" in *Afrika N'Ko: Debating the African Colonial Library*, edited by Mamadou Diawara, Mamadou Diouf and Jean-Bernard Ouédraogo (Présence Africaine, 2022), he recently devoted an article to Hountondji's work: "Actualités et spectralités de Paulin J. Hountondji. Introduction à 'Des 'Socrate' par milliers ?' de Paulin J. Hountondji" (*Politika*, 2024).

Sammy Baloji lives and works between Lubumbashi and Brussels. He started in September 2019 his PhD artistic research project, "Contemporary Kasala and Lukasa: towards a Reconfiguration of Identity and Geopolitics," at Sint Lucas Antwerpen. A Chevalier des Arts et des Lettres (France), he has received numerous fellowships, awards and distinctions, notably at the African Photography Encounters of Bamako and the Dakar Biennale, and was a laureate of the Rolex Mentor and Protégé Arts Initiative. In 2019–2020, he was a resident of the French Academy of Rome – Villa Medici. Since 2018, he teaches at the Sommerakademie in Salzburg. Sammy Baloji co-founded in 2008 the Rencontres Picha/Biennale de Lubumbashi.

Marie-Aude Fouéré is a senior lecturer in social and cultural anthropology at the École des hautes études en sciences sociales (EHESS). She was IFRA-Nairobi's in-house researcher from 2011 to 2014 and its director from 2018 to 2022. Her research interests cover vernacular historiographies and the social and political uses of the past in contemporary Tanzania, focusing on the time of Ujamaa and the figure of Julius Nyerere as well as on the revolution of 1964 in Zanzibar. She (co-)edited numerous volumes, including *Remembering Julius Nyerere in Tanzania (*Mkuki na Nyota, Africae, 2014), *Social Memory, Silenced Voices, and Political Struggles* (Mkuki na Nyota, 2018) about today's memories of the revolution in Zanzibar with William C. Bissell, *Kenya in Motion: 2000-2020* (Africae, 2021) with Christian Thibon and Marie-Emmanuelle Pommerolle, and *Across the Waves: Strategies of Belonging in Indian Island Societies* (Brill, 2022) with Iain Walker.
ORCID: https://orcid.org/0000-0002-7565-4231

Pierre-Philippe Fraiture is professor of French studies at the University of Warwick, where he teaches postcolonial literatures. He is a member of the European Research Council-funded project "Philosophy and Genre: Creating a Textual Basis for African Philosophy" (2020–25). His most recent publications include *Unfinished Histories: Empire and Postcolonial Resonance in Central Africa and Belgium* (Leuven University Press, 2022), *Past Imperfect: Time and African Decolonization, 1945-1960* (Liverpool University Press, 2021), *The Mudimbe Reader* (Virginia University Press, edited with Daniel Orrells, 2016), and *V.Y. Mudimbe: Undisciplined Africanism* (Liverpool University Press, 2013). He is currently working on the notion of extractivism in Congolese art and literature.

Kai Kresse is professor of social and cultural anthropology at Freie Universität Berlin and Vice-Director of Leibniz-Zentrum Moderner Orient (ZMO). His book publications include *Philosophising in Mombasa: Knowledge, Islam, and Intellectual Practice on the Swahili Coast* (Edinburgh University Press for the IAI, 2007), *Swahili Muslim Publics and Postcolonial Experience* (Indiana University Press, 2018; Mkuki na Nyota, 2019), and numerous edited volumes, including *Rethinking Sage Philosophy: Interdisciplinary Perspectives on and beyond H. Odera Oruka*, with Oriare Nyarwath (Lexington Books, 2023), and *Thinking the Re-thinking of the World: Decolonial Challenges to the Humanities and Social Sciences from Africa, Asia and the Middle East*, with Abdoulaye Sounaye (de Gruyter, 2022).

Maëline Le Lay is a CNRS research fellow and a scholar of African literatures, posted at THALIM research center in Paris, formerly at IFRA-Nairobi (2018–21). Her research focuses on literature and performance in Africa's Great Lakes region, in conflict and post-conflict situations (Democratic Republic of Congo, Burundi) and in a post-genocide society (Rwanda). She was Co-I of the AHRC Network project: "Stages of Violence. Rwanda, Kenya and Northern Ireland" (2021–24), with Bobby Smith (University of Warwick). Some of her publications include the edition of two collections of texts from Africa's Great Lakes region published in 2019 (*Au-dessous du volcan. Rencontres littéraires de Goma; Chroniques des Grands Lacs*, edited with Dominique Ranaivoson) and a slam poetry collection from Goma (*Slamer pour résister ! Anthologie du slam à Goma*, Africae, 2024). ORCID: https://orcid.org/0000-0002-6838-3875

Emelyn Lih is completing a PhD at New York University's Department of French Literature, Thought and Culture. Her dissertation examines a series of formally innovative autobiographical projects in twentieth-century French prose, focusing on the relationship between autobiography and history in the work of Blaise Cendrars, Michel Leiris, Claude Simon, and Annie Ernaux. She has published multiple articles on the work of Claude Simon, and she is also active as a translator.

Francis Owakah is the Coordinator of the Centre for Human Rights and Peace and a senior lecturer in the Department of Philosophy and Religious Studies of the University of Nairobi where he lectures philosophy and human rights. His research interests include African humanism, African ontology, global ethics and minority rights. He also works on the history of philosophy in Africa and knowledge production. He notably published "Indigenous Knowledge: An Exposition of Sage Philosophy and Oral Literature Projects in Kenya," in *Rethinking Sage Philosophy: Interdisciplinary Perspectives on and beyond H. Odera Oruka, edited by* Kai Kresse and Oriare Nyarwath (Lexington Books, 2023), and "Terrorism, Anti-Terror War and Minority Rights: The Case of the Boni of Coastal Kenya," in *The Role of Philosophy in the African Context: Traditions, Challenges and Perspectives,* edited by Stephen Okello (Urbaniana University Press, 2019). ORCID: https://orcid.org/0000-0002-1499-5251

Alex Nelungo Wanjala is a senior lecturer in the Department of Literature and French at the University of Nairobi. His research interests include postcolonial theory, cultural studies, comparative literature, and African literature in French and English expression. He is the Editor-in Chief of *The Nairobi Journal of Literature*, Co-Editor of *Matatu: Journal for African Culture and Society*, and regional editor for East Africa of the journal *Tydskrif vir Letterkunde*. He is also the current Chairperson of The Association for Commonwealth Literature and Language Studies (ACLALS). ORCID: https://orcid.org/0000-0002-0609-5982

Preface

Marie-Aude Fouéré and Karori Mbugua

This edited volume stems from an international symposium held at the University of Nairobi in 2019, which brought together leading scholars in African Studies, and African Philosophy in particular. The symposium was titled "Thinking Africa with Mudimbe" and focused on the work of the Congolese writer, cultural and literary critic, philologist and philosopher, V.Y. Mudimbe. On that occasion, speakers, organisers and the public gathered at the University of Nairobi (UoN) as part of an institutional and intellectual collaboration between the French Institute for Research in Africa (IFRA-Nairobi) and the Department of Philosophy and Religious Studies. This symposium was included in a larger research programme for knowledge dissemination, "Intellectuals from Africa and the diaspora: how African thinking about Africa is being reinvented," which focused on two prominent thinkers from Eastern and Central Africa: Kenyan writer Ngũgĩ wa Thiong'o, and Mudimbe. Its aim was to debate, in Africa, the relevance of their thoughts and revisit the traces and legacy they had left, especially for the decolonisation of knowledge and the grounding of the humanities and social sciences in African epistemologies.

The Mudimbe symposium in Nairobi was grounded in the idea that, due to its scope and depth, Mudimbe's work should be seen as inescapable, primarily because of its call for a radical epistemic change. It is a call for decolonising thought, decolonising knowledge production and management, decolonising the ways in which the world has been understood and studied, and decolonising the types of questions we ask about it and how we answer them. Mudimbe tells us how we could change the conditions of possibility of thinking, that is, to refer to a Foucauldian phrasing, of what we can see and what we can say. We first need to assess how much Western thinking shaped and influenced African societies and individuals during colonisation but also after colonisation—looking carefully at the concepts used, the questions asked, the answers brought, the objectives given, and who was considered legitimate to speak and to think, and who was not. Mudimbe speaks of an "epistemic cage" (1988, 77) in which Africans were enclosed and are still enclosed; other authors refer to the "colonial intimacy" that shaped both the colonisers and the colonised, yet within a situation of colonial oppression. Hence a call for decolonisation that concerns the former colonisers as much as the formerly colonised.

According to Mudimbe, we can free ourselves from the epistemic cage by thinking against the cage and from outside the cage. For this epistemic agency to be possible, new questions need to be raised, new theoretical foundations imagined, new conceptual frames and instruments invented which should be grounded in an African epistemological locus. But "what is to be done?" in practical ways, asked philosopher Paulin Hountondji in 1989, to accomplish Mudimbe's programmatic vision? (Apter 1992: 89). This is a question which a younger generation of African intellectuals have embraced, revealing how much Mudimbe's critical work stimulated transformative and liberating thinking about Africa. In a way, this book is an attempt to answer the question posed by Hountondji and is a testimony to the heuristic value of Mudimbe's work and the richness of his thought.

This collection is very much the product of a joint effort between IFRA-Nairobi and staff at the Department of Philosophy and Religious Studies at the University of Nairobi, supported by the Institut Français in Paris. Without the enthusiastic engagement of Reginald Oduor, Oriare Nyarwath and Francis Owakah, the Mudimbe symposium would never have happened, and this volume would not have seen the light of the day. We warmly thank them. Salim Abdelmadjid from Université Toulouse Jean Jaurès in France and Kai Kresse from the Leibniz-Zentrum Moderner Orient in Germany are also thanked for facilitating the links between IFRA-Nairobi and the University of Nairobi philosophers.

All IFRA-Nairobi staff and researchers were involved in this project and we wish to thank them, too. Among them, Maëline Le Lay was in charge of organising a successful roundtable discussion on Mudimbe at the Alliance Française de Nairobi, together with her colleague Pierre Boizette, in order to reach out to a non-academic public. Both had been deeply involved in a sister-event on Ngũgĩ wa Thiong'o organised in Goma, DRC, a few months before the Nairobi symposium, discussing his programmatic ideas about the use of African languages for enabling an Afrophone and Africa-grounded epistemic emancipation.

References

Apter, Andrew. 1992. "Que Faire? Reconsidering Inventions of Africa." *Critical Inquiry* 19, no. 1: 87–104. https://doi.org/10.1086/448664.

Mudimbe, V.Y. 1988. *The Invention of Africa. Philosophy, Gnosis and the Order of Knowledge*. Bloomington and Indianapolis, IN: Indiana University Press; London: James Currey.

Introduction: Thinking Africa with V.Y. Mudimbe

Salim Abdelmadjid, Marie-Aude Fouéré, Maëline Le Lay

The philosophical and literary work of V.Y. Mudimbe provides us with a decisive critical foundation for thinking Africa.[1] From the time of *L'autre face du royaume. Une introduction à la critique des langages en folie* (1973), and his later works such as *L'odeur du père. Essai sur des limites de la science et de la vie en Afrique Noire* (1982), *The Invention of Africa. Gnosis, Philosophy and the Order of Knowledge* (1988), and *The Idea of Africa* (1994), Mudimbe has shown that Africa as we know it today is the product of an exogenous, asymmetrical historical construction, of extreme violence, that has constitutionally biased the supposedly scientific knowledge about African societies. In his view, Africa therefore requires a theoretical reappropriation by Africans, inseparable from the practical reappropriation in the liberation struggles.

These premises—the scientific value and emancipatory power of Mudimbe's epistemological critique, and its necessity for the epistemic de-asymmetrisation to be pursued—were the starting point for the organisation of the symposium "Thinking Africa with Mudimbe" at the University of Nairobi in 2019, of which this book is an extension.[2] In addition to the chapters by researchers in philosophy (Salim Abdelmadjid, Francis

1. The French version of this introduction can be found in the digital version of this book, available online in the "Africae Studies" series on OpenEdition Books ("Introduction: Penser l'Afrique avec V.Y. Mudimbe." https://books.openedition.org/africae/7142).

2. The symposium was the result of a collaboration between the University of Nairobi's Department of Philosophy and Religious Studies and the Institut français de recherche en Afrique (IFRA), Nairobi. It was organised by Marie-Aude Fouéré, Maëline Le Lay and Karori Mbugua at the University of Nairobi on 17 December 2019. It included the following discussions: Francis E.A. Owakah (Philosophy, University of Nairobi), "Introducing Mudimbe to East Africa: The Good, the Fun and the Ugly"; Pierre-Philippe Fraiture (Literature, University of Warwick, United Kingdom), "V.Y. Mudimbe's Modernities?"; Kai Kresse (Institute of Social & Cultural Anthropology, Leibniz-Zentrum Moderner Orient, Germany), "Entanglement and Critique: Eurocentrism, Africanism—and Beyond? Thinking Mudimbe"; Oriare Nyarwath (Philosophy, University of Nairobi), "Beyond the Invented Africa"; Reginald M.J. Oduor (Philosophy, University of Nairobi), "The Relevance of V.Y. Mudimbe's *The Invention of Africa* to Future Directions in the Humanities and Social Sciences"; Salim Abdelmadjid (Philosophy, Université Toulouse Jean Jaurès, France), "Reading V.Y. Mudimbe towards a Concept of Africa."

Owakah, and Kai Kresse who is also an anthropologist) and literature (Pierre-Philippe Fraiture and Alex Nelungo Wanjala), the book features an interview by Maëline Le Lay of the visual artist and video maker Sammy Baloji, whose installation "A Blueprint for Toads and Snakes," partly influenced by Mudimbe's thinking, was showcased at the symposium.[3] The book also includes a previously unpublished translation, by Emelyn Lih, of an excerpt from Mudimbe's autobiography *Les Corps glorieux des mots et des êtres. Esquisse d'un jardin africain à la bénédictine*,[4] which will allow us to hear his voice, will resonate with several chapters of the book, and will also introduce a lesser-known facet of Mudimbe in the English-speaking context, as not all his literary works have been translated.

In comparison to the importance we attribute to it, Mudimbe's work is not yet sufficiently well known in France and Kenya, which are the first two countries of reference for this book. In France, the recent translation of *The Invention of Africa*, which was published by Présence africaine under the title *L'invention de l'Afrique. Gnose, philosophie et ordre de la connaissance* (2021), and the publication, also by Présence africaine, of the collective work *Afrika N'Ko* (Diawara, Diouf, and Ouedraogo 2022), subtitled *La bibliothèque coloniale en débat* (*Debating the African Colonial Library* in the English version), have brought new attention to Mudimbe's thinking. This last work invites us on a "quest to establish plurality in theoretical perspectives" (ibid., 34), which is necessary to "deconstruct conceptual and political systems founded on slavery, colonization and contemporary forms of domination" (ibid., 39). In the English-speaking world, the recent translation by Jonathan Adjemian of *L'odeur du père* (1982) under the title *The Scent of the Father: Essay on the Limits of Life and Science in Sub-Saharan Africa* (Mudimbe 2023), as well as the volume *Africa Beyond Inventions: Essays in Honour of V.Y. Mudimbe* edited by Zubairu Wai (2024), are other signs of the growing recognition of Mudimbe's work. It is our hope that this volume will contribute to its dissemination.

---

3. The installation was exhibited at the Alliance Française de Nairobi from 16 to 20 December 2019. The symposium and installation were accompanied by a public debate held on 16 December entitled "Thinking Africa through the works of the philosopher V.Y. Mudimbe" organised at the Alliance Française de Nairobi by Maëline Le Lay, moderated by Pierre Boizette, and with contributions by Sammy Baloji, Kai Kresse, Pierre-Philippe Fraiture, and Reginald M.J. Oduor.

4. This can be translated as: *The Glorious Bodies of Words and Beings. Sketch of an African Benedictine Garden.*

1. Thinking and knowing Africa with V.Y. Mudimbe

What does "thinking Africa" mean, and why "thinking Africa?" In Mudimbe's work, these questions inseparably arise for the purpose of "knowing Africa." On the one hand, this link is obvious. It has to do with the complementary relationship between thought and knowledge: it is necessary to think a thing—not just to conceive it, but to grasp its meaning—in order to know it; and it is necessary to know a thing—not just to know it exists, but to have studied it—in order to think it. But, on the other hand, the link between "thinking Africa" and "knowing Africa" has been deeply problematic. The relationship between knowledge and power, historically carried out in the case of Africa as a relationship between discourses claiming to be scientific about Africa and colonialism, explains the need to liberate thinking about Africa from these discourses and, to do this, to think critically about knowledge of Africa and ways of knowing about Africa, starting with what Mudimbe calls "the colonial library"[5] and with the colonial categories of knowledge.

Mudimbe is at the heart of this tension between thinking and knowing Africa. Right from *L'autre face du royaume* (1973) and *L'odeur du père* (1982), he has made the possibility of knowing Africa conditional on understanding its meaning, and to that end on deconstructing the colonial idea of Africa, which was a negation of the meaning and understanding of the real Africa. "[A] Western epistemological order," Mudimbe wrote in *The Invention of Africa* and *The Idea of Africa* (Mudimbe 1994, xv), has made Africa an ensemble of "'fantasies' and 'constructs'" (ibid.) that have been laid over reality: Africa has been conceived of as primitive, exotic and immobile, frozen in the repetition of tradition, without history. "(...) under the guise of discovering and speaking Africa," colonial sciences, ethnology in particular, only presented Africa "through a distorting prism" (Mudimbe 2023 [1982], 8). Subjected to the colonial matrix and the Western *episteme*, these sciences have failed, according to Mudimbe,

5. Mudimbe gives the following definition in *The Idea of Africa*: "It was, I think, fifteenth- and sixteenth-century Europe that invented the savage as a representation of its own negated double. Exploiting travelers' and explorers' writings, at the end of the nineteenth century a 'colonial library' begins to take shape. It represents a body of knowledge constructed with the explicit purpose of faithfully translating and deciphering the African object. Indeed, it fulfilled a political project in which, supposedly, the object unveils its being, its secrets, and its potential to a master who could, finally, domesticate it. Certainly, the depth as well as the ambition of the colonial library disseminates the concept of deviation as the best symbol of the idea of Africa. I do refer to this colonial library, which beyond its adjustments and arrangements offers traces or reflections of a longer tradition. In fact, I have tried to circumvent its epistemological violence by including its nightmares as well as the fragile presuppositions of its ponderous knowledge." (Mudimbe 1994, xii).

to create a real knowledge of Africa. Instead, "a paradigm of [essentialised] difference" (Mudimbe 1994, xii) from Europe has prevailed: Africa is what Europe, and more broadly the West, is not; it is conceptually, to use Mudimbe's words, its "negated double" (ibid.). According to him, getting rid of the Western epistemic order requires us to think Africa, which includes criticising this order and, so as to do that, studying it, but also, following the well-understood complementarity of thought and knowledge, studying Africa itself in the diversity of its singular situations.

Mudimbe's proposal to take Africa itself as the subject of philosophical reflection constitutes a decisive contribution to the contemporary field of African philosophy,[6] following a generation which, for reasons that history explains,[7] had above all been primarily concerned with the very definition of African philosophy, notably within the framework of the contradiction between ethnophilosophy[8] and "rational, or theoretical, or critical, or professional philosophy"[9] (Fløistad 1987, 1), and with the directly political question of emancipation and affirmation.[10] Mudimbe

6. The emergence of the field of African philosophy is often dated to 1945, with the publication of *La philosophie bantoue* by Placide Tempels—translated into English as *Bantu Philosophy* in 1959. In this book, Tempels, who was a Belgian missionary in the Congo (now the Democratic Republic of Congo), claimed to set out, on the basis of his observations of Congolese society, what we could call the "system of thought" or "worldview" of that society, and even, according to the title of the book, of any "Bantu" society, with the aim of contributing to the colonial administration of the Congolese population (Tempels 1945). Dating the emergence of the field of African philosophy to the publication of *La philosophie bantoue* is obviously problematic. Firstly, we can confidently assume that there was philosophy in Africa before 1945. Secondly, it is astonishing to date the emergence of the field of African philosophy to the publication of a book whose author is not African. Thirdly, philosophy does not consist of collective "systems of thought" or "worldviews." Finally, and most importantly, it seems impossible to date appearance to the publication of a book whose author sees its function as contributing to the colonial oppression of Africans.

7. In the African context of the post-Second World War era, then of independence, the priority was to demonstrate the existence of an African philosophy and thereby provide, against the colonial negation of the very ability of Africans to philosophise and therefore of the very possibility of an African philosophy, further proof of the humanity commonly shared by Africans and colonisers.

8. "Ethnophilosophy" refers to the practice, initiated by Tempels in *La philosophie bantoue* (1945), of extracting a "worldview" from the observation of a society.

9. Represented notably by Fabien Eboussi Boulaga in "Le Bantou problématique" (1968), by Marcien Towa in *Essai sur la problématique philosophique dans l'Afrique actuelle* (1971), and by Paulin Jidenu Hountondji in *Sur la "philosophie africaine"* (1977)—translated into English in 1983 under the title *African Philosophy: Myth and Reality* . Hountondji and Towa created the concept of ethnophilosophy, which they criticise.

10. See Salim Abdelmadjid's chapter. Of course, Africa as such had already been constantly taken as a subject for philosophical reflection, "at least implicitly, in the history of pan-Africanism, eminently during independences, for example in Fanon or

calls for us to start again from the empirical reality—which he also calls, in French, "*la chose du texte*" in *The Invention of Africa* (1988)—based on an inner, intimate knowledge of that reality. In his view, we should use *gnosis* as our fulcrum: that is, a wide-ranging ensemble of knowledge immersed in African realities, practices and ways of life, quite distinct from Western "*doxa* or opinion" (Mudimbe 1988, ix) or from "*episteme*, understood as both science and general intellectual configuration" (ibid.). *Gnosis* is thus a "methodological tool" (ibid.) or an epistemic matrix, different from Western *episteme* without being totally separated from it, which would make it possible to study and reflect on African situations and experiences.[11]

Taking Africa itself as the subject of philosophical reflection does not mean reducing it to itself so as to study it in isolation, which would be tantamount to abstracting it. It means, on the contrary, since Africa is in the world and this is part of its definition, to think and study it within the horizon of the world.[12] Mudimbe's work therefore by definition goes beyond the boundaries of African studies. Historically, it is part of an intellectual context in which the epistemological foundations of colonial knowledge and its epistemic effects in all regions of the world were radically called into question. Mudimbe's critique of Africanism is thus inseparable from Edward Said's critique of orientalism in *Orientalism* (1978). They actually both draw on the thinking of Michel Foucault, in particular on his thematisation of the relations between knowledge and power, his concept of *episteme*, and his archaeological approach to exploring the foundations of knowledge (Alix 2008,[13] Bisanswa 2000, Mangeon 2006). In *The Idea of Latin America* (2005), Walter Mignolo makes explicit his association with Mudimbe's critique, his colleague at Duke University, of the colonial construction and essentialisation of extra-European areas.[14]

Nkrumah among so many; but the explicit and properly philosophical nature of the position of the question ["What is Africa?"] set Mudimbe apart" in the contemporary history of African philosophy.

11. *Gnosis* also has an "esoteric dimension" (Mangeon 2013, our translation), as Mudimbe makes clear from the outset (Mudimbe 1988, ix).

12. For many intellectuals who worked with Mudimbe or have been inspired by him, Africa is even the place from which to think the world (see e.g. Jewsiewicki 1996, Mbembe & Sarr 2017).

13. See also Alix (2022).

14. See also Walter Mignolo's recent article "Africa in the Colonial Horizon of Western Modernity: 1652-2000" (Mignolo 2022), which begins: "I would like to take this opportunity to honor the legacy of Valentin Y. Mudimbe's *The Invention of Africa: Gnosis, Philosophy, and the Order of Knowledge* (1988)."

2. Who is V.Y. Mudimbe?

Valentin-Yves Mudimbe was born in 1941 in the Congo, then colonised by Belgium (now the Democratic Republic of the Congo), in Jadotville (now Likasi), in the province of Katanga, in the southeast of the country. He received a Catholic education, studying at the minor seminary and then the major seminary, and intending to become a priest. In 1960, he took up the Benedictine habit and was sent to the monastery of Gihindamuyaga in Rwanda. He left the monastery in 1962, distraught by the ethnic massacres that were shaking Rwanda at the time. He studied Romance philology at the University of Lovanium in Léopoldville (Kinshasa) and obtained a doctorate in French linguistics at the Catholic University of Louvain in Belgium. What he called his "intellectual odyssey" in *Parables and Fables* (Mudimbe 1991a, ix) began, between the University of Nanterre in Paris, where he taught as a lecturer just after May 1968, and Louvain, where he continued to visit the library regularly. He was subsequently appointed professor in the Department of Romance Philology at the National University of Zaire (UNAZA) in Lubumbashi, and Dean of the Faculty of Letters from 1972 to 1974. In 1980, faced with Mobutu's dictatorship and attempts to intimidate him, Mudimbe went into exile in Europe and then the United States. He taught at Haverford University, Stanford University, and then Duke University until his retirement in the mid-2010s (Amuri-Mpala Lutebele 2009; Kishiba Fitula 2021). In the 1970s, because of Mobutu's policy of so-called "authenticity" and the injunction to "Zairianise" the country, including proper names, Valentin-Yves Mudimbe changed his first name to Vumbi Yoka. Since then, he has signed his writings "V.Y. Mudimbe."

Mudimbe's work belongs to several fields, mainly philosophy and literature, African studies and postcolonial studies, and covers several domains, notably epistemology, history and politics. We have mentioned several works of philosophy. Among his many works of literature, we can mention *Déchirures*, a collection of poems published in 1971, of which, to our knowledge, there is no English translation;[15] *Entre les eaux*, a novel published in 1973, translated into English as *Between Tides* in 1991; *Shaba deux. Les carnets de Mère Marie-Gertrude* in 1989, about the Kolwezi wars, of which, to our knowledge, there is no complete English translation.

The richness and singularity of Mudimbe's work have prompted numerous studies and commentaries. There is therefore an extensive bibliography on Mudimbe which explores the different facets of his

15. The title of this collection can be translated as *Tears*. These are not the tears which flow down our cheeks, but those which tear pages and muscles.

philosophical and literary work. This bibliography is difficult to access, however, notably because of the linguistic polarity of the international academic field. Indeed, the exegeses of his philosophical texts come mainly from the English-speaking academic field, while his literary writings are mostly analysed within the French-speaking field. Works in French include: *V.Y. Mudimbe ou le discours, l'écart et l'écriture*[16] by Bernard Mouralis in 1988; the collective work *L'Afrique au miroir des littératures. Mélanges offerts à V.Y. Mudimbe,*[17] co-edited by Mukala Kadima-Nzuji and Sélom Komlan Gbanou in 2003; *V.Y. Mudimbe et la ré-invention de l'Afrique. Poétique et politique de la décolonisation des sciences humaines*[18] by Kasereka Kavwahirehi in 2006; or Jean-Pierre Bekolo's lengthy interview with Mudimbe, "*Les choses et les mots de Mudimbe*," in 2015, filmed at the thinker's home, which provides a vivid insight into Mudimbe's thinking in his teeming intellectual environment. Among the works offering a general study of Mudimbe's work and trajectory, we can cite those by some contributors of this present volume: the special issue "Reading Mudimbe" in the *Journal of African Cultural Studies* coordinated by Kai Kresse in 2005, *V.Y. Mudimbe: Undisciplined Africanism* by Pierre-Philippe Fraiture in 2013,[19] and *The Mudimbe Reader* edited by Pierre-Philippe Fraiture and Daniel Orrells in 2016.

3. Reading and discussing Mudimbe in Kenya

Although it is not a central part of teaching at Kenyan universities, Mudimbe's work is known to a significant number of academics, in particular philosophers, who use it in their own works and teach it to their students. Since the beginning of the 1990s, Dismas Masolo in particular has contributed to the reception of Mudimbe in Kenya, most notably at the University of Nairobi. He did so especially through his university courses, his article "An Archaeology of African Knowledge. A Discussion of V.Y. Mudimbe" published in *Callaloo* in 1991, and his book *African Philosophy in Search of Identity*, published in 1994,[20] as the chapters by Francis Owakah and Alex Nelungo Wanjala confirm. The structuring concepts elaborated in

16. This can be translated as *V.Y. Mudimbe or Discourse, Distance and Writing.*

17. This can be translated as *Africa in the Mirror of Literatures. Collected Works in Honour of V.Y. Mudimbe.*

18. This can be translated as *V.Y. Mudimbe and the Reinvention of Africa. Poetics and Politics of the Decolonisation of the Human Sciences.*

19. On the notion of "indiscipline" in Mudimbe's work, see also, in French, Mangeon (2008).

20. See in particular "V.Y. Mudimbe: An Archaeology of African Knowledge" (Masolo 2011, 178-93).

The Invention of Africa and *The Idea of Africa*, starting with the "invention" and "idea" of Africa, as well as "gnosis" and the "colonial library," have been reappropriated and debated. They can also inspire criticisms of a way of thinking that is sometimes found to be too abstract, insufficiently anchored in local practice and theory, or not sufficiently attentive to the political potential of cultural belongings. Mudimbe's extensive use of a European academic body of knowledge might also be viewed as an internal epistemic contradiction for a philosopher who calls for emancipation from the European *episteme*. This interpretation of Mudimbe in Kenya may have been influenced by a certain ethnophilosophical understanding of African philosophy, as embodied by John Samuel Mbiti, whose famous *African Religions and Philosophy* (1969) has had an intellectual and even institutional influence in the Department of Philosophy and Religious Studies at the University of Nairobi; or by Henry Odera Oruka's proposition of "Sage Philosophy"[21] (Odera Oruka 1990).

However, just as Mudimbe's philosophical work, most of which was written in English, remains at a distance from French-speaking readers, his literary work, which is celebrated in the Democratic Republic of Congo (DRC) where he first trained in the literary circles he ran at the time[22] (and where his books are considered "classics" and studied in the country's schools[23]), and which is also acclaimed by international critics, is still hard for English-speaking readers to gain access to, and is therefore still relatively unknown. These two restrictions on how Mudimbe is received betray an unfortunate compartmentalisation of academic knowledge on Africa—one that echoes the linguistic polarisation of African studies that was inherited from the colonial division of the continent, as well

21. Odera Oruka defined "Sage Philosophy" as such: "What is sage philosophy and how can one distinguish this from other forms of philosophy that are available in Africa? These other forms include professional philosophical texts (works of academics and students formally trained in philosophy), nationalist-ideological theories and ethnographical studies of traditional African beliefs labelled as "philosophy" (ethnophilosophy). Sage philosophy becomes a fourth trend in this list. [...] Sage philosophy consists of the expressed thoughts of wise men and women in any given community and is a way of thinking and explaining the world that fluctuates between *popular wisdom* (well-known communal maxims, aphorisms and general commonsense truths) and *didactic wisdom* (an expounded wisdom and a rational thought of some given individuals within a community). While popular wisdom is often conformist, didactic wisdom is at times critical of the communal set-up and popular wisdom." (Odera Oruka 1991, 33).

22. See Le Lay (2014, particularly chapter 1.4 "L'École littéraire de la Kasapa", 54–63).

23. Isidore Ndaywel è Nziem underlines that in the DRC, Mudimbe's name "is more alive than ever, in the world of the youth and at university (...), a name that people learn to know in school textbooks and encyclopedias of literature, a name that is quoted with pride (...)." (1996, 272, our translation)

as disciplinary divisions, and reveals the extent of the fragmentation of the field of African studies. In this respect, Mudimbe's work stands out as a fundamental point of reference for unifying and redefining African studies. It gives us a bridge between both French-speaking and English-speaking academic fields, but also between disciplines, not just philosophy and literature but also the humanities and social sciences, notably history and anthropology. It recognises Africa as a subject, with a method that is constructivist and critical of colonialism and of its epistemic and political effects, and with the aim of contributing to the epistemological liberation of African studies from what remains colonial within them.

In expressing an epistemological critique that could emancipate knowledge, Mudimbe can be compared to the Kenyan novelist Ngũgĩ wa Thiong'o,[24] who, from the same generation, published an essay in 1986 with the evocative title *Decolonising the Mind: The Politics of Language in African Literature*. It was with the idea of revisiting the works and influence of these two great thinkers on Africa that the research dissemination programme "Intellectuals from Africa and the diaspora: how African thought on Africa is being reinvented" (*Intellectuels d'Afrique et de la diaspora: comment se réinvente la pensée africaine sur l'Afrique*) was conceived, incorporating a cross-referenced, multi-sited perspective between Kenya and the DRC. Created within IFRA-Nairobi and with financial support from the Institut Français in Paris, the programme was developed in partnership with the Institut Français in Goma for the DRC component, and with the University of Nairobi's Department of Philosophy and Religious Studies for the Kenya component. The aim was to encourage exchanges between academics and intellectuals, African and European, on the contribution, reception, and significance of the works of Mudimbe and Ngũgĩ for Africa in general, and in particular for the two countries concerned. A series of events was also organised, on Ngũgĩ in Goma in June 2019[25] and on Mudimbe in

---

24. Ngũgĩ wa Thiong'o is a Kenyan writer, born in 1938, now internationally recognised as a classic. In 1986, he published *Decolonising the Mind. The Politics of Language in African Literature*, translated into French in 2011 under the title *Décoloniser l'esprit*. In this essay, Ngũgĩ wa Thiong'o reflects on his experience as a writer, theatre-maker and academic in a recently decolonised country. He shares his awareness of the alienation experienced by Africans who have opted for the language of the coloniser as their official, national, or teaching language.

25. A round table on the work of Ngũgĩ wa Thiong'o was organised at the Institut français in Goma on 12 June 2019, and a theatrical adaptation of Mark Twain's pamphlet *King Leopold's Soliloquy*—translated in French by Jean-Pierre Orban and directed by Patrick Zézé and Jean-Pierre Orban—performed there on 11 June 2019: https://f.hypotheses.org/wp-content/blogs.dir/1864/files/2019/06/Autour-de-Ngugi_doc-de-comm-Goma_juin-2019.pdf. An interview with Ngũgĩ wa Thiong'o by Maëline Le Lay in Nairobi in March 2019 is available on Youtube: "Decolonizing the Mind with

Nairobi in December 2019, with the view of participating in the linguistic decompartmentalisation of their respective receptions.

Given the audiences for their works, the two thinkers are eminent representatives of the Kenyan and Congolese intellectual contexts: revisiting their works was relevant to a project that sought to increase awareness of these contexts on both sides of the territorial and linguistic borders. Mirroring Mudimbe and Ngũgĩ within the framework of an exchange between Kenya and the DRC also contributed to the same objective of reflecting on the decolonisation of thought (Kavwahirehi 2006) and "undiscipline" (Fraiture 2013), as the two thinkers are also authors. Mudimbe and Ngũgĩ share a questioning of the conditions of independence of thought in Africa, and thus of emancipation from colonial epistemic domination. What they also have in common is the heuristic richness of an intellectual enterprise combining literature (more so in the case of Ngũgĩ) and philosophy (more so in the case of Mudimbe), as well as a central reflection on the language of thought and writing—English and Gikuyu for Ngũgĩ, French and English for Mudimbe. Lastly, Mudimbe and Ngũgĩ are both bearers and defenders—each in their own way and with their own tools—of an emancipatory, pan-Africanist, democratic, socialist, and internationalist political project, rooted in a violent experience of resistance to neocolonial dictatorship: prison and exile for Ngũgĩ during the dictatorship of Daniel arap Moi, and exile for Mudimbe during that of Mobutu Sese Seko. In fact, being of the same generation (Ngũgĩ was born in 1938, Mudimbe in 1941), the two thinkers have witnessed common events and situations on the continent, from colonialism to the independence struggles, and from political independence to neocolonialism and the fight for real independence.

4. From the symposium to the book

Mudimbe's problematisation of Euro-American and African academic cooperation as early as *L'odeur du père* was a guiding principle for conceiving and putting in place the "Intellectuals from Africa and the diaspora" programme in general, and for organising the symposium on Mudimbe in Nairobi in particular. This excerpt from the book (Mudimbe 2023 [1982], 82–84) sets forth in clear terms the main requirements—"creativity, an enduring spirit, and rigour"—put forward by Mudimbe to make fair

Ngũgĩ wa Thiong'o " (Published online by IFRA Nairobi on 7 October 2019, 13'). https://www.youtube.com/watch?v=eXq8AurffeQ.

and reciprocal cooperation possible, against what remains of colonial asymmetry:

> "What could cooperation between Euro-American and African universities mean? The answer is simple: in my opinion, what matters is that African universities find their own path. This path should respond to the needs of the evolution (I prefer 'evolution' to 'development,' because of the latter's economico-rational implications; evolution implies only change, whatever it may be) and the authenticity (in the original sense of the term) of African societies. True interuniversity cooperation can occur only within this framework, and has three principal requirements: creativity, an enduring spirit, and rigor [...].[26]
> Based on these three requirements, any operational model of interuniversity cooperation between Africa and Euro-America should answer at least to the following conditions:
> —In all fields affected by cooperation, the offer must respond and correspond to the demand. Up until today, as we know all too well, the demand has been conditioned by the offer, in keeping with the simple formula of difficult times: we settle for fish, because there is no more meat.
> —Scientific and cultural demands must take priority over economic imperatives. This means the impact of 'political tactics' on the material chosen for cooperation must be limited as much as possible.
> —Reciprocity must be the norm. In other words, there must really be cooperation: that is to say, exchange on all levels rather than 'assistance,' technical or otherwise."

Although reciprocity was limited by the prior nature of the "Intellectuals from Africa and the diaspora" programme, the Mudimbe symposium

---

26. Mudimbe goes on to define these three requirements: "Creativity—but starting from the fundamental basis of African culture. As Joseph Ki-Zerbo puts it: "Culture is the most immediate and most important dimension of independence ... There is no conscious nation without national culture ... In the end, the African soul will dissolve if the elites of the continent continue to refuse their past, to fear immersion into the masses and preach cultural exodus ... For my part, I have no doubt: if African culture and history were to become the order and site according to which the present and future were thought in African universities, we would be able to substitute values that are more attentive to the real flourishing of humanity for the eminently castrating norm of immediate profitability at all costs, which so violently marks universities in Africa. / Enduring spirit—this is at once faith in the social, scientific, and spiritual mission of the university ("I will live; even if I must die, I will continue on") and, through it, a critical openness to all possibilities. In sum, every university must think itself and its future in terms of its social and political possibilities, beginning with its essential mission—which is, as is sometimes forgotten, to train and produce true men and women of science. / Finally, rigor—a scientific rigor that is a serious exercise of "freedom," a refusal of paths traced once and for all, a permanent questioning of what has been learned, and a dialectical overcoming of knowledge. But also a political rigor that is both a calm analysis of the social and economic structures that "condition" the university as a social organization, and a fervent but critical attention to its hopes and needs." (Mudimbe 2023 [1982], 83)

was organised with philosophers from the Department of Philosophy and Religious Studies at the University of Nairobi. With the participants, including the foreigners supported by IFRA-Nairobi, in this symposium hosted by the University of Nairobi, as well as with the authors of the chapters of this volume—which we are honoured to co-publish with the East African publishing house *Twaweza Communications*—we have made a conscious effort to design with balance the scientific and editorial apparatus of this collective work on Mudimbe. This effort is now open to the reader's criticism.

Centring cooperation between a French institution based in Kenya and a Kenyan institution on the work of Mudimbe—mirroring that of Ngũgĩ—, or, in other words, on a set of reflections on the origin and significance of asymmetries of all kinds (political, institutional, economic, social, epistemic, etc.) resulting from colonial oppression, and on the need to overcome them, is a way of responding to Ngũgĩ's call for the decolonisation of thought, which also reflects Mudimbe's position. This exhortation concerns not only African thinkers and institutions—as the contributions of the Kenyan philosophers and the symposium audience attest[27]—but also—and absolutely—Western thinkers and institutions, including teaching and research institutions.

In a quotation from *The Invention of Africa*, Mudimbe uses the metaphor of the epistemic "cage" (Mudimbe 1988, 64) to describe the hold of sedimented ideas about Africa, from which it is necessary to free oneself. Are we here, in spite of ourselves, re-enacting the "trick" whose power Mudimbe denounces in *The Scent of the Father*? "(…) for Africa, to truly escape from the West presupposes an exact appreciation of the price we have to pay to detach ourselves from it; it presupposes knowing to what extent the West, perhaps insidiously, has drawn close to us; it implies a knowledge, in that which permits us to think against the West, of all that remains Western; and a determination of the extent to which our recourse against it is still possibly one of the tricks it directs against us, while it waits for us, immobile and elsewhere" (Mudimbe 2023 [1982], xvi). We refuse to believe that the absence of relations between the regions of the world is the solution to the problem of asymmetry and a remedy for this trick. The symposium and this book bear witness to this. We have attempted to face the neocolonial problem in practice and in our field, by confronting its asymmetries of domination, and to extricate ourselves from the epistemic classificatory dichotomies that historically correspond to them. This

27. We would especially like to thank Garnette Oluoch-Olunya and Mohamed Bakari for their interventions.

decompartmentalisation has been achieved in terms of discipline, by combining philosophy and literature; in terms of language, by navigating from English to French back and forth; and in terms of participation, by bringing together contributors from Africa and Europe. Nothing has been completed yet in the effort to combat the fragmentation of the field of African studies and to liberate African studies epistemologically from what is still colonial in them, but studying the works of Mudimbe and other African thinkers like Ngũgĩ is making a contribution.

5. The chapters

This volume comprises chapters covering different dimensions of Mudimbe's work, but without any claim to exhaustiveness or agreement between them.[28] It is intended as a modest contribution to Mudimbe studies and their dissemination, and hence to the fields in which these studies take part, such as philosophy, literature, the social sciences, African studies, and postcolonial and decolonial studies.

The book opens with Francis Owakah's chapter, "Introducing V.Y. Mudimbe in East Africa: My Experience at the University of Nairobi," which plunges us into the introduction of Mudimbe's work in the Department of Philosophy and Religious Studies at the University of Nairobi, where the author studied before becoming a professor of philosophy himself. Owakah's description of and reflection on the context in which Mudimbe's work was received reveal, in particular: the importance of Masolo for the introduction of Mudimbe into the Kenyan and wider East African philosophical and intellectual field; the importance of reading Mudimbe for two decisive openings, on the one hand to the human and social sciences, to the question of their articulation with philosophy and to the problem of their application in Africa, and on the other hand to contemporary French philosophy and hence to the fundamental problem for the unity of the field of African philosophy of the link between its Anglophone and Francophone expressions.

Kai Kresse's chapter, "Africanism and beyond? Re-reading Mudimbe in Context Today," extends this contextualisation by discussing the relevance of Mudimbe's critique of Africanism in relation to other African thinkers of his generation and as a reference point for a younger generation of intellectuals in African philosophy and African studies calling for radical epistemic changes. Highlighting Mudimbe's critical insight into the entanglement of Africanism in Eurocentrism and its intellectual and

28. These chapters have been reviewed by the three scientific editors of this book as well as by external reviewers chosen by the publisher.

political violent effects, Kresse shows that the philosopher elaborated erudite constructive ideas for overcoming Africanism, but not practical tools that could readily be applied. The author discusses this lack of a practical path to intellectual decolonisation by drawing from the work of three major African philosophers—Paulin Hountondji, Kwasi Wiredu, and Henry Odera Oruka—as well as by immersing the reader in classroom debates with his own students in African studies. In spite of this, Kresse argues, recent critical approaches are pushing Mudimbe's emancipatory project further in new and inventive ways. Referring to Felwine Sarr's book *Afrotopia*, Kresse sheds light on the clear goals and concrete tasks which an Afrophone and Africa-centred rewriting of the humanities and social sciences from Africa could turn to.

Alex Nelungo Wanjala's chapter, "Interrogating an African *Gnosis* in the Analysis of Kenyan Literature," takes us from philosophy to literature, applying the concept of *gnosis* to Kenyan literature in the search for an African *gnosis* there. Differentiating between Ngũgĩ wa Thiong'o and Grace Ogot, Wanjala wonders, with Spivak, whether African *gnosis* is more likely to be found in African writers who are not caught up in the "double take" characteristic of subaltern intellectuals. This chapter brings us face to face with the difficult Mudimbian concept of *gnosis*, also forces us to confront the Mudimbian problematisation of authenticity.

In Mudimbe's work, this is inseparable from a problematisation of modernity, which Pierre-Philippe Fraiture addresses in an original way in his chapter, "V.Y. Mudimbe's Modernities: Towards a Temporal and Spatial Excavation of (Neo)colonialism." He examines the notion of modernity in a selection of Mudimbe's works. Whilst loosely relying on the two cardinal concepts developed by Reinhart Koselleck—experience and expectation—, Fraiture sets out to explore (neo)colonial temporal politics and the factors behind the *modern* spatialisation of time in sub-Saharan Africa and the Congo in particular. Mudimbe's work offers a diagnosis of colonialism and neocolonialism over the *longue durée* and can also be interpreted as an outright rejection of historical and ontological determinism. *Via* Michel de Certeau's "walking rhetoric," the first part analyses how Mudimbe appraises the spatio-temporal implications of the missionary evangelisation of the former colonised Congo. The second part focuses on Mudimbe's attempts to come to terms with the legacies of Western modernity, challenge the epistemological violence of the Enlightenment, and question the basis of African neocolonialism. The final part of this chapter briefly assesses the role ascribed to African intellectual resources—and African philosophy—in Mudimbe's ongoing critique of Western extroversion.

As we wanted to include a text by Mudimbe himself in this volume, we have chosen an extract from a relatively under-studied book by Mudimbe, now out of print, published in Montreal in 1994, *Les Corps glorieux des mots et des êtres. Esquisse d'un jardin africain à la bénédictine*. It is both an intellectual autobiography and a sociohistorical essay about Mudimbe's "conversion"—religious, but also intellectual, subjective, and intimate—, which, as an "attempt at self-understanding, or better, self-acceptance of his present in the light of his childhood and past," is at the same time an "act of courage, lucidity, and historical and political awareness" (Kavwahirehi 1998, 124, our translation). The book provides very specific information on religious education and the monastery as alienating devices that frame and shape individuals from an early age. The story alternates between vivid descriptions of the transformation of the structural frameworks of everyday existence and more analytical passages showing a certain distance from emotions, without erasing affects such as bitterness or even sarcasm towards the domestication of bodies and minds. About this piece, Pierre Halen aptly notes that it "illustrates quite well the journey of a critic in search, less of knowledge about Africa, than of the conditions in which knowledge is sought about Africa and, necessarily, *for* Africa" (2014, 255, our translation). His autobiography shows how Mudimbe's religious education not only deeply shaped his mind but also influenced his philosophy. More precisely, this personal text reflects his existential conflict between criticism of institutionalised religion and a more individual, even intimate, experience of God. This tension is evident in his novels (whose titles betray it), as shown by Nadia Yala Kisukidi (2013). To our knowledge, this is the first time that an extract from *Les Corps glorieux des mots et des êtres* has been translated into English, here by Emelyn Lih. It resonates in particular with Pierre-Philippe Fraiture's chapter and Maëline Le Lay's interview of Sammy Baloji, illustrating, in a language that blends intimacy and analytical distance, a colonial topography that orders places according to the principles of separation and hierarchy, and captures the effects of colonisation, particularly by missionary and Catholic, on African subjectivities—in this case, that of Mudimbe.

The copresence of literature and philosophy in Mudimbe's work makes the possibility of its artistic reception all the more obvious. Sammy Baloji willingly agreed to discuss and explain how his art may have been inspired by, or even derived from, Mudimbe's thinking. In the conversation between the artist and Maëline Le Lay, "Comparing Viewpoints to Depict the Stratified Memory of a Territory Forged by Colonial Policy," reflections on the politics of building and planning in the colonial cities—in this case

Elisabethville, the copper capital, which would become Lubumbashi, in the mining province of Katanga, the home region of Baloji and Mudimbe—are intertwined. The discussions also address the way the artist portrays the memory of this place, and questions the ties of continuity or rupture from one era to the next. Baloji repeatedly reminds us how much reading Mudimbe echoes his creative research. He finds his own artistic technique of collage, montage, and juxtaposition in the philosopher's method of comparing very different documents and sources on the same subject. In the interview, the artist offers a political and historical interpretation of the city of Lubumbashi in the light of Mudimbe's thought. Using maps, it shows how, during the colonial era, urban planning was used to domesticate and convert culture, and how the areas where Europeans and Congolese lived and were kept separate from each other were designed and organised. Like the extract from *Les Corps glorieux des mots et des êtres*, the interview is published in the original French, to convey the meaning of the conversation as accurately as possible, and in English to make it available to English-speaking readers.

The texts by Pierre-Philippe Fraiture, V.Y. Mudimbe, Sammy Baloji, and Maëline Le Lay bring to light an important aspect of Mudimbe's thinking, whose archaeological method might lead one to believe in the primacy of temporality and history: for him, these are inseparable from spatiality and geography.[29] This explains why, in order to think Africa and its history, Mudimbe needed a different logic from that of the modern philosophies of history, which are excessively based on temporality. Salim Abdelmadjid's chapter, "Africa and Dialectics: Reading V.Y. Mudimbe Towards a Concept of Africa," can be read in relation to this idea. In line with Mudimbe's position of Africa as a subject of thought, and with this book's proposition to think Africa with Mudimbe, Abdelmadjid proposes to read Mudimbe's work in light of the question "What is Africa?" and with a view to a philosophical concept of Africa. In particular, he explains how Mudimbe helps to problematise both the unity of Africa—the justification of which is a priority condition for a concept of Africa—and—this is the meaning of the expression "Africa and dialectics"—the logic and method necessary to think this unity.

29. See the conclusion of *The Invention of Africa*: "The Geography of a Discourse" (Mudimbe 1988, 187–200).

References

Alix, Florian. 2008. "Foucault déplacé: réécriture chez E.W. Said et V.Y. Mudimbe." *Malfini: Publication exploratoire des espaces francophones* ("Discours"). http://malfini.ens-lyon.fr/document.php?id=124 [archive].

Alix, Florian. 2022. *L'essai postcolonial: Poétique de l'entreglose.* Paris: Karthala.

Amuri-Mpala Lutebele, Maurice. 2009. "La querelle littéraire de Lubumbashi: Mudimbe contre Ngal." *Études littéraires africaines*, no. 27 (Special Issue: "Lubumbashi, épicentre littéraire"): 28–35. https://doi.org/10.7202/1034303ar.

Bisanswa, Justin K. 2000. "V.Y. Mudimbe : réflexion sur les sciences humaines et sociales en Afrique." *Cahiers d'Études africaines*, no. 160: 705–22. https://doi.org/10.4000/etudesafricaines.45.

Bisanswa, Justin K., ed. 2013. *Entre inscriptions et prescriptions, V.Y. Mudimbe et l'engendrement de la parole.* Paris: Honoré Champion.

Diawara, Mamadou, Mamadou Diouf, and Jean-Bernard Ouédraogo, eds. 2022. *Africa N'Ko. La bibliothèque coloniale en débat.* Paris: Présence africaine.

Eboussi Boulaga, Fabien. 1968. "Le Bantou problématique." *Présence africaine*, no. 66: 4–40. https://www.jstor.org/stable/24348583.

Fløistad, Guttorm. 1987. "Introduction." In *Contemporary Philosophy. A New Survey.* Vol. 5: African Philosophy, edited by Guttorm Fløistad, 1–7. Dordrecht-Boston-Lancaster: Martinus Nijhoff.

Fraiture, Pierre-Philippe. 2013. *V.Y. Mudimbe: Undisciplined Africanism.* Liverpool: Liverpool University Press.

Fraiture, Pierre-Philippe, and Daniel Orrells, eds. 2016. *The Mudimbe Reader.* Charlottesville: University of Virginia Press.

Halen, Pierre. 2014. "V.Y. Mudimbe, jardinier de l'histoire: Les mémoires d'une modernité." *Canadian Journal of African Studies / Revue canadienne des études africaines* 30, no. 2: 248–56. https://doi.org/10.1080/00083968.1996.10804418.

Hountondji, Paulin J. 1977. *Sur la "philosophie africaine."* Paris: Maspero.

Hountondji, Paulin J. 1983. *African Philosophy: Myth and Reality.* Bloomington and Indianapolis, IN: Indiana University Press; .

Jewsiewicki, Bogumil. 1996. "Des vies et des savoirs "avec" et "en dehors" de l'Afrique." *Canadian Journal of African Studies / Revue canadienne des études africaines* 30, no. 2: 234–35. https://doi.org/10.1080/00083968.1996.10804416.

Kadima-Nzuji, Mukala, and Sélom Komlan Gbanou, eds. 2003. *L'Afrique au miroir des littératures. Mélanges offerts à V.Y. Mudimbe.* Paris: L'Harmattan.

Kavwahirehi, Kasereka. 2006. *V.Y. Mudimbe et la ré-invention de l'Afrique. Poétique et politique de la décolonisation des sciences humaines.* Amsterdam and New York: Rodopi.

Kavwahirehi, Kasereka M. 1998. "'Reprendre' ou des (en)jeux d'une conscience historique et politique. À propos de 'Les Corps glorieux des mots et des êtres' de Valentin Y. Mudimbe." *Présence africaine*, no. 157: 123–40. https://www.jstor.org/stable/24352049.

Kishiba Fitula, Gilbert, ed. 2021. *V.Y. Mudimbe: appropriations, transmissions, reconsidérations.* Preface by Guy Mbuyi Kabunda. With the collaboration of Germain Ngoie Tshibambe and Antoine Tshitungu Kongolo, Paris: Éditions du Cygne.

Kisukidi, Nadia Yala. 2013. "Du christianisme comme "expérience de conflit."" *ThéoRèmes*, no. 4. https://doi.org/10.4000/theoremes.470.

Kresse, Kai, ed. 2005. "'Reading Mudimbe'—An Introduction." *Journal of African Cultural Studies* 17, no. 1: 1–19. https://www.jstor.org/stable/4141300.

Le Lay, Maëline. 2014. *"La parole construit le pays". Théâtre, langues et didactisme au Katanga (République démocratique du Congo).* Francophonies. Paris: Honoré Champion.

Mangeon, Anthony. 2006. "Maîtrise et déformation : les lumières diffractées." *Labyrinthe*, no. 24: 63–83. https://doi.org/10.4000/labyrinthe.1249.

Mangeon, Anthony. 2008. "Indiscipline et transformation du savoir : les stratégies d'Alain Leroy Locke et V.Y. Mudimbe." In *Littératures, savoirs et enseignement*, edited by Musanji Ngalasso-Mwatha, Virginia Coulon and Alain Ricard, 177–86. Pessac: Presses universitaires de Bordeaux. https://doi.org/10.4000/books.pub.43052.

Mangeon, Anthony. 2013. "La 'gnose africaine' de Valentin-Yves Mudimbe." In *Entre inscriptions et prescriptions, V.Y. Mudimbe et l'engendrement de la parole,* edited by J. Bisanswa, 47–56. Paris: Honoré Champion. https://hal.science/hal-03160083/document.

Masolo, Dismas A. 1991. "An Archaeology of African Knowledge: A Discussion of V.Y. Mudimbe." *Callaloo* 14, no. 4: 998–1011. https://doi.org/10.2307/2931218.

Masolo, Dismas A. 2011. *African Philosophy in Search of Identity.* Nairobi, Kampala, Dar es Salaam, Kigali: East African Educational Publishers Ltd.

Mbembe, Achille, and Felwine Sarr, eds. 2017. *Écrire l'Afrique-Monde.* Paris: Philippe Rey/Jimsaan.

Mbiti, John Samuel. 1969. *African Religions and Philosophy.* Nairobi, Ibadan, London: Heinemann.

Mignolo, Walter. 2005. *The Idea of Latin America.* Malden, Oxford, Victoria: Blackwell Publishing.

Mignolo, Walter. 2022. "Africa in the Colonial Horizon of Western Modernity 1652–2000." *Global Africa*, no. 1: 50–64. https://doi.org/10.57832/wfcn-zb53.

Mouralis, Bernard. 1988. V.Y. *Mudimbe ou le discours, l'écart et l'écriture.* Paris: Présence africaine.

Mudimbe, V.Y. 1971. *Déchirures.* Kinshasa: Éditions du Mont Noir.

Mudimbe, V.Y. 1973. *Entre les eaux. Dieu, un prêtre, la révolution*. Paris: Présence africaine.

Mudimbe, V.Y. 1973. *L'autre face du royaume. Une introduction à la critique des langages en folie*. Lausanne: L'Âge d'Homme.

Mudimbe, V.Y. 1982. *L'odeur du père. Essai sur des limites de la science et de la vie en Afrique noire*. Paris: Présence africaine.

Mudimbe, V.Y. 1988. *The Invention of Africa. Gnosis, Philosophy and the Order of Knowledge*. Bloomington and Indianapolis, IN: Indiana University Press; London: James Currey.

Mudimbe, V.Y. 1989. *Shaba deux. Les carnets de Mère Marie-Gertrude*. Paris: Présence africaine.

Mudimbe, V.Y. 1991a. *Parables and Fables. Exegesis, Textuality and Politics in Central Africa*. Madison: The University of Wisconsin Press.

Mudimbe, V.Y. 1991b. *Between Tides*. Translated by Stephen Becker. New York: Simon and Schuster.

Mudimbe, V.Y. 1994. *The Idea of Africa*. Bloomington and Indianapolis, IN: Indiana University Press; London: James Currey.

Mudimbe, V.Y. 1994. *Les Corps glorieux des mots et des êtres. Esquisse d'un jardin africain à la bénédictine*. Paris: Présence africaine; Montréal: Humanitas.

Mudimbe, V.Y. 2021. *L'invention de l'Afrique. Gnose, philosophie et ordre de la connaissance*. Translated by Laurent Vannini. Paris: Présence africaine.

Mudimbe, V.Y. 2023. *The Scent of the Father: Essay on the Limits of Life and Science in Sub-Saharan Africa*. Translated by Jonathan Adjemian. Cambridge and Hoboken, NJ: Polity Press.

Ngũgĩ wa Thiong'o. 1986. *Decolonising the Mind. The Politics of Language in African Literature*. London: James Currey. Nairobi, Portsmouth: Heinemann. Harare: Zimbabwe Publishing House.

Ngũgĩ wa Thiong'o. 2019. "Decolonizing the Mind with Ngũgĩ wa Thiong'o." Interview by Maëline Le Lay. Nairobi: French Embassy in Kenya, IFRA, Masegor, SCAC, Giladi Film. Published online by IFRA Nairobi on 7 October 2019. https://www.youtube.com/watch?v=eXq8AurffeQ.

Ndaywel è Nziem, Isidore. 1996. "Quand Mudimbe et Vansina se répondent en écho pour célébrer l'Afrique: de l'africanisme à la mondialisation ?" *Canadian Journal of African Studies/Revue canadienne des études africaines* 30, no. 2: 272–79. https://doi.org/10.1080/00083968.1996.10804421.

Odera Oruka, Henry. 1990. *Sage Philosophy. Indigenous Thinkers and Modern Debate on African Philosophy*. Leiden: E.J. Brill. https://doi.org/10.1163/9789004452268.

Odera Oruka, Henry. 1991. *Sage Philosophy. Indigenous Thinkers and Modern Debate on African Philosophy*. Nairobi: Acts Press, African Centre for Technology Studies.

Said, Edward. 1978. *Orientalism*. New York City: Pantheon Books.

Tempels, Placide. 1945. *La philosophie bantoue*. Translated from Dutch into French by Antoine Rubbens. Elisabethville: Lovania.

Tempels, Placide. 1959. *Bantu Philosophy*. Translated from French and Dutch into English by Colin King. Paris: Présence africaine.

Towa, Marcien. 1971. *Essai sur la problématique philosophique dans l'Afrique actuelle*. Yaoundé: Clé. [Archive]

Wai, Zubairu. 2024. *Africa Beyond Inventions. Essays in Honour of V.Y. Mudimbe*. Cham: Palgrave Macmillan.

Introducing V.Y. Mudimbe in East Africa

My Experience at the University of Nairobi

Francis Owakah

Introduction

In this chapter I seek to recount the introduction of the work of V.Y. Mudimbe into the East African intellectual landscape and the impact it had on the ways in which the knowledge of Africa was approached and understood in philosophy and the social and human sciences. I specifically focus on the case of the University of Nairobi in the early 1990s, when I was both a student and a staff member in the Department of Philosophy. The extension from this department to East Africa is only a hypothesis, addressed firstly to my colleagues in neighbouring countries, based on the observation that the University of Nairobi has a longer tradition of Philosophy than its East African sister universities, such as Makerere in Uganda and Dar es Salaam in Tanzania which have for some time welcomed faculty trained at the University of Nairobi.[1]

So how did we discover Mudimbe there? And how have his writings influenced our reflections and debates? To answer these questions, I will retrace the ways in which we, students of philosophy, and myself in particular, concretely received and understood his thinking (1), by relating and comparing it to the works of other influential authors—of African literature, history and philosophy, but not exclusively—, some of whom we already knew at the time, and some of whom we discovered or got to know better through reading Mudimbe (2).

1. Encounter with Mudimbe's philosophy

In 1990, after I graduated with a Bachelor of Arts (Hons) degree from the University of Nairobi, I was admitted for a Master of Arts (MA) degree in the Department of Philosophy as a student but also as part of the Department's staff development programme in anticipation of the double

1. The Universities of Rwanda, Burundi, and Southern Sudan are relatively new entrants in philosophy teaching and research.

intake of students expected that year. The country was phasing out the 'A' Level programme, hence admitting the last cohort of Form 6 students to university. Meanwhile, the first 'O' level (Form 4) students were sitting their final examinations in readiness to join the university. This situation created a need for more faculty members to handle the expected high teaching load.

The University of Nairobi MA syllabus required that students take and pass coursework before embarking on writing a Master thesis (this option was referred to as "coursework and thesis," as opposed to "thesis only," or "coursework and project"). This task required students to acquaint themselves with the major texts in their field of study, and conceptualise, write and defend a thesis on a topic of their choice. The defense normally took place before a panel of scholars, some drawn from a discipline other than the one the students were enrolled in. Only after passing the two examinations—coursework and thesis—could a student qualify for the award of the degree of MA in Philosophy.

The first semester was dedicated to coursework which included courses in Logic, Metaphysics, Ethics & Social Philosophy, and Philosophy in Africa. Prof. D.A. Masolo was then in charge of the last one. It was he who introduced us to Mudimbe. Masolo was born and brought up during British colonial rule in Kenya, where he began his research on the socio-historical roots of philosophical traditions and on the contribution of African philosophies to world philosophy. He has, since then, become a philosopher of international repute, currently teaching at the University of Louisville in the United States, and is particularly important in the field of African philosophy, notably for his famous *African Philosophy in Search of Identity* in 1994 (Masolo 1994), where Mudimbe appears in the acknowledgements, and where he wrote about him in the very first chapter: "Mudimbe's work is a powerful genealogy of African *episteme* as a product of a complex interplay of different forms of Western power, political and cognitive, which, in Mudimbe's view, succeeded in alienating and objectifying Africans as 'the other.' We strongly share this view." (Masolo 2011, 2).

I remember that during our first session in class, Masolo assigned us to read and individually make a presentation on *The Invention of Africa: Gnosis, Philosophy and the Order of Knowledge*. Reading it was, more than anything else, to experience a writing style that seemed at times exploratory, dense and erudite, and at other times abstruse and obscure. The language appeared heavy at first, with a mixture of English, French, Greek and Latin concepts. The sentences were long and winding, with multiple citations to explain every idea under analysis. Just reading the title was difficult! The closest I had ever encountered such was in the works of Paulin Hountondji, the philosopher and politician from Benin considered one of the founders of the field of African philosophy alongside authors like Kenyan Henry Odera Oruka and Ghanaian Kwasi Wiredu. But patiently reading Mudimbe revealed an unmistakably expansive thinker, whose work involved varied and complex methodologies, and was inflected with a touch of audacity and generosity. The content of the book, which redefined the thinking of and interaction with colonial discourse and in this respect could not fail to resonate deeply with the intellectual experience of Kenyan students of philosophy, was extraordinarily diverse and wide-ranging in the intellectual and historical questions it posed and engaged with, astonishingly contributing to a broad spectrum of disciplines in what today is known as African Studies.

To make reading Mudimbe easier, Prof. Masolo shared with the class an article he had authored and published in *Callaloo*: "An Archaeology of African Knowledge: A Discussion of V.Y. Mudimbe" (Masolo 1991). This article was illuminating because it summarised the arguments and positions Mudimbe had developed in *The Invention of Africa*. It presented the debates in a less complicated language, contextualised the arguments and made them more familiar. It acted as a preface to understanding Mudimbe. The class enjoyed the debates as they were presented. I were now ready to plunge into Mudimbe's writings in depth.

In *The Invention of Africa*, I discovered how Mudimbe makes use of the archaeological approach to texts to explain the invention of the primitive and savage African. This notion of a primitive and savage African has been maintained in history, and Mudimbe's work provides explanations for its creation and persistence. I debated the notion thoroughly in class, notably through Chapter One of the book, titled "Discourse of Power and Knowledge of Otherness." Mudimbe points out at the outset that, "although in African history the colonial experience represents but a brief moment from the perspective of today, this moment is still charged and controversial, since, to say the least, it signified a new historical form and the possibility of radically new types of discourses on African traditions and cultures" (Mudimbe 1988). Mudimbe rightly observes that the colonial project was not only meant to dominate and exploit, but also to redesign, reorganise and rearrange Africa in a different structure, easily understandable to the Western interpreters, and, in sum, to "transform non-European areas into fundamentally European constructs" (ibid.). The discourse inventing and constructing the rival images of the primitive and the civilised is the discourse within which Africa as we know it today was formed, within the womb of colonialism.

2. Mudimbe in the intellectual landscape at the University of Nairobi in the early 1990s

The University of Nairobi had just turned twenty in the 1990s. Because the British colonised Kenya, the British tradition still dominated many spheres of Kenyan life, including academia. The Kenyan educational system mirrored the British system, as it still does, and English was the official language, as it still is. The intellectual landscape was littered with mostly Anglophone literature, with limited translations of texts in other languages.

During our undergraduate studies, we read the works of Robin Horton, Robert Redfield and Ferdinand Tönnies, three notable scholars in sociology and cultural anthropology who were usually referenced in developing the thesis of a cultural divide between the West and Africa. As MA students, we could still remember their texts in great detail, and often quoted them in our essays. We also knew of E.E. Evans-Pritchard, the renowned British anthropologist who studied South Sudanese societies such as the Nuer, the Azande and the Dinka, and appeared different because of his sympathetic descriptions of these societies and their socio-religious experiences (Evans-Pritchard 1973), and because of his view of social anthropology as a humanistic rather than a strictly distanced and objective study of society. But for his role in shifting the focus of anthropology from the study of the function of rituals in society only to an examination of the meaning ascribed to rituals by members of that society, "we," the progressive students in Nairobi, still disliked him. Based on such claims regarding meaning over function, Prof. Casper Odegi Awuondo, the late, a sociologist who was teaching in the Department of Sociology, would even strictly distinguish anthropology from sociology by claiming that the former is a colonial science through and through, while sociology was not.

We were also familiar with the works of thinkers such as the philosophers Hegel and Marx, sociologist Max Weber, and eminent scholars such as Issa Shivji from Tanzania and Andrew Gunder Frank from Germany who were Marxist thinkers addressing issues such as class struggle and relations of dependency within the world system. We had encountered Okot p'Bitek, the Ugandan poet of international repute, who was a vocal critic of Western culture; and Mudimbe's radical reading and deconstruction of Western thought on Africa obviously echoed the works of Okot p'Bitek which we had studied during our classes, notably the famous *Song of Lawino* (1966) and *African Religions in Western Scholarship* (p'Bitek 1970) where he argues that "Western scholars have never been interested in African religions *per se*. Their works have all been part and parcel of some controversy or debate in the Western world" (p'Bitek 2011).

All these figures contributed to our intellectual background for understanding class and racial relations through critical theory, and many of them acted for us as role models. Mudimbe not only added to this background but brought in new ways of approaching the relations between the West and Africa through his archaeology of knowledge on Africa. Through the exploration of Western discourses and claims about Africa and the impact these had in creating Africa as "the other" in Western views, Mudimbe was highlighting different historical processes such as the undermining of African history, the primitivisation of Africans and the self-aggrandisement of Europe, that we could thus advantageously integrate into our reflections and debates. For us, the way he was laying bare the colonial project by linking philosophy and history to better dig into Western discourse on Africa was an eye-opener. His approach and positions not only set a new mood in the intellectual discussions in Kenya but provided alternative critical reading of history besides that provided by Kenyan thinker Ali Mazrui, for instance, at the time a prominent intellectual figure in the East African intellectual landscape, the editor of the eighth volume, *Africa since 1935*, of UNESCO's *General History of Africa* in 1993, and who was also writing on North-South relations.

In addition to encouraging us to read our main references and view Black-White racial relations in a new way, Mudimbe also opened up new domains for us, beginning with contemporary French philosophy. For students of philosophy in the late 1980s, the most famous translation from French was *Bantu Philosophy* by a Belgian missionary in the Congo, Placide Tempels. It is through Mudimbe that I was exposed to the works by French philosophers hitherto unknown to us. Among them, the first who comes to mind, given Mudimbe's archaeological method, is Foucault, who was not only studied in our philosophy classes but also in the Departments of Literature, Political Science and History. Foucault's theory of power and knowledge, as borrowed by Mudimbe to develop his approach on the Western invention of Africa, was immediately convincing to us; and we also immediately understood how we could apply it to our contemporary situation, to show how power penetrates the entire social body not only through open authority, but also through hidden mechanisms. For instance, we could immediately understand that the domination of this Western epistemology had been and was being made possible through "*dispositifs*" found in institutions such as education, the church, family, media, or law, which all served to transmit the values and interests of the colonial state.

Strangely enough—given the fact that Mudimbe referred to him in only three pages of *The Invention of Africa*, to elaborate on his theories— the author I discovered in the debates generated by my reading of Mudimbe who made an impression on me the most was Althusser. We had read and discussed Marx extensively; we saw the analogy between colonisation and colonial discourse on the one hand, and, on the other hand, economy and ideology; and we articulated, in the analysis of the relations between Africa and Europe, Mudimbe's archaeology of the invention of Africa and the Marxian explanation of the relation between economy and ideology. In such a reflection, Althusser's interpretation of the Marxian concept of ideology was very useful, as was, more specifically, the concept of "ideological state apparatuses" (Althusser 2001) that we could relate to Foucault's "*dispositifs*." The reading of Mudimbe, Foucault and Althusser was also very useful to apply to the African past and present situation, following the suggestion by Masolo in his article, "Marx's concept of *false consciousness*" (Masolo 1991, 1003).

Conclusion

It is difficult to pin down a writer of Mudimbe's stature. I will simply stress, to conclude, four points which have struck me in particular. Firstly, he harshly attacks colonial, racial, ethnic, and religious discourses, and their impact on post-colonial Africa and on post-colonial relations between Africa and Europe, and more broadly the West.

Secondly, he is one of the major critics of essentialism as found in the construction of the notions of "black" and of a "primitive" Africa. The combination of essentialisation and of opposition of "the other" and "the same" has structured the colonial discourse on Africa and shaped, until now, the relation between Europe and Africa, and the relation between whites and blacks, separating and hierarchising a supposedly logical white and European thought and a supposedly illogical black and African thought, a supposedly historical Europe and a supposedly ahistorical Africa. The archaeology of such a discourse by Mudimbe has had for us a powerful critical effect on any essentialist stance, in the domains of African philosophy and African studies, among others.

Thirdly, he helps to demonstrate the role of ideology in creating a discourse on "otherness." Because colonialism did not just represent a physical occupation of Africa, but also sought to replace African culture with a "superior" Western culture enshrined in Christianity, it involved the exploitation not only of African people and natural resources, but also of African spiritual heritages. This was not a historical accident but a clearly laid out programme that began many years before the advent of colonialism involving physical occupation (Bulhan 2015).

And lastly, Mudimbe seeks to reconstruct the thinking of African reality using an African *episteme* and, through a critique of the classics ranging from philosophy and anthropology to comparative literature, he provides new directions in the social sciences and humanities so that they could contribute to an independent African knowledge, that is, founded on, as Masolo says, an "authentic African epistemological locus" (Masolo 1991, 1004).

Reading Mudimbe, one is thus presented with tough questions that still stand in the way of such a new epistemological order for Africa. How do we define what is authentic? How should this be appropriated in African thinking? Who is defining the acceptance? Which instruments are being used to judge acceptance or non-acceptance? And who is setting the standards and instruments? These are crucial questions that still need to be addressed in today's Africa.

References

Althusser, Louis. 2001. "Ideology and Ideological State Apparatus (Notes Towards an Investigation)." In *Lenin and Philosophy and Other Essays*, trans. B. Brewster. New York: Monthly Review Press.

Bulhan, Hussein A. 2015. "Stages of Colonialism in Africa: From Occupation of Land to Occupation of Being." *Journal of Social and Political Psychology* 3, no. 1. https://doi.org/10.5964/jspp.v3i1.143.

Evans-Pritchard, Edward Evan. 1940. *The Nuer: A Description of the Modes of Livelihood and Political Institutions of a Nilotic People.* Oxford, Clarendon Press.

Evans-Pritchard, Edward Evan. 1973. "Genesis of a Social Anthropologist." *The New Diffusionist* 2, no. 10: 14–20.

Masolo, D.A. 1991. "An Archaeology of African Knowledge: A Discussion of V.Y. Mudimbe." *Callaloo* 14, no. 4: 998–1011. https://doi.org/10.2307/2931218.

Masolo, D.A. 1994. *African Philosophy in Search of Identity.* Bloomington, IN: Indiana University Press; Edinburgh: Edinburgh University Press.

Masolo, D.A. 2011. *African Philosophy in Search of Identity.* Nairobi, Kampala, Dar es Salaam, Kigali: East African Educational Publishers Ltd.

Mazrui, Ali A. 1993, ed. *Africa since 1935, General History of Africa VIII.* Paris: Unesco; Berkeley, CA: University of California Press; London: Heinemann Educational Books. https://unesdoc.unesco.org/ark:/48223/pf0000184297.

Mudimbe, V.Y. 1988. *The Invention of Africa: Gnosis, Philosophy and the Order of Knowledge*. Bloomington and Indianapolis, IN: Indiana University Press; London: James Currey.

p'Bitek, Okot. 1966. *Song of Lawino: A Lament*. N.p. [Uganda]: East African Publishing House.

p'Bitek, Okot. 1970. *African Religions in Western Scholarship*. Kampala, Nairobi, Dar es Salaam: East African Literature Bureau.

p'Bitek, Okot. 2011. *Decolonizing African Religions: A Short History of African Religion in Western Scholarship*. New York: Diasporic Africa Press.

Africanism and Beyond?

Re-reading Mudimbe in Context Today

Kai Kresse[1]

> "Mudimbe (...) adopts a wide variety of disciplinary approaches—linguistic, archaeological, anthropological, literary, and philosophic—to delineate the figures of the Black subject within the Western archive. By this broad trajectory, he reveals a mode of philosophical problematization which appears to be at first quite unsettling, but which (...) by the sheer breadth of its conceptuality, announces many possibilities for African philosophy." (Osha 2011, 195)

What can thinking and conducting research beyond Africanism really mean, and how can it bring forward the agenda of African philosophy and research on African intellectual culture most productively? Taking V.Y. Mudimbe's classic programmatic position as an exemplary reference point, this essay discusses his work with a view to its merits and limitations, in context with other African thinkers of his generation. On this basis, it seeks to sensitise the reader to certain challenges and questions that need to be addressed. The critique of Africanism—ultimately with the goal of overcoming it—is at the core of V.Y. Mudimbe's project, and has also been a central task for African philosophy on the whole to work through. Africanism is largely characterised as a Eurocentric representation of Africa (African history, and the African experience more generally), along the lines in which Orientalism refers to a distorting representation of the non-European "other" by Europeans, marking a Eurocentric project that needs to be critically reflected (Said 1978), and revised. V.Y. Mudimbe, one of the most well-known African philosophers of the postcolonial

1. Acknowledgements: I am grateful to the editors and the Nairobi conference organisers for their invitation to participate in this project, for discussions during our meetings, and for their feedback on a first draft. I also thank Schirin Amir-Moazami for inviting me to present on Mudimbe and Africanism, in her lecture series on the 40th anniversary of Edward Said's *Orientalism* at Freie Universität Berlin in 2018. There and here I built also on passages and ideas presented earlier on in Paris, at an EHESS-Columbia-UCAD summer school on epistemology of area studies and global studies, following an invitation by Rémy Bazenguissa-Ganga and Salim Abdelmadjid. I thank the organisers and participants, especially Hady Ba, Bado Ndoye and Houfrane Ahamed for rich and stimulating discussions. For related discussions more generally, I also thank Reginald Oduor and Abdoulaye Sounaye and the participating colleagues—often spread out across continents—of the Working Group Thinkers and Theorizing from the South based at Leibniz-Zentrum Moderner Orient (ZMO).

 41

era (next to Paulin Hountondji, Kwasi Wiredu, Henry Odera Oruka and others), was trained within the colonially established missionary system of education in the Catholic Belgian Congo, excelled within it and continued to do so far beyond it, as an increasingly refined and independent scholar. The ongoing relevance of a critique of Africanism today is reflected and echoed in current calls for the decolonisation of knowledge, now (more urgently than before) by a younger generation. Parallel calls for a recentring of knowledge in the humanities and social sciences seek to place African epistemologies at the core. This resonates well with Mudimbe's position, as I discuss in the concluding part of this essay.

The fact that Mudimbe, while engaged in a project of liberating critique, is himself entangled in those epistemic power-knowledge relations that he criticises and works through, exemplifies aspects of the global setting we are all part of. Therefore, what has been perceived as Mudimbe's "reliance on European thinkers" and intellectual history (Fraiture and Orrells 2016, xxxix) is part of a wider, more general and ongoing structural historical reliance or intellectual "scientific dependency" (Hountondji 1990), of Africa on the West—an intellectual entanglement. What is well understood is Mudimbe's programmatic insight that, due to interweaving histories of power and knowledge, European conceptual frames are commonly at the basis of (self)interpretations and understandings of what it means to be "African." Mudimbe goes far in showing this in his work, notably in *The Invention of Africa* (Mudimbe, 1988) and *The Idea of Africa* (Mudimbe, 1994), and the question emerges: if these dynamics are at the core of Africanism, how may it be possible to get beyond? Mudimbe himself is demanding a shift to Africa-centred notions, frames and keywords, as conceptual anchors that help build the pathway for a new intellectual agency that is liberated and able to engage actively in the future, because it is based and grounded in African epistemologies and histories of thought. Yet the empirically-based processes of what the concrete work leading us there entails are not laid out by him, neither the specific terms that guide it forward. Mudimbe, as a foundational thinker, is concerned with reflections on the terms of the conditions of possibility here, and less with the concrete realisation of such an overcoming of Africanism.[2] This then seems to be the set task for African and Africanist scholars of the younger generation.

2. My own work—as an Africanist anthropologist concerned with intellectual history, philosophical thought, and critical debate within the living dynamics of societies in Africa today—has attempted to identify and provide some tasks and fields for research that could be valuable here. I seek to bring that into the discussion here as well, also in terms of a general argument for a complementary collaboration between philosophical (and literary) and anthropological positions.

Mudimbe's critique of Africanism, as a set of sustained Eurocentric and thus distorted discourses about Africa, follows a Foucauldian approach, and Mudimbe's writing—in these two major Anglophone books of his—lays bare and works through the continent's long-ongoing historical processes of entanglements in Eurocentric visions and narratives. Mudimbe was indeed uniquely qualified for such work, as a philologist (drawing ably from Greek and Latin), as a historian of ideas, a life-long student of philosophy, and an avid reader of modern anthropological writings in French and English. According to Mudimbe's account, such entanglements seem all-encompassing and almost unsurmountable. Mudimbe himself suggests this, when calling "even the most Afrocentric approaches" somewhat trapped within the Western *episteme*, in the introductions to both *The Invention of Africa* and *The Idea of Africa* (1988, x; 1994, xv). With this in mind, I also discuss constructive visions and pathways for overcoming Africanism by Mudimbe, and by some of his academic counterparts and contemporaries.

Indeed, other prominent African philosophers of Mudimbe's generation, like Paulin Hountondji (from Benin), Kwasi Wiredu (from Ghana), and Henry Odera Oruka (from Kenya), also critically engaged with these fundamental dynamics of colonially forged conceptual entanglements, and sought pathways for decolonisation, addressing them in different ways (e.g. Wiredu 1996; Odera Oruka 1991). Here, I use their works as complementary reference points for discussion. Overall, I seek to connect this discussion to ongoing pressing concerns about the need for conceptual decolonisation and the overcoming of Eurocentrism. Thus, one question for discussion is, how far can *thinking with Mudimbe* today help us to truly overcome Eurocentrism? Here, I argue that while being fundamentally important and enabling, thinking with Mudimbe may not be able to take us far enough. Mudimbe's thinking enables us to see (and his biography helps us to understand) the postcolonial intellectual entanglements that need to be overcome. It also gives us pointers and criteria for the envisaged process, but the actual constructive work forward needs to be conducted from another position, working with specific African epistemes to shape specific Afrophone and/or Africa-centred conceptual anchors for general reflection (on being human, social, etc.) for all to draw from.

My discussion here draws from my own experiences over the years: as a teacher of students in anthropology, philosophy, and African studies, teaching Mudimbe in courses on African philosophy and anthropology, rereading and discussing his work in class. As a researcher who has been working at the intersection of anthropology and African philosophy, particularly with a view to Swahili thinkers, their texts, and related empirical processes and performances of knowledge, debate, and critique on the Kenyan Kiswahili coast (e.g. Kresse 2007; 2008; 2009; 2018). I drew inspiration from Mudimbe, next to Odera Oruka and Hountondji, but also from anthropologists who studied local thinkers and social forms and paradigms of knowledge, like Karin Barber, Michael Lambek, Wyatt MacGaffey, John Janzen, Johannes Fabian, and others.[3] Their research shows that anthropology, historically a major culprit in the constitution of Africanism, can be practised in ways that work towards its overcoming.[4]

***

Now, why is it that reading Mudimbe and engaging with his work has been stimulating to others? The answer is rather straightforward, I think, along two lines. On the one hand, the fundamental issues of Africanism and its entanglements in Eurocentric assumptions have not yet been resolved. On the other hand, within the humanities and social sciences, calls and pressures abound, for fundamental reorientation and conceptual transformations along the lines of decolonising scholarship (e.g. Diagne and Amselle 2018; Ndlovu-Gasheni 2018; Grosz-Ngaté 2020). In this vein, putting Africa and its own conceptual resources and potentials at the centre of such endeavours resonates much with Mudimbe's central concern. Hereby, the fundamental task of "rewriting the humanities and social sciences from Africa" (Sarr 2019a) and other regions of the so-called "global South," as an alternative epistemological locus to a dominant Eurocentric one, is a foundational desideratum at the core of the envisaged transformations of academia (also Sarr 2019b; Diouf 2015; Pollock 2015). This task can directly be connected to, and built upon, Mudimbe who demanded an alternative epistemological locus from Africa to be established and thought with. For projects taking on such a task of fundamental rethinking or rewriting, the appeal is to build, appropriate, and use, in the words of Mudimbe, an African epistemological order (instead of a Western one) at the centre not only of African studies (1988, x-xi) but also more generally of Africa-based research and theorising. The goal is to build a well-grounded vision, engaged in thinking through what it means to be human or social in the world today, from Africa. In this way, Mudimbe can also be seen to contribute directly to the related project of

3. See for instance Barber (2007); Lambek (1993); Janzen (1992); MacGaffey (2000); Fabian (1996).

4. My thoughts here also go back to and build on an earlier lecture series and publication effort on "Reading Mudimbe" (Kresse 2005), which I coorganised with Louis Brenner at the School of Oriental and African Studies (SOAS) in London, in 2001.

"provincializing Europe," relativising its hegemonic position and its impact across the world (Chakrabarty 2007, Introduction).

This chapter discusses these core programmatic ideas and concerns vis-à-vis selected counterparts and peers of Mudimbe in the field of African philosophy, especially Paulin Hountondji and his take on Africanism as problematic discourse; and Kwasi Wiredu and Ngũgĩ wa Thiong'o and their projects of conceptual decolonisation (in theory and practice). An intermediary section, on "struggling with Mudimbe," then looks at entanglements of Mudimbe's work (e.g. van Binsbergen 2005), and at challenges that students and other readers are facing when reading his work. In the concluding part and as an outlook, I discuss the bottom line of these reflections in relation to Felwine Sarr's recent calls for an Afrotopia and the rewriting of the humanities from Africa (Sarr 2019a; 2019b). In programmatic terms, the latter may be seen to take off where Mudimbe ends, with the constructive work of conceptual key terms, genres, authors, and narratives that promise to provide alternative Africa-grounded conceptual frameworks with which to think and orient oneself in the world more widely.

1. Mudimbe's programmatic critique of Africanism

Mudimbe was inspired by Foucault's archaeology of knowledge and his critique of knowledge-power relations. Building on this approach, he studied the history of knowledge production about and the representation of "Africa," largely *to* a wider (Western) world *by* a wider (Western) world—what he qualifies as "Africanism" (1988, ix; xi; also 1994). In more general and generic terms, he also qualified Africanism as "knowledge about Africa" (1994, 38), and "the body of discourses on and about Africa" (1994, 39). The meaningful connotations of Africanism that Mudimbe finds important to introduce and keep in play, when summarising his project conceptually, are about the dynamic historical dimensions of processes, origins and contexts that play a role in the building and constitution of knowledge, taking both epistemological and social dimensions on board. He is interested in keeping in view the conditions of possibility of knowledge and experience, while exploring also the power dynamics at work in the determination of meaning and (mis)representation.[5] Here, Mudimbe looks at the *longue-durée* of knowledge production and knowledge-power relations, starting

5. These are the relevant expressions from the Introduction to *The Invention of Africa* (1988): "the larger body of knowledge on Africa" (1988, ix)—with a view to the conditions of possibility; pointing to "sociohistorical origins but also epistemological contexts" (ix); "discourses on African societies, cultures, peoples as signs of something else" (ix); project "a sort of archaeology of African gnosis" (x); "foundations of

from the consultation of ancient Greek and Latin sources and working his way through the Renaissance to colonial history and its postcolonial aftermath. He does so by means of an eclectic critical survey, discussing the representation of Africa in relation to relevant projects and periods of external domination since the Greek and Roman empires.

Pierre-Philippe Fraiture, in his comprehensive study of Mudimbe's oeuvre, calls Mudimbe's critique of Africanism "the African equivalent of Orientalism" and Said's critique of it (2013, 8)—and an attentive critical comparative study between the two might be a rewarding project indeed.[6] Fraiture himself has called his book on Mudimbe "Undisciplined Africanism" to denote the scope and fundamental character of Mudimbe's overall work, as writer, cultural and literary critic, philologist, and philosopher who draws eclectically from his vast training in these various overlapping fields (also including anthropology and theology). It is challenging to understand Mudimbe's writing, as his contextualisations within Greek and Latin history, and also other references to European modern and premodern writers are often difficult to grasp. The same applies to his reflections upon specific debates among African intellectuals, or on the (colonial and early postcolonial) Congolese situation in which African and colonial theologians and missionary scholars take on a central role. Most readers are not familiar with all the aspects of the large scope of Mudimbe's knowledge repertoire and writing, including poetry and fiction.

In the introduction to *The Invention of Africa*, Mudimbe announces a study of "the theme of the foundations of discourses about Africa" (1988, xi); he states that the book "is only a critical synthesis of the complex questions about knowledge and power in and on Africa" (ibid.). His central conceptual point of concern, also constituting the main conceptual challenge to research in the field, is about the fundamental entanglements of Africanism (and, as we shall see below, even Afrocentrism) in Eurocentrism. He puts this major programmatic point forward in the following lines, flagged up verbatim, as part of the introduction to both *The Invention of Africa* (1988) as well as its sequel, *The Idea of Africa* (1994):

> "Western interpreters as well as African analysts, have been using categories and conceptual systems which depend on a Western epistemological order. Even in the most explicitly 'Afrocentric' descriptions, models of analysis explicitly or implicitly, knowingly or unknowingly, refer to the same order." (1988, x;1994, xv)

---

discourses about Africa" (xi); "systematically promoting a gnosis" out of which "arose both African discourses on otherness and ideologies of alterity" (xi).

6. Indeed, in part this has been pursued already; see Alix (2014). I am grateful to the editors for pointing this out.

"What does this mean for the field of African studies?" is the big question added to this directly afterwards (only) in *The Idea of Africa*, while *The Invention of Africa* proceeds in asking:

> "Does this mean that African *Weltanschauungen* and traditional systems of thought are unthinkable and cannot be made explicit within the framework of their own rationality? My own claim is that *thus far* the ways in which they have been evaluated and the means used to explain them relate to theories and methods whose constraints, rules, and systems of operation suppose *a non-African epistemological locus*." (1988, x; my emphasis)

With a view to the focus of discussion here, this last half-sentence is crucial, and its significance can hardly be overestimated. This statement points to the fundamental task to develop, establish, and cultivate the use of Africa-centered epistemological frameworks and reference points for research on (specific) African worldviews, religions and philosophies that are embedded within particular regional and trans-regional intellectual histories. These are themselves grounded in specific lifeworlds and their respective conceptual frameworks and regional languages, which constitute the channels for expression and fundamental reflection, and which could thus provide the basis (and conceptual resources) for the envisaged future kind of analytic language that Mudimbe calls for.

Notably, the next step, seen from the perspective of historical and anthropological research on socially embedded intellectual histories and intellectual practices, would be to provide accounts of any empirically known Africa-centered epistemological spaces in the past and present, and to show that (and how) they have been in use and changed (over time), in specific regional socio-historical settings in Africa. With this in mind (as I understand it), Mudimbe pointed at times to meaningful recent Africanist research in anthropology and history, weaving these references into his lines of argument. Following from Mudimbe's quote above, what is needed within interdisciplinary research in the wider field of African philosophy and African studies, is identifying, building, and using such epistemological spaces as resources that can provide frameworks, key terms, and cornerstones for the development and cultivation of new (or renewed) and more adequate analytic languages. This then could feed into, and underpin, a self-sustained and Africa-centred building of theory and method, within contemporary, postcolonial academic practice. This would, as I think he is saying, be truly liberating in perspective, as the criterion of being grounded in an African epistemological locus would be fulfilled.

The subtitle of *The Invention of Africa* is "gnosis, philosophy and the order of knowledge," and the use of "gnosis" as a key term—denoting a wider and blurred semantic field of knowledge and inquiry that is distinct from *doxa* (opinion) and *episteme* (science)[7]—is characterised by Mudimbe "as a methodological tool" (1988, ix). It is meant to assist in clarifying the conditions of possibility of philosophy within the "larger body of knowledge on Africa called 'Africanism'" (1988, ix). He employs "gnosis" with a heuristic impetus in mind, as the term is under-determined and thus useful when searching for the relevant meanings and associations of terms and practices in concrete socially shaped fields of knowledge in practice.[8] Using "gnosis" in this process avoids the common usage of dominant Eurocentric terms, like "philosophy" or "religion," that are already determined by Western criteria and categories. In this way, keeping the analytic language more open and under-determined so that the internal dynamics of subfields of knowledge and aspects of meaning can be more clearly identified and understood in the process, is pursued by Mudimbe as a heuristic strategy. Having clarified these basic goals and intentions in Mudimbe's programmatic approach to overcome Africanism, let us now turn to Paulin Hountondji and his elaborations on related matters.

2. "Africanism," extraversion and beyond—Hountondji

Before Mudimbe's critique of Africanism that he presented in *The Invention of Africa* and pushed further in *The Idea of Africa*, prominent academic coverage of this term was not easily found. Yet one important problematisation and critique of Africanism that preceded Mudimbe's was brought forward by Paulin Hountondji who had a critical point to make, in a longer-term perspective, when sketching out a generic characterisation of "Africanism" in the writings that later constituted his book *African Philosophy: Myth and Reality* (1996; originally written in French and published in 1976). Africanism is, as he elaborates, "the straight and narrow path" (1996, 52–3) of a restrictive and externally imposed and ideologically motivated paradigm of studying Africa, initiated as part of Western colonial projects of subjection and exploitation. The school of "ethnophilosophy" had taken on this paradigm, and thus saw Africa and Africans characterised by

7. "Gnosis" (in the subtitle) "means seeking to know, inquiry, methods of knowing investigation and even acquaintance with someone. (…) is different from *doxa* or opinion (…) and (…) cannot be confused with *episteme*, understood as both science and general intellectual configuration" (Mudimbe 1988, ix).

8. On the field of "knowledge in practice" in anthropological research, using these broad analytic terms for similar reasons with which Mudimbe prefers "gnosis" here, see Lambek (1993); Kresse and Marchand (2009). In my own work, I have specifically focused on the social dynamics of the cultivation and negotiation of knowledge, and forms and genres of "intellectual practice" in everyday Swahili lifeworlds, see Kresse (2007) and Kresse (2018).

a "collective, immutable system of thought in eternal opposition to that of Europe" (52). According to Hountondji, this constituted a fundamental—and fundamentally mistaken—"myth" of African philosophy, and as such a "theoretical impasse" (ibid.). The pursuit of studying African cultures and societies in such a vein would be a self-alienating enterprise engaged in a fictitious dialogue dominated by outsiders (more so, the former colonising powers), and responding to external demands upon how Africa should be represented and represent itself. Such a mistaken orientation is what Hountondji then calls "extraversion" (1996, 45; also 1990). With a view of the field of African philosophy, the project of "ethnophilosophical description" that follows such an essentialist approach marked by Africanism, in Hountondji's view, is restricting Africans further as it binds them to specific descriptions of similar kind (Yoruba, Zulu, Swahili etc.) and thus perpetuates the dominance of external demands upon them. Hountondji calls upon those who seek to build and shape African philosophy as a field of study (and, more generally, research and science in and on Africa on the whole) to overcome such dynamics of extraversion (Hountondji 1990).[9]

Following Hountondji, African philosophy needed to liberate itself from such restrictions and develop self-centred debates, thus replacing extraversion with introversion, internal pluralism, and cultivating open debates and discussions among insiders. Indeed, the "reality" of African philosophy that Hountondji invokes in his book title, *African Philosophy: Myth and Reality*, refers to the existence of African philosophy as an internal discourse, "a literature produced by Africans and dealing with philosophical problems" (1996, 63). The conception of philosophy to be practised from here onwards is, in principle, liberating, as self-reliant (in terms of the determination of its goals and questions), and critically engaged. With this argument, Hountondji sought to show a real and recommendable alternative to the way in which ethnophilosophy pursued a descriptive and essentialising approach that followed the paradigm of Africanism which was simplifying, reductionist, and ultimately untenable. Like Orientalism, Africanism needed to be overcome. This could be achieved, according to Hountondji, when decisive conceptual agency was taken over from within Africa (and when a focus on such conceptual agency was taken as a guideline) both in African philosophy and African studies more widely, as self-determined fields of scholarly engagement.[10]

9. On the challenge and pathway to overcome extraversion, thinking with Hountondji, see also Duebgen and Skupien (2019, Chapter 6).

10. In later essays, Hountondji elaborates further on how, in the ongoing postcolonial era, the dynamics of extraversion have continued to be in play. This can be seen in the domination of research and scholarship by external interests, thus perpetuating

It is noteworthy, at this point, to remark upon certain parallels of thinking here, between Hountondji and Mudimbe, both in the ways that they frame their work of fundamental critique and in their visions for a way forward. Hountondji himself tried to implement such a pathway in practical terms, when taking over political responsibility as a minister of education for Benin for a while. Also in a different role, as a senior researcher and coordinator for a subsequent interdisciplinary research project that sought to collect, survey and discuss the varieties of traditions (i.e. histories and genres) of knowledge, science and literacy in Africa, Hountondji formulated a constructive guideline for people to work with, so as not to be trapped (Hountondji 1997). Researchers on such traditions, he advised, needed to make sure they studied "endogenous knowledge," i.e. knowledge that was seen and accepted as such from within the internal dynamics of the perspective of the community or society that was being studied—from the perspective of an "African epistemological locus," as one could say in Mudimbe's terms. Hountondji contrasted "endogenous" with "indigenous"—a term he regarded as suspicious as entangled in reductionist and demeaning connotations of earlier extroverted discourses and their terminology (like "native," or "primitive"). He also argued that it should be the "internal pluralisms" within African societies and cultures that needed to be focused upon and attended to (i.e. understood) in research, for it is in these dynamic fields of challenges and responses where the exchange of relevant arguments and the refinement of theoretical and practical conceptions actually takes place (1996, 165; also 1983). Following such a perspective, then, research "beyond Africanism" needed to be developed, built, and cultivated along these lines, namely with a view to the social, discursive, and conceptual dynamics from within.

If such a pathway for the overcoming of Africanism was to include liberating and decolonising aspects (as argued and recounted here), let us see how this relates to the task of conceptual decolonisation, as discussed by the Ghanaian philosopher Kwasi Wiredu (1996).

3. Two sides of conceptual decolonisation—Wiredu

Kwasi Wiredu's essay, "The need for conceptual decolonization in African philosophy" (Wiredu 1996), can be regarded as a central pillar and reference point for the project of decolonising African philosophy in the

---

the "scientific dependency" of Africa vis-à-vis the West (Hountondji 1990). While Hountondji admits that it is difficult to see how this could be fully overcome, politically, economically, and institutionally, he insists that the possible pathway should be through introversion.

postcolonial era. In it, Wiredu lays out two fundamental tasks for such a project in relation to each other. First, the required work of critique, as a kind of "negative" occupation of clearing the thickets of intellectual entanglement; and second, the constructive and thus "positive" visionary work of shaping new conceptual pathways and possibilities while drawing from old resources that are being reappropriated. With an emphasis on these two complementary aspects, and the "positive" aspects building on the "negative" ones. This is how Wiredu phrased the task in his own words:

> "By conceptual decolonization I mean two complementary things. On the *negative* side, I mean avoiding or reversing through a critical conceptual self-awareness the unexamined assimilation in our thought (that is, in the thought of contemporary African philosophers) of the conceptual frameworks embedded in the foreign philosophical traditions that have had an impact on African life and thought. And, on the *positive* side, I mean exploiting as much as is judicious the resources of our own indigenous conceptual schemes in our philosophical meditations on even the most technical problems of contemporary philosophy. The *negative* is, of course, only the reverse side of the *positive*. But I cite it first because the necessity for decolonization was brought upon us in the first place by the historical superimposition of foreign categories of thought on African thought systems through colonialism." (Wiredu 1996, 136; my emphasis)

The overall goal for Wiredu here is to work out a perspective for the liberation of African philosophical thinking in academic practice. This has, he argued, thus far been constrained and obstructed through the (ongoing) effects of imposed structures, categories, and connotations of the former colonial languages that still dominate higher education and research. Wiredu shows how African academic philosophy has been reliant upon and thus constrained by the central dominance of Europhone concepts and their connotations.[11] He points to a range of fundamental semantic differences between these concepts and their counterparts in Akan (his own language) that have led thinkers astray, along pathways of interpretation that have no grounding in African conceptual frameworks and their contextual realities—people's lifeworlds. In the context of this discussion, he also points to aspects of untranslatability—e.g. of Descartes' dictum "cogito ergo sum" that has no meaningful equivalent in the Akan language, because (like in many other African languages) "being" cannot be thought of as abstract and separate from concrete ways of being positioned in time and place.

11. See also his comments during my interviews with him on related matters (Kresse and Wiredu 2000); for another critique of the dominance of Europhone discourse in African philosophy, criticising Mudimbe and Appiah, see Ousmane Kane's "Non-Europhone Intellectuals" (Kane 2012).

It is remarkable that Wiredu, otherwise a rather conservative and by no means radical thinker, can be seen here to advocate a fundamental turn for postcolonial African philosophy to take the language question on board. He demands that philosophical thinking needs to take African language concepts and categories as its starting point—which is something that he himself until then had rarely done in his own work (and that he was not able to make the basis of his work, for much of his career). This simple and basic but fundamentally crucial point, of consciously and confidently taking one's own conceptual framework—instead of a Western Europhone one—as the starting point and mediating platform for reflection and theorising, must be seen, one could argue, as a precondition in order to be able to develop a strong sense of intellectual empowerment and liberation. In this way then, being able to work within the scenario of a more self-reliant pathway and framework for reflexive thought processes, drawing creative stimulation from Afrophone concepts and reference-points, ultimately leads to a different status of more intellectual (and scientific) independence. This is a "positive" and constructive response then, to overcome the "scientific dependency" scenario that Hountondji sketched out (as mentioned above), now more than forty years ago, for research and science in Africa, a dependency that has been ongoing. The implementation of an Afrophone conceptual centricity, as advocated by Wiredu in principle, thus can be seen as one way of switching the African-based scientific discourse to an introversion, away from the paradigm of Western-dominated extraversion, as discussed by Hountondji (1990; 1997).

4. Using African mother tongues for decolonising the mind—Ngũgĩ

On a level of political activism and critique, and from another complementary angle based in the study of African literatures, the relevance of a self-centred Afrophone discourse is also illustrated in Ngũgĩ wa Thiongo's influential project of "Decolonising the mind," which he has pursued persistently and successfully since the 1970s (e.g. Ngũgĩ 1981; 1986). Cultivating a programme for a socially and politically engaged Afrophone tradition of creative writing—by switching from English to his mother tongue Kikuyu as a Kenyan author—his case has proven the practical relevance and political significance of using an African language. For, as soon as his Kikuyu writings (first plays, then novels) became publicly visible, he was arrested and detained for working against the interests of the postcolonial state, and his works were banned. Notably, his writings had not really become more critical or radical than when written in English. But they had become widely accessible to a popular audience of common people, ordinary Kenyans whom he sought to address. With that, his writings had become truly dangerous to the postcolonial ruling elite—and indeed, the fictional freedom fighter hero Matigari, from his novel of the same name, was searched for by the Kenyan police.

Ngũgĩ's case has become paradigmatic for a specific pathway of Africa-centered postcolonial critique, and it has had inspirational value far beyond the field of literature—for the humanities and social sciences, and for philosophy itself. Engaging in such a project ultimately includes a commitment to proper mutual recognition between all languages involved (and their speakers), based in the global North or South, and it reflects a commitment to the vision of further intellectual exchange of mutual benefit in the future. More recently, Ngũgĩ challenged African philosophers directly, for not having put in enough effort into the active, foundational and creative use of African languages in African philosophy (Ngũgĩ 2013). The lack of such engagements, it can be argued—also with Mudimbe's desideratum of an African epistemological locus in mind—has been delaying the cultivation of Afrophone philosophical thinking and thereby to some extent obstructing the production of modern academic African philosophical literature in African languages (see also Rettova 2007 and Jeffers 2013, for efforts in this direction).[12] With a view to Mudimbe's critique with which I started this essay, of the lack of African discourses being grounded in an Africa-centred conceptual space, we can point to Ngũgĩ as an example—a particularly well-known one—that illustrates a politically conscious position of such a desirable conceptual self-centredness. In Ngũgĩ's case, this is demonstrated by an African intellectual who speaks in his mother tongue to an audience that far exceeds the number of speakers of the language he uses. Maybe, in some sense, Ngũgĩ and his decisive commitment to his own language, as an enabling conceptual reservoir (with a history) to be relearned and reshaped in order to be used to address challenges (and build visions, questions, and proposals in response), and to be translated and mediated across the world (Ngũgĩ 1981; 1993), can be seen as a possible role-model case for what Mudimbe anticipated with a view to the task, and the need, to take African epistemological loci as self-centred and self-conscious starting points for future endeavours in African philosophy.

12. Following a different pathway to make a related point, a study of Yoruba key concepts for knowledge and belief (along the lines of Quine's ordinary language philosophy) has shown the creative and critical potential of Yoruba language use in direct comparison with English (Hallen and Sodipo 1997; orig. 1986).

If then Ngũgĩ and his project can be seen to represent in some way also the realisation of a vision that Mudimbe had in mind, we could also see, earlier on, that the programmatic agendas of both Hountondji and Wiredu overlap in central terms with that of Mudimbe. And even though their ways of presenting their arguments, their reference points, their writing styles, and their scholarly affiliations are quite different from Mudimbe's, there is a clear consensus (or shared basic concern) among them that fundamental conceptual independence and self-reliance need to be fought and struggled for by African philosophers, as a priority without which fairly little can be said to have been achieved overall.

In the end, it seems, such a goal can only be realised by commitment to the priority of endogenous knowledge, language, and specific regional and local forms of expression, genres of discourse that represent and reflect intellectual histories, and that are themselves embedded in complex social histories. Mudimbe's work, then, encourages and pushes us (researchers working on, and thinking with Africa) to pursue further research constructively along those lines, exploring the existent diverse and dynamic traditions of African knowledge and intellectual practice and portraying them as rich and productive resources to think with, in the present. His work of critique, as I understand it, has cleared a good deal of the obstructive historical thickets and thereby provided important pathways for such kind of research. This, then, is dedicated to the understanding of the complex specifics of regional intellectual traditions, practices, and thinkers, while keeping the shared experiences and interests of Africa in mind.

For my own work that engages with knowledge, thinkers, and intellectual practice on the East African Swahili coast (e.g. Kresse 2007; 2009; 2018), Mudimbe's work has been a stimulating reference point, together with the writings of Hountondji and Wiredu. Mudimbe's emphasis on (need for, and the relevance of a) reversal from a focus on European to Africa-centred conceptual frameworks to guide empirically-based research and provide grounding, can hardly be overstated. It should appeal especially to the younger generation of African scholars today, those who are engaged in seeking to rewrite, enrich, and augment the field of African philosophy and intellectual history from particular regional perspectives, yet with a view to the whole.

However, it is also understandable how Mudimbe's writing has led to critique, too, for Mudimbe has not really pursued that kind of research himself. He has neither engaged closely with Afrophone texts (or concepts) in context, nor with regionally grounded religious or political practices. And, as conceptual reference points for him, as philosophical thinkers to provide guidance, he has confined himself almost exclusively to proponents of schools of European philosophy. So, when critics remark upon that as indications of ongoing reliance of a Europhone intellectual on Eurocentric thought (e.g. Kane 2012)—in tension with his goal as sketched out above—this aversion has to be understood and seen in this context.

5. An Afrotopia and the rewriting of the humanities —Sarr

Before a conclusion, it is beneficial to look at some continuities and overlaps (but also differences) between Mudimbe, one of the most senior African thinkers providing foundational conceptual grounding for the younger generation of thinkers today, and Felwine Sarr, a Senegalese proponent of that younger generation, who has recently engaged in programmatic considerations that resemble (or share certain features with) Mudimbe's basic terms and demands. For Sarr, more than thirty years on from the publication of *The Invention of Africa*, the vision of an intellectually liberated Africa does not seem so fundamentally different from the way in which Mudimbe (back then, in the 1980s) emphasised the need to establish "an African epistemological locus" at the centre of scholarship and all intellectual endeavours. But while for Mudimbe this seemed to remain a general reference point as part of a programmatic outlook to a future that was anticipated, for Felwine Sarr and his visions of an "Afrotopia" (laid out in a book of the same name) and a fundamentally revised and transformed project of global humanities, concrete tasks and goals as subfields and sub-projects are invoked and sketched out. These include understanding and rehabilitating African values and humanisms that are grounded in regional social histories; a critical theoretical rethinking of African cosmologies; aspirations to universal relevance, based on a critical self-consciousness, through the realisation of Africa's own potential (Sarr 2019a). These create, one could say, in their mutual intersection, the idea (or should I say "invention") of a newly grounded and somewhat self-recreated continent, proud and confident, intellectually able and versatile. In this vision, Africa roots its liberating project of building its future in a consciousness of the past, and of living traditions as resource for the present.

Sarr flags up the rewriting of the humanities from "Africa," as a realisable project that is in reach (Sarr 2019b). He sketches this out, to be pursued around an Africa-centred epistemological reference point for the transformative process of overcoming Eurocentrism. This is something that Mudimbe did not and perhaps could not do, and the difference in outlook and coverage taken on by these two thinkers of different generations is notable. The youthful Sarr, in a bold and visionary mode, sketched out a scenario of what an intellectually liberated Africa can look like, as an Afrotopia, and what it should build upon; he aims at pointing to Africa's possibilities and exploring its resources. In contrast, Mudimbe, as someone who biographically underwent existential processes of colonial education, postcolonial liberation and re-repression, and in the more doubting and perhaps realistic mode of a skeptic (who may like to see himself disproved), lays out multiple layers of historical entanglements and conceptual distortions that unavoidably characterise Africa's modern, postcolonial heritage. Yet seen in the bigger picture, both Sarr and Mudimbe can be seen to share basic goals and principles regarding the overcoming of external epistemic dominance, Africanism.

6. Interjection: Dimensions of struggling with Mudimbe

For many readers, dealing with Mudimbe's theoretical texts constitutes a struggle, as these are dense and full of diverse and wide-ranging references to Western (and other) intellectual history across the centuries, and written in long-winded and difficult language, making them at times almost inaccessible. In turn, readers may feel overawed and unable (or unwilling) to work them through more closely. This effect, that I experienced with students in classes and seminars, is regrettable, as Mudimbe's texts are unique in the way they take on challenges and work through some of the thickets of intellectual entanglements and the resulting (mis)representation of Africa.

Another dimension of struggling with Mudimbe has been through a critical engagement with his biographical entanglement in Eurocentric intellectual history. Mudimbe has been characterised as an "unhomely scholar" (Fraiture 2013, 182), an intellectual who spent long phases in exile—first in Belgium, and later on in the USA. His biographic trajectory has been determined by ongoing, overlapping and intersecting processes which in some ways also pushed tensions and self-contradictions. Taken out of his homely family background for educational purposes at a young age (undergoing schooling, missionary education, philosophical and theological studies and a phase of priesthood), Mudimbe's own experience also stands for a generation of this type of "clerical intellectuals" (van Binsbergen 2005). These were produced within the Belgian colonial system, and their sense of a meaningful connection to the conceptual frameworks of their surrounding African languages and historic religion was often fundamentally shaken (see also Fraiture and Orrells 2016). This is a sense also expressed by Mudimbe himself, in his novels and autobiographical writings.[13]

A critical reading of Mudimbe, portraying him as a biographically entangled African intellectual with an inadvertently Eurocentric perspective, was put forward by Wim van Binsbergen, who himself has a special biographical position of expertise in traditions of knowledge and their practice in Africa, having been initiated as a healer and diviner (*isangoma*) during his long-term fieldwork experiences in Zambia and Botswana (van Binsbergen 2003, 155–94).[14] Focusing on Mudimbe's *Tales of Faith: Religion as political performance in Central Africa* (1997), van Binsbergen argues that Mudimbe's account follows a Western epistemic perspective and thereby partly obstructs the view upon socially relevant historical African systems and practices of meaning (van Binsbergen 2005). He criticises Mudimbe for not providing more engagement with "African historical religion" as practised by ordinary people on the ground when discussing political ideology and religious practice in Central Africa (and he also disagrees with Mudimbe's selection of sources). Could this be seen to connect back to Mudimbe's own skeptical statement (quoted above) that it may seem almost impossible for contemporary African thinkers to position themselves outside the Western *episteme*?

The fundamental skepticism expressed by Mudimbe, about the dilemma of being stuck in Western epistemic dominance, seems somewhat confirmed here, illustrating a fundamental challenge that he himself could not fully resolve.[15] Yet in specific chapters of *The Invention of Africa* (i.e. The Patience of Philosophy) and *The Idea of Africa* (i.e. *Reprendre*), Mudimbe points to relevant research in African studies from a range of different disciplines, centring around endogenous forms and processes of knowledge, as a way forward. These make it possible, in his view, for readers to see a more appropriate and complex picture of African cultures and societies, and he recommends these studies for their potential to contribute to the envisaged shift of paradigms, from a Western to an Africa-centric one, overcoming Africanism.

Let me briefly connect these observations to my experience of teaching (that is, discussing the readings of) Mudimbe's project of addressing the

13. I am not so familiar with these, but I thank the editors for pointing this out.

14. He had dropped his disciplinary preference for anthropology in favour of a professorship on intercultural philosophy (in Rotterdam).

15. In contrast, as an anthropologist van Binsbergen was able to acquire a body of endogenous knowledge during extensive fieldwork interactions, which he uses as a kind of Africa-centered resource also for his own critical engagements.

challenge of Africanism. Discussions of *The Invention of Africa* in the classroom were usually tough going. Mudimbe's theoretical orientations are diverse and demanding, and the historical range covered may seem overwhelming (from Herodotus via Latin and early Italian and Portuguese travellers to missionary and colonial authors of Francophone and Anglophone kinds, to the African-American thinkers of the 19th and 20th centuries, and finally the early participants in the debate over African philosophy). While students were intrigued and animated when discussing the programmatic introduction and the quotation presented above, they were often asking why the argument built and presented by Mudimbe in the lengthy and testing chapters of the book were not more accessible and explicit. The bottom line that class discussions arrived at (the last time I read Mudimbe with students at Columbia University) was that he needed to be seen as a central figure for the historically grounded and ongoing critique of the processes of constitution of knowledge about "Africa," pushing his readers to see the necessary long-term histories and effects of power-knowledge relationships. Mudimbe was admired for the conceptual approach of fundamental critique, the Foucauldian kind of archaeology of knowledge on Africanism worked through in response, the historical scope of his work, and the sensitivity with which he presented authors and their arguments in his accounts.

Yet there was also a shared sense that, while a critical historical account was delivered and a theoretical approach for further critique and actual reform and transformation of African studies was presented by him, it was not part of Mudimbe's own agenda to conduct fieldwork, empirical research in African contexts, or to engage in textual studies of living oral discourses in African languages (or archival readings in them). In class, we ended with open-ended discussions as to how far Mudimbe's work itself may have prepared, encouraged, or even pushed for such research to take place—and here opinions differed. Mudimbe was seen as an immensely impressive critic, a versatile reader, and a documenter of vast historical materials that concerned the distorted perspective of Africanism by students who managed to get a grip on the difficult readings that his writings represented. However, some students regretted that his accounts gave us little insight into the empirical universes of the internal dynamics of the contestations and negotiations of knowledge in Africa, of its forms, genres, and languages—even though he sensitised his readers so much to these aspects. In other words, Mudimbe, in class discussions, was recognised as a historian, philosopher, and highly intellectually versatile cultural critic—giving inspiration and guidance. But the guidance given seemed articulated largely by means of reference to Western thinkers and conceptual paradigms; it did not explore the specifics, or the variety, or the complex internal dynamics of African epistemes.

But not only students have struggled with reading Mudimbe, some professors have done so too. Henry Odera Oruka (1944–95), the influential Kenyan philosopher who pushed for fieldwork on African philosophical traditions with his sage philosophy project (Odera Oruka 1990-1991), can be invoked as an example of how even senior academic figures too struggled to understand Mudimbe's writings. Odera Oruka was unhappy with Mudimbe's project, as far as he understood it. However, judging from Odera Oruka's few published sentences of critique, it seems he may not have understood him too well. Neither did he realise that his own sage philosophy project could be seen as a complementary constructive part to Mudimbe's project of critique. In his essay, "African philosophy in the 1990s," he even attacked Mudimbe as a "grand ethnophilosopher" (1997, 113) and accused him of "imperializing scholarship" (ibid., 112). To me it seems that Mudimbe's critique of the colonising structure of essentialising knowledge of Africa led Odera Oruka to have the impression that it was Mudimbe who was advocating an essentialising perspective.[16]

Conclusion: Beyond Africanism

While working to prepare a pathway for subsequent research on Africa that could follow Africa-centred paradigms, Mudimbe's concern may not have been to work out specific approaches that he or others could use for constructive empirically based research—perhaps this would have been beyond the limits of what he could do. Working toward the goal of overcoming Africanism by means of critique, he can be seen, I think, to be establishing a new starting point for others (the next generation), to enable them to go further. It is intriguing to see how Mudimbe, as a prominent figure advocating and pushing for a fundamental critique of colonial effects, on conceptual frameworks and the organisation of lived realities, has himself been existentially entangled, by way of his own biographical trajectory, in possibly unresolvable dynamics of self-positioning. Laying out the scope and dimensions of Africanism as part of his critique and with a view to its overcoming, he does not himself engage in concrete

16. Mudimbe may have been seen by Odera Oruka as taking a position that not only identifies and critiques, but also itself actively takes on and perpetuates a mechanism of "othering," of essential difference. It seems to me that Odera Oruka here was irritated by an approach and a project that did not make sense to him at first glance, and which he did not seek to understand further. Mudimbe's thinking is more complex and demanding than Oruka saw and acknowledged here. On rethinking Odera Oruka, see Kresse and Nyarwath (in press).

steps forward as part of such overcoming but in some ways even seems to perpetuate a conceptual reliance upon Western epistemes. In conclusion, an overlapping interest among all authors treated here—Hountondji, Wiredu, Ngũgĩ and Sarr—seems to lie in the fact that they address the shared fundamental dilemma of Africanism that Mudimbe outlined for us: how to overcome, and move beyond, the dominance of a Western epistemological order? The quest for a foundational basis for self-reliant and independent thinking and philosophising in and from Africa is shared. And while Mudimbe has not shown himself engaged in research on (or with) African languages in his academic works (as far as I know), this certainly is within the central scope of his interest, and as we have seen, he has been supporting research in that direction.[17]

In the preface to *The Idea of Africa*, Mudimbe states that "the intellectual space covered outlines Africa as a paradigm of difference" (1994, xii). Taking *Africa as a paradigm of difference*, then, is made productive as an understanding of what Africanism means. In related terms, Mudimbe comments on the ambivalence of the "colonial library," as both an outcome of and a resource for the construction of such a paradigm of difference. This is something that he needed to work through in order to capture the workings of Africanism. Mudimbe explains that he "tried to circumvent its epistemological violence by including its nightmares as well as the fragile presuppositions of its ponderous knowledge" (1994, xii), acknowledging that in the wider pool of resources that constitute the colonial library, remnants of Africa's valuable knowledge may also be found—thus we must not simply dismiss these sources and leave them aside.[18]

With a view to the outcome of his own critical interrogation, Mudimbe points to the existential meaning and limitations of his struggle. He hopes (he writes) that readers agree "that the task of bringing philosophy to some of its own limits and metaphors in social science, and that of philosophy's ambiguous contacts with unphilosophical discourses" justify his commitment "to what it essentially means to be an *African* and a *philosopher* today" (1988, xi). This has to be struggled with, and one needs to critically come to terms with. Yet the historical entanglements, collective, individual and biographical, and in terms of fields and disciplines, may

17. Ousmane Kane (2012) has raised harsh criticism of Mudimbe as an exclusively Europhone-oriented intellectual—too harsh, in my view, as he did not acknowledge the relevance that Mudimbe's critique has (or can have) for the work on Afrophone intellectual traditions.

18. I am thinking here, for example, of the missionary sources on Central Kongo that became central resources for conceptually oriented historical studies by Janzen and MacGaffey (1974), which they also continued to conduct individually.

be impossible to resolve: for Mudimbe; for the disciplines; and for us. The pathway is, as Mudimbe shows, to constructively engage with these entanglements from where we are positioned, as scholars, and as individuals with our own respective biographical trajectories, and our abilities and limitations, based either in the global North or South.

The "wider authority" (also in the envisioned constructive project) that Mudimbe prefers to invoke, consists in, as he says, "intellectual discourses as a critical library." Mudimbe also seeks to invoke (prefaced by an "if I could"), "the experience of rejected forms of wisdom which are not part of the structures of political power and scientific knowledge" (1988, x–xi). This, as I understand, should be a resource for critical, empirically-based reconstructive research on African knowledge and conceptual frameworks—which themselves can then become resources and provide guidelines for us to think with today. The fact that he injects the phrase "if I could" to me highlights his admirable humility as an intellectual, a consciousness of his own limitations. As discussed above, he may not be the one best equipped to pursue these empirically-based pathways of research; but he is sensitive to their relevance and identifies them as crucial. And this is indeed where a general demand exists, for interdisciplinary research, between history, anthropology, and literary studies. Also, for the wider project of "re-writing the humanities from Africa" that Felwine Sarr is pushing for, there is need for complementary collaboration between different intellectual traditions and institutional resources from the global South and the North, in order to transform the humanities globally, into a richer, more diverse and fairly balanced, and more accessible shared resource for human beings from anywhere (Pollock 2015). In this way, I think, Mudimbe can be understood as also being highly constructive. He does point us the right way, sensitively and with a perceptive view to the actual challenges and complexities that need to be worked through and overcome.

To conclude, Mudimbe has contributed fundamentally to both the *critical* and the *constructive* venture of the project of building a pathway for overcoming Africanism, and for transforming the study of Africa and its intellectual traditions and knowledge-oriented practices toward a more Africa-centred scholarship. On the level of the fundamental critique of Africanism, a Eurocentric force to be overcome—what Wiredu called the "negative" aspect of conceptual decolonisation and liberation—Mudimbe, able and trained like no other African philosopher in terms of breadth and depth of Western scholarship, did work through the effects and repercussions of the colonial library and its historical antecedents on the image of Africa within Western-dominated scholarship. And he did so in a manner that showed this ground covered. This then has enabled (and continues to enable) others to concentrate on more substantial, and construct, empirically-based and regionally-grounded work on/in Africa, and forward-looking tasks. If it seems that Mudimbe has less to offer on this second level, in constructive terms, what Wiredu called the "positive" aspect of working on Africa-centric conceptualisation and building Africa-centric theory, we should acknowledge that without his fundamental groundwork the conceptual thickets of Africanist entanglements could not be cleared in the same way—nor could the sowing of new seeds and plants to come be prepared in the same way. We also need to understand that for such anticipated work of sowing and planting, different and complementary sets of qualifications and expertise are needed in order to go ahead and take conceptual liberation and new substantial contributions of Africa-centred theory forward. Those, like Sarr, now working constructively, creatively, and collaboratively on wide-ranging projects along such lines, owe much to the enabling work by those of the older generation and especially Mudimbe—who personally experienced Africa's problematic transformation from colonial to postcolonial challenges and dilemmas—clearing thickets and the creating spaces for them to do so.

References

Alix, Florian. 2008. "Foucault déplacé: réécriture chez E.W. Said et V.Y. Mudimbe." *Malfini: Publication exploratoire des espaces francophones*. http://malfini.ens-lyon.fr/document.php?id=124 [archive].

Barber, Karin 2007. *The Anthropology of Texts, Persons and Publics: Oral and Written Culture in Africa and Beyond*. New Departures in Anthropology. Cambridge: Cambridge University Press. https://doi.org/10.1017/CBO9780511619656.

Diagne, Souleymane Bachir, and Jean-Loup Amselle. 2020 [2018]. *In Search of Africa(s)*. London: Polity Press.

Diouf, Mamadou 2017. "Humanities after Apartheid." *Comparative Studies of South Asia, Africa, and the Middle East* 37, no. 1: 117–20. https://doi.org/10.1215/1089201x-3821357.

Duebgen, Franziska, and Stefan Skupien. 2019. *Paulin Hountondji: African Philosophy as Critical Universalism*. London: Palgrave Pivot. https://doi.org/10.1007/978-3-030-01995-2.

Fabian, Johannes. 1996. *Remembering the Present: Painting and Popular History in Zaire*. Berkeley, CA: University of California Press.

Fraiture, Pierre-Philippe. 2013. *V.Y. Mudimbe: Undisciplined Africanism*. Liverpool: Liverpool University Press.

Fraiture, Pierre-Philippe, and Daniel Orrells, eds. 2016. *The Mudimbe Reader*. Charlottesville: University of Virginia Press.

Grosz-Ngaté, Maria. 2020. "Knowledge and Power: Perspectives on the Production and Decolonization of African/ist Knowledges." *African Studies Review* 63, no. 4: 689–718. https://doi.org/10.1017/asr.2020.102.

Hountondji, Paulin J. 1996 [1976]. *African Philosophy: Myth and Reality.* Bloomington, IN: Indiana University Press.

Hountondji, Paulin J. 1983. "Reason and Tradition." in *Philosophy and Cultures*, edited by H. Odera Oruka and D.A. Masolo, 132–39. Nairobi: Bookwise.

Hountondji, Paulin J. 1990. "Scientific Dependence in Africa Today." *Research in African Literatures* 21, no. 3: 5–15. https://www.jstor.org/stable/3819631.

Hountondji, P.J., ed. 1997. *Endogenous Knowledge: Research Trails.* Dakar: CODESRIA. https://doi.org/10.57054/codesria.pub.382.

Janzen, John M. 1992. *Ngoma: Discourses of Healing in Central and Southern Africa.* Berkeley, CA: University of California Press.

Janzen, John M., and Wyatt MacGaffey. 1974. *An Anthology of Kongo Religion: Primary Texts from Lower Zaire.* Lawrence, KS: University of Kansas Press.

Jeffers, Chike, ed. 2013. *Listening to Ourselves: A Multilingual Anthology of African Philosophy*. Albany, NY: SUNY University Press.

Kane, Ousmane Oumar. 2012. *Non-europhone Intellectuals.* Dakar: CODESRIA. https://doi.org/10.57054/codesria.pub.84.

Kresse, Kai. 2007. *Philosophizing in Mombasa: Knowledge, Islam, and Intellectual Practice on the Swahili Coast.* Edinburgh: Edinburgh University Press.

Kresse, Kai. 2009. "Knowledge and Intellectual Practice in a Swahili Context: 'Wisdom' and the Social Dimensions of Knowledge." *Africa: Journal of the International African Institute* 79, no. 1: 148–67. https://doi.org/10.3366/E000197200800065X.

Kresse, Kai. 2018. *Swahili Muslim Publics and Postcolonial Experience.* Bloomington, IN: Indiana University Press.

Kresse, Kai, ed. 2005. "Reading Mudimbe. Special Issue." *Journal of African Cultural Studies* 17, no. 1. https://www.jstor.org/stable/i388500.

Kresse, Kai, and Trevor H.J. Marchand, eds. 2009. "Knowledge in Practice: Expertise and the Transmission of Knowledge in Africa. Special Issue." *Africa: Journal of the International African Institute* 79, no. 11. https://www.cambridge.org/core/journals/africa/issue/CDC208A412EA24686C93A2D015A0689A.

Kresse, Kai, and Oriare Nyarwath, eds. 2022. *Re-thinking Sage Philosophy: Interdisciplinary Perspectives*. Lanham: Lexington Books.

Kresse, Kai, and Kwasi Wiredu. 2000. "Language Matters!" *Polylog: Forum for Intercultural Philosophy* 2. http://them.polylog.org/2/dwk-en.htm [archive].

Lambek, Michael. 1993. *Knowledge and Practice in Mayotte: Local Discourses of Islam, Sorcery and Spirit Possession*. Toronto: Toronto University Press.

MacGaffey, Wyatt. 2000. *Kongo Political Culture: The Conceptual Challenge of the Particular.* Bloomington, IN: Indiana University Press.

Mudimbe, V.Y. 1988. *The Invention of Africa. Gnosis, Philosophy and the Order of Knowledge*. Bloomington and Indianapolis, IN: Indiana University Press; London: James Currey.

Mudimbe, V.Y. 1994. *The Idea of Africa.* Bloomington, IN: Indiana University Press.

Mudimbe, V.Y. 1997. *Tales of Faith: Religion as Political Performance in Central Africa.* London. Bloomsbury Publishing.

Ndlovu-Gatsheni, Sabelo J. 2018. *Epistemic Freedom in Africa: Deprovincialization and Decolonization*. London: Routledge. https://doi.org/10.4324/9780429492204.

Ngũgĩ wa Thiong'o. 1981. *Writers in Politics*. Nairobi: Heinemann.

Ngũgĩ wa Thiong'o. 1986. *Decolonizing the Mind*. Nairobi: Heinemann.

Ngũgĩ wa Thiong'o. 1993. *Moving the Centre: The Struggle for Cultural Freedoms*. Nairobi: East African Educational Publishers.

Ngũgĩ wa Thiong'o. 2013. "Tongue and Pen: A Challenge to Philosophers from Africa." *Journal of African Cultural Studies* 25, no. 2: 158–63. https://doi.org/10.1080/13696815.2013.789251.

Odera Oruka, Henry. 1990/1991. *Sage Philosophy Indigenous Thinkers and Modern Debate on African Philosophy*. Leiden: Brill; Nairobi: ACTS Press. https://doi.org/10.1163/9789004452268.

Odera Oruka, Henry. 1997. "African Philosophy in the 1990s." In *Sagacious Reasoning: Henry Odera Oruka in memoriam*, edited by Anke Graness and Kai Kresse, 101–18. Frankfurt: Peter Lang.

Osha, Sanya. 2011. *Postethnophilosophy*. Amsterdam: Rodopi.

Pollock, Sheldon. 2017. "The Columbia Global Humanities Project." *Comparative Studies of South Asia, Africa, and the Middle East* 37, no. 1: 113–116. https://doi.org/10.1215/1089201x-3821345.

Rettova, Alena. 2007. *Afrophone Philosophies: Myth or Reality*. Prague: Zdenek Susa.

Sarr, Felwine. 2019a. *Afrotopia*. Minneapolis, MN: University of Minnesota Press.

Sarr, Felwine. 2019b. "Rewriting the Humanities from Africa: Toward an Ecology of Knowledge" (manuscript). First Berlin Southern Theory Lecture, 11 Dec. 2019. Berlin, Ethnologisches Museum. Published online by Leibniz-Zentrum Moderner Orient on 19 December 2019. https://youtu.be/eU3U4ExAsdI?si=JuL3hZhGHzR_fKow.

Van Binsbergen, Wim M.J. 2003. *Intercultural Encounters: African and Anthropological Lessons Towards a Philosophy of Interculturality.* Berlin: Lit-Verlag.

Van Binsbergen, Wim M.J. 2005. "'An Incomprehensible Miracle': Central African Clerical Intellectualism versus African Historical Religion,' *Journal of African Cultural Studies* 17, no. 1: 11–65. https://www.jstor.org/stable/4141301.

Wiredu, Kwasi. 1996. "The Need for Conceptual Decolonization in African Philosophy." In *Cultural Universals and Particulars*, 136–44. Bloomington, IN: Indiana University Press.

Interrogating an African *Gnosis* in the Analysis of Kenyan Literature

Alex Nelungo Wanjala

Introduction

V.Y. Mudimbe analyses "knowledge on Africa" (Mudimbe 1988, ix) as a social construct arising from a discourse on and about the continent and its people; and examines texts generated by thinkers and scholars in various fields such as anthropology, theology, history, literature and philosophy, in a quest to determine the meaning of that knowledge. In relation to that, he also analyses "African knowledge" (Mudimbe 1988, ix) or what he terms "African *gnosis*" (Mudimbe 1988, ix).[1] As he states:

> "J. Fabian used the notion of *gnosis* in his analysis of a charismatic African movement [...]. [T]he wider frame [of this notion] seems better suited to the range of problems addressed, all of which are based on a preliminary question: to what extent can one speak of an African knowledge, and in what sense? Etymologically, *gnosis* is related to *gnosko*, which in the ancient Greek means "to know." Specifically, *gnosis* means seeking to know, inquiry, methods of knowing, investigation, and even acquaintance with someone. Often the word is used in a more specialized sense, that of higher and esoteric knowledge, and thus it refers to a structured, common, and conventional knowledge, but one strictly under the control of specific procedures for its use as well as its transmission. *Gnosis* is, consequently, different from *doxa*, or opinion, and on the other hand, cannot be confused with *episteme*, or general intellectual configuration." (Mudimbe 1988, ix).

In Mudimbe's deployment of the term *gnosis*, we observe his desire to go deeper than simple conventional knowledge in or about Africa, in order to encompass an understanding and evaluation of the cultural and intellectual conditions of possibility of this knowledge.

1. *The Invention of Africa* begins with the problem of defining "African Philosophy" within the strict confines and historical traditions of the academic discipline of Philosophy. According to Mudimbe, the only way "the defined framework of the discipline" would apply to "African traditional systems of thought," would be either "metaphorically, or [...] from a historicist perspective" (Mudimbe 1988, ix). He thus introduces the notion of African *gnosis* to address the problems of defining, more generally, African knowledge.

Given Africa's history, an analysis of African knowledge through the consideration of an African *gnosis* should notably address this question: "How can one reconcile the demands of an identity and the credibility of a claim to knowledge with the process of refounding and reassuming an interrupted historicity within the representations?" (Mudimbe 1988, 183). Such an approach would act as a pathway to what Mudimbe refers to as *la chose du texte*: "that which is out there in the African traditions, insistent and discreet, determining the traditions yet independent from them" (Mudimbe 1988, 183). Using this approach to explore literary texts remains rare in academic treatises on Kenyan literature, hence my attempt in this chapter.

Mudimbe demonstrates that the idea of Africa has emerged through a discourse that mainly responds to the ideological interests of the various practitioners that have focused upon the subject (Mudimbe 1988, 1994). Placing Western researchers who depicted Africans as primitive savages at one extreme, and African "traditionalists" who perceive precolonial Africa as having had its own approach to knowledge at the other, Mudimbe illustrates how in the contemporary period there has developed a middle ground comprising intellectuals who have attempted to use a sympathetic approach to understanding the African subject—via an interrogation of African traditional practices in a manner that Ali Mazrui (2005) has termed the retraditionalisation of Africa—and the academics from Africa who have engaged in classical philosophical practices to address concerns related to the continent. Mudimbe, who is not swayed by the notion that Africa may have had an existing philosophy that would need to be recovered, and who also does not believe in the superiority of Western philosophy, instead chooses as his method for examining representational discourse a middle ground between Claude Lévi-Strauss' method of studying non-Western societies, and Michel Foucault's archaeology of knowledge. He states that one of the objectives of his study is "to think about and propose reasonable modalities for the integration of African civilisations into modernity, this in accordance with critical thinking and scientific reason, for the purpose of the liberation of man" (Mudimbe 1988, 175). D.A. Masolo sums up Mudimbe's approach thus:

> "The neostructuralism of Foucault which Mudimbe endorses has been a milestone in giving a counterposition to this "Westernization" by offering a softer version of relativism which encourages contact rather than estrangement between diverse rationalities or cultural perspectives. And one important way in which they do this is to eliminate the gap between the "rational" and the "irrational" by defining knowledge as paradigms of discourses and representations." (Masolo 1991, 1009)

Given the dearth of scholarship that uses Mudimbe's ideas in the field of East African literature in general and Kenyan literature in particular, I believe it is useful to make an attempt at a preliminary investigation on how his approach can be used to interrogate the African *gnosis* presented and the discourse expressed in our literature. To do so, I will focus on Ngũgĩ wa Thiong'o, Kenya's leading author nominated several times for the Nobel Prize, and Grace Ogot, one of Kenya's best-known female writers who published several novels and short stories, both in English and Dholuo.

1. Ngũgĩ wa Thiong'o's *Matigari*

Ngũgĩ's writing career began in the early sixties with the publication of his first novel *Weep Not, Child* (1964). The novel was quite successful and was followed shortly thereafter by *The River Between* (1965) and *A Grain of Wheat* (1967). These three novels provided a foundational narrative of the colonial period and of decolonisation in Kenya, and gave a vivid description of the socioeconomic and cultural changes experienced by members of the Agikuyu community. They also reflected Ngũgĩ's education at Makerere University, in Uganda, where he was trained as part of Africa's emerging intellectual elite, studying the classics of English literature, writing compositions and essays for his coursework and short stories for magazines such as *Penpoint*, a student magazine. It is therefore no surprise that Ngũgĩ's earlier novels were written in the modernist tradition of Western literature, although they contributed to establishing an African tradition of novel writing (Wanjala, 2003). With a view to analysing an African *gnosis*, one could therefore draw a parallel between what Mudimbe describes as the foundation of African philosophical practice—that fitted quite comfortably into the mainstream of Western philosophy—and Ngũgĩ's early novels, which rely on a Western aesthetic in delivering an African perspective on history.

Ngũgĩ's trilogy was followed by the publication of an anthology of short stories, *Secret Lives, and Other Stories* (1975), and after a hiatus of ten years, the publication of his fourth novel, *Petals of Blood* (1977). The novel marked a shift in focus from his earlier novels, in that it demonstrates the betrayal of the dreams of independence through the actions of fellow Africans who belong to the ruling elite and the intellectual classes. In doing so, Ngũgĩ depicted what Phyllis Taoua has described as "the postcolonial condition" (Taoua 2009). This shift is quite significant for African literature, as it signals a form of class struggle in post-independence African society, and the commitment of the writer to the masses. In Ngũgĩ's own words, as documented in Carol Sicherman's *Ngugi wa Thiong'o: The Making of a Rebel*:

> "Previously there was a tendency to have peasant and worker characters but give them the vacillating mentality and world outlook of the petite bourgeoisie. This is evident especially in my portrayal of peasant characters in *A Grain of Wheat*. What I have tried to do in *Petals of Blood* is to depict peasant and worker characters in their world outlook and also in their own view of classes and their relationships within their struggle, and especially as a people capable of freeing themselves from the clutches of their enemies, because this is historically true." (Sicherman 1990, 25)

We could thus surmise that in his fourth novel, Ngũgĩ mobilised the modernist framework of socialist realism to articulate issues that resonated with the postcolonial Kenyan society at large. These issues are similar to the neo-Marxist ideology developed in the 1970s by African philosophers such as Paulin Hountondji who, according to Mudimbe, would come up with "ideological clarification in order to oppose illusions, mystifications and lies that continue to exist in Africa and about Africa," promote a "true understanding of the best in international philosophy, including Marxism (...)" and eventually undertake "a paradoxical task—stepping out of philosophy in order to meet and have dialogue with social reality" (Mudimbe 1988, 168).

Ngũgĩ's work as a playwright led him to work closely with members of his ethnic community on the development of the arts as a means of depicting social realities. After the formation of a cultural centre in his home village of Kamiriithu, Ngũgĩ started working with the locals to produce plays in Gĩkũyũ that addressed issues close to the plight of workers and peasants, and revised the official versions of history that had been promoted during colonial times and also in the postcolonial period. He announced during the launch of his fourth novel, in the presence of his mother, that his future writing would be in Gĩkũyũ so that his works would be understandable to peasants like her. Since that time, which coincided with the production of the play in Gĩkũyũ *Ngaahika Ndeenda* (*I will Marry When I Want*), Ngũgĩ's novels, such as *Caitaani Mutharabaini* (1980), *Matigari ma Njiruungi* (1986), *Murogi wa Kagogo* (2004), *Kenda Muiyuru* (2018), have all been written and published in Gĩkũyũ first, then translated into other languages.

For the purposes of this chapter, I will focus on one of Ngũgĩ's novels that was originally published in Gĩkũyũ, *Matigari* (1987)—originally published as *Matigari ma Njiruungi* (1986)—and interrogate the African *gnosis* depicted through the text. *Matigari* stylistically merges a Gĩkũyũ oral narrative about an old man named Ndiiro with biblical allegory through a messianic character who has come to deliver the masses from social evils, in order to depict the betrayal of independence by the current leadership of an African country, and the need for a revolution to achieve the goals of the struggle for independence. As Gbemisola Adeoti explains:

> "Matigari is like the old man, Ndiiro, who in the traditional story that inspired the novel looms large in his simultaneous presence and absence as 'a force, a god, a destiny.' But apart from the traditional source, Ngũgĩ draws on the biblical framework on the second coming of Jesus Christ. According to the scripture, Jesus, after his death, resurrection and ascension to heaven is expected to come back to redeem the world. The triumphant return of Matigari from the forest, wearing the belt of peace, recreates in him a messianic figure; a prince of peace. The biblical allusion is central to the plot and the characterisation in the novel as Matigari embodies hope and courage for the oppressed in his quest for truth and justice." (Adeoti 2016, 9)

Ngũgĩ, in an interview with Maya Jaggi (1989), explains that the character Matigari, should not be seen as an individual, but as a representative character, just like Ndiiro in the oral narrative on which the novel is partly based. *Matigari* could also represent a collectivity, which in this case could be seen as the workers, the peasants, or the Mau Mau who fought for Kenya's independence. In a related manner, *Matigari* is not meant to cover a specific period or space either. Using such literary features of orality, the novel could be seen as narrating the perpetual quest for truth and justice by a collective, who in this instance seek to find an end to neocolonialism in a postcolonial African society. In posing such a view, it is evident that Ngũgĩ attempted to articulate African mythology and Marxism.

This position is affirmed by Simon Gikandi, who explains that the meaning of the word *Matigari* in Gĩkũyũ popular culture shifted, from referring to dregs or leftovers, to signifying metaphorically, during the Mau Mau struggle, those who had left to the forest and engaged in Kenya's liberation struggle; and then the fighters who had not returned from the forest after independence. According to Gikandi, the post-independence period saw a growing disenchantment in which those fighters acquired a mythical status and were perceived as potential saviours, who would return and rescue the masses from their current predicament. Their second coming would thus in a way be the fulfilment of a messianic prophecy. As such, according to Gikandi, the word *Matigari* by the late 1960s had taken on a revolutionary significance; that of the reversal of the betrayal of independence by returnee Mau Mau fighters (Gikandi 1991, 162).

Therefore, the title of the novel is not used to simply name a character, but to describe an event, related not only to Kenya's history, but also to its future. This helps our understanding of Ngũgĩ's statement in the interview cited earlier: we can only grasp the meaning of the text if we read it not only through the lenses of realism, but also by cultivating an understanding of the literary features of African oral narratives. Gikandi goes on in his essay to examine whether Ngũgĩ, in his writing of *Matigari* in Gĩkũyũ, achieves an epistemological break from the tradition in which his previous novels were framed. He establishes that Ngũgĩ attempts to strike a balance between the realism of historical representation, the reason fighters went to the forest, the current postcolonial situation, and Matigari's mythical powers that enable him to be at several places and be multiple personalities within the narrative. Gikandi also describes how Ngũgĩ uses simple language, ostensibly to appeal to his target audience, the masses rather than the intellectual classes. He points out that this simplification of language is only a difficulty in the translated version of the text, and that the problems of translation are also evident in the very meaning of the text: even the meaning of the title changes, from describing "Matigari" as an event in which the "remnants" from past struggles provide hope for future liberation in the Gĩkũyũ original, to that of naming "Matigari" as an individual character in the English translation, who might have the power to provide some hope for the future, but does not pose the same threat to the current political establishment. Gikandi thus sees a paradox in the translated version of the text, which negates the authority of the original text:

> "Implicit in this dilemma is the problem of what I will call the epistemology of translation. Simply put, the relation between *Matigari Ma Njiruungi* and *Matigari* is not one of equality: the two texts function in a political situation where English is more powerful than Gĩkũyũ. If Ngũgĩ's intention was to make the Gĩkũyũ text the great original to which all translations would be subordinated, this intention is defeated not only by the political repression of *Matigari Ma Njiruungi*, but by the act of translation itself. In short, the eloquent English translation of *Matigari Ma Njiruungi* defeats Ngũgĩ's intention of restoring the primacy of African language as the mediator of an African experience." (Gikandi 1991,166)

This observation aptly illustrates the bind identified by Mudimbe when interrogating African *gnosis*: the distortion of African realities and meanings expressed in foreign asymmetric discourses. However, the problem of interrogating an African *gnosis* from a discursive reading of *Matigari* is not only limited to the losses arising from translation. There are several other factors, such as the period of history covered in the novel, which is fairly recent. The knowledge revealed in the narrative of *Matigari* does not contain any specificities that would be tied to an ontology of the Agikuyu community. Rather, it is based on Western constructs regarding class and revolutions, imported into the oral narrative structure of the novel, then tied in with another Western construct of biblical allusion.

Through this continued exploitation of the tenets of Marxism and of a Christian worldview, Ngũgĩ unconsciously sticks to Western aesthetic forms. We could thus place his philosophical position in his writing of *Matigari* on the same plane as that of his novels written in English. In regard to whether *la chose du texte* is revealed, the answer is therefore negative. Despite the incorporation of some aspects of a Kenyan oral narrative, Ngũgĩ's *Matigari* is a neo-Marxist novel shaped by Western philosophical, political and religious categories.

2. Grace Ogot's *The Strange Bride*

The second writer that I will focus on when interrogating the existence of an African *gnosis* in Kenyan literature is Grace Ogot. Her publishing career ran in tandem with Ngũgĩ's: she started writing and publishing in English—her first novel was *The Promised Land* in 1966—before moving on to write in a local language, Dholuo, with the same desire to communicate with the previous generations and with the masses. Ogot's publications in Dholuo include texts such as *Ber Wat* (1981), *Aloo Kod Apul-Apul* (1981), *Miaha* (1983). Some of her works were published after she passed away in 2015. These include *Simbi Nyaima—The Lake that Sank* (2018), *The Royal Bead* (2018), *Princess Nyilaak* (2018); novels that are based on Luo traditional oral narratives.

The Promised Land appeared shortly after the publication of Ngũgĩ's first two novels. Both Ngũgĩ and Ogot were driven by the same impulses in writing their early novels: "Ogot suggests that a kind of regional nationalism inspired them both when they were made aware at the 1962 Makerere conference on African literature of the relative 'literary barrenness' of East Africa" (Stratton 1994, 59). Ogot's first novel is set in the colonial period, just after the Second World War. It gives a realistic depiction of Luo traditional life at the time and goes a long way to describe Luo culture in an ethnographic manner. It also grafts elements of the oral tale into its narration, and privileges preternatural elements to advance its plot (Wanjala 2007). In grafting the oral tale to a form that is alien to it (the novel), Ogot marked a first in Kenyan literature: publishing a novel that appealed to both the masses and the literary elite.

Paradoxically, the critical reception of *The Promised Land* was not a warm one. As a result, her subsequent short novel *The Graduate* (1980) was quite different in style and content. But it is only through her third novel *Miaha* (1983), that Ogot finally achieved her dream of writing in

Dholuo. *Miaha* is based on a Luo myth that describes how the people of the community of Got Owaga, who originally lived in harmony with nature and with their deity Were Nyakalaga, under the kind and benevolent leadership of a village chief known as Were Ochak, fell from grace due to the "evil" machinations of Nyawir, a young bride who was betrothed to and married Owiny, one of Were Ochak's sons. The novel describes how, because of Nyawir's interference, Were Nyakalaga, who interacted directly with the community, was annoyed and moved away from the hill that he inhabited to a far-off mountain where he could no longer be physically accessed. This marked the end of the idyllic life led by the members of the community: whereas hard work had been done using an automatic hoe and an automatic axe provided by their deity, they now had to use physical force to cultivate their land and build their houses. *Miaha* was thus based on an explanatory tale explaining the roots of Luo traditions and culture. An analysis of the English translation of the novel, titled *The Strange Bride* (1989), would demonstrate how Ogot managed, through interpreting a Luo myth, to give details on traditional Luo culture concerning events such as birth, courtship, betrayal, marriage, and on various rituals undertaken in the everyday lives of the members of the community (Wanjala A.N. 2016). Such details give the novel its aspect of realism and help in the preservation of the cultural memory of the community.

In presenting us with these explanations regarding Luo culture; by focusing on this village named Got Owaga, metonymy for Luoland; by incorporating in her writing, elements derived from orality such as a tale that incorporates the belief in the supernatural; by eschewing aspects of historicity related to a Western worldview; by bringing out the consciousness of the subaltern classes in Kenya as to the origins of their societies and how they entered into an African "modernity"; the novel "locks out the European tradition even while exploiting the written form" (Wanjala A.N. 2016, 169), Ogot contributes to an African *gnosis à la* Mudimbe, and *Miaha*, and *The Strange Bride* can be said to expose *la chose du texte.*

Conclusion

In this chapter, I have attempted a reading of the novels of two iconic writers from Kenya, in a manner that relates their literary work to Mudimbe's quest for an African *gnosis*. There may be many reasons why Ogot's novels, especially those written in Dholuo, seem to come closest, one of them being that Ogot does not belong to the class of intellectuals who have received a Western education from the early years up to university level. As Gayatri Spivak demonstrates in *An Aesthetic Education in the Era of*

Globalization (2012), such intellectual trajectories lead scholars, writers and critics to have a "double take" that is subconsciously manifest in their writing. She prescribes that they must "learn to unlearn" in order to speak to or for the subaltern (Spivak, 1988). However, writers such as Ogot are not given prominence by the critical establishment; their works are not placed within the literary canon of African literature. There is therefore a need to give serious attention to literary texts that attempt to present an indigenous African worldview, without locking them out for addressing what has been viewed as a "closed past."

My analysis is by no means conclusive, as there are many texts by Mudimbe, Ngũgĩ and Ogot which have not been considered in this chapter, such as the recent novels written in African languages: *Kenda Muiyuru* (2018) by Ngũgĩ, *Simbi Nyaima—The Lake that Sank* (2018), *The Royal Bead* (2018), and *Princess Nyilaak* (2018) by Ogot. It is my hope that this expository study will give other researchers the impetus to engage in similar studies on those novels, in order to establish whether or not they bring out the African voice.

References

Adeoti, Gbemisola. 2016. "Demystifying the Future in Africa's (Un) vanishing Past: A Study of Ngugi wa Thiong'o's Novels." *Africa Development / Afrique et Développement* 41, no. 2: 1–22. https://www.ajol.info/index.php/ad/article/view/163577.

Gikandi, Simon. 1991."The Epistemology of Translation: Ngũgĩ, Matigari and the Politics of Language." *Research in African Literatures* 22, no. 4: 161–67. https://www.jstor.org/stable/3820365.

Mazrui, Ali A. 2005. "The Re-invention of Africa: Edward Said, V. Y Mudimbe, and beyond." *Research in African Literatures*, 36, no. 3: 68–82. https://www.jstor.org/stable/3821364.

Mudimbe, V.Y. 1988. *The Invention of Africa: Gnosis, Philosophy and the Order of Knowledge*. Indianapolis and Bloomington, IN: Indiana University Press; London: James Currey.

Mudimbe, V.Y. 1994. *The Idea of Africa*. Indianapolis and Bloomington, IN: Indiana University Press.

Masolo, D.A. 1991. "An Archaeology of African Knowledge: A Discussion of V.Y. Mudimbe." *Callaloo*, 14, no. 4: 998–1011. https://doi.org/10.2307/2931218.

Ngũgĩ wa Thiong'o. 1986. *Matigari Ma Njiruungi*. Nairobi: East African Educational Publishers.

Ngũgĩ wa Thiong'o. 1964. *Weep Not, Child*. London: Heinemann.

Ngũgĩ wa Thiong'o. 1965. *The River Between*. London: Heinemann.

Ngũgĩ wa Thiong'o. 1967. *A Grain of Wheat*. London: Heinemann.

Ngũgĩ wa Thiong'o. 1977. *Petals of Blood*. London: Heinemann.

Ngũgĩ wa Thiong'o. 1987. *Matigari*. London: Heinemann.

Ngũgĩ wa Thiong'o, Jaggi Maya. 1989. "Matigari as Myth and History." *Third World Quarterly* 11, no. 4: 241–51.

Ogot, Grace. 1966. *The Promised Land*. Nairobi: East African Educational Publishers.

Ogot, Grace. 1989. *The Strange Bride*. Nairobi: East African Educational Publishers.

Sicherman, Carol. 1998. "Revolutionizing the Literature Curriculum at the University of East Africa: Literature and the Soul of the Nation." *Research in African Literatures* 29, no. 3: 129–48. https://www.jstor.org/stable/3820624.

Sicherman, Carol. 1990. *Ngugi wa Thiong'o The Making of a Rebel: A Source Book in Kenyan Literature and Resistance*. Kent: Hans Zell Publishers.

Spivak, Gayatri Chakravorty. 2012. *An Aesthetic Education in the Era of Globalization*. Cambridge, MA: Harvard University Press.

Spivak, Gayatri Chakravorty. 1988. "Can the Subaltern Speak?" In *Marxism and the Interpretation of Culture*, edited by Cary Nelson and Lawrence Grossberg 271–313. Champaign, IL: University of Illinois Press.

Stratton, Florence. 1994. *Contemporary African Literature and the Politics of Gender*. New York: Routledge. https://doi.org/10.4324/9781003070924.

Taoua, Phyllis. 2009. "The Postcolonial Condition." In *The Cambridge Companion to the African Novel*, edited by Abiola Irele, 209–26. Cambridge: Cambridge University Press. [Archive]

Wanjala, Alex N. 2015. "Rerouting the Postcolonial from an East African Perspective." *Eastern African Literary and Cultural Studies* 2, no. 1-2: 54–63. https://doi.org/10.1080/23277408.2016.1183300.

Wanjala, Alex N. 2016. "Historiography or Imagination? The Documentation of Traditional Luo Cultural Memory in Kenyan Fiction." In *The Language Loss of the Indigenous*, edited by G.N. Devy, Geoffrey V. Davis, and K.K. Chakravarty, 159–82. London and New York: Routledge. https://doi.org/10.4324/9781315645810.

Wanjala, Alex N. 2007. "Grace Ogot's *The Promised Land* as a Pioneer Feminist Text." *The Nairobi Journal of Literature*, no. 5: 44–52. http://erepository.uonbi.ac.ke/handle/11295/40134.

Wanjala, Chris. 2003. "The Growth of a Literary Tradition in East Africa." An Inaugural Lecture Delivered at the University of Nairobi.

V.Y. Mudimbe's Modernities

Towards a Temporal and Spatial Excavation of (Neo)colonialism

Pierre-Philippe Fraiture

Born in 1941 in the industrial heartland of the former Belgian Congo, V.Y. Mudimbe is well-placed to comment on the *modern* implications of (neo) colonialism. Indeed, it would not be an exaggeration to say that from the late 1960s to the late 1990s, his work was overwhelmingly concerned with modernity: African modernity but also, and perhaps more significantly, Western modernity and its effects on Africa and African modernisation. From a definitional point of view, modernity, the concept, remains elusive (see, Eze 1997a; Geschiere et al. 2008; Probst et al. 2002; Táíwò 2010). Raymond Williams suggests that from the 18th century onwards, modernity was used as a quasi-synonym for "civilization," defined here as:

> "a specific combination of the ideas of a process and an achieved condition. It has behind it the general spirit of the Enlightenment, with its emphasis on secular and progressive human self-development. Civilization expressed this sense of historical process, but also celebrated the associated sense of *modernity*: an achieved condition of refinement and order." (Williams 1985, 43; my emphasis)

Williams' definition resonates with Mudimbe's own appraisal of the way in which this "achieved condition," and its inherent "Eurocentrism," was employed to colonise sub-Saharan Africa and implement an all-encompassing process of civilisational realignment:

> "Because of the colonializing structure, a dichotomizing system has emerged, and with it a great number of current paradigmatic oppositions have developed: traditional versus modern; oral versus written and printed; agrarian and customary communities versus urban and industrialized civilization; subsistence economies versus highly productive economies. In Africa a great deal of attention is generally given to the evolution implied and promised by the passage from the former paradigms to the latter." (Mudimbe 1988, 4)

Mudimbe's work has thus been traversed by modernity-related questions and has been punctuated by his own dogged exploration of modernity as a useful instrument to understand the alienating, destructive *and* transformative effects of colonialism. His most famous book, *The Invention of Africa*, is from the outset concerned with the far-reaching cultural consequences of colonialism for the Africa of the late 1980s. He contends here that the encounter of "the so-called African tradition and the projected modernity of colonialism" has generated the emergence of an "intermediate space" which:

> "... could be viewed as the major signifier of underdevelopment. It reveals the strong tension between a modernity that often is an illusion of development, and a tradition that sometimes reflects a poor image of a mythical past. It also unveils the empirical evidence of this tension by showing concrete examples of developmental failures such as demographic imbalance, extraordinarily high birth rates, progressive disintegration of the classic family structure, illiteracy, severe social and economic disparities, dictatorial regimes functioning under the cathartic name of democracy, the breakdown of religious traditions, the constitution of syncretic churches, etc." (Mudimbe 1988, 5)

My own approach to modernity—and, ultimately, to the connections between temporality and spatiality in Mudimbe's work—will rely on the theoretical framework established by the German historian Reinhart Koselleck (1923–2006). This choice might be somewhat surprising for Koselleck, after all, is *not* a historian of Africa and is a scholar who barely mentioned the colonial past in his books. He is chiefly remembered for his work on German history. However, it is important to signal that Koselleck belonged to what has been labelled the "skeptical generation," i.e. to a generation of German scholars who:

> "grew up in postwar Germany, after the experiences of National Socialism, Hitlerjugend, war, captivity, assisting in the defense against allied bombings, or of the total breakdown in May 1945. Due to their experiences [...] members of the 'skeptical generation' were characterized by a critical, skeptical, and distrustful attitude toward political ideology and long-term social planning [...]." (Olsen 2012, 14)

For the purposes of this chapter, I shall therefore refer to the conceptual framework developed by Koselleck to come to terms with (German) modernity in *Futures Past: On the Semantics of Historical Time*. This book, first published in German in 1983 and then translated into English, was part of a larger project—a lifelong project it must be added (see Koselleck's *Begriffsgeschichte* [conceptual history])—to explore the interface between semantics (and semantic mutations) and the emergence of new political concepts in Germany from the 17th to the 19th century. In this research, Koselleck argues that the period spanning from 1750 to 1850—what he calls *Sattelzeit* (literally "saddle time" or threshold)—coincided with a high degree of semantic shifts (and conceptual inventiveness) which were concomitant with the emergence of a new secular political modernity (*Neuzeit*). During this transitionary period, history and historical time acquired new meanings. For the first time ever, history became "temporalized"—wurde *verzeitlicht*—(Koselleck 2010, 362), that is, secularised and freed from the religious and eschatological logic on which it had hitherto been predicated. Gradually, this process of secularisation modified how one would henceforth relate to the past, present and future. Increasingly, the future would become synonymous with progress (worldly progress) and history, as a discipline, would be understood as a technology to relocate "past and future [...] with respect with each other" (Koselleck 2004, 4).

My main contention here is that modern imperialism, a process that gained significant momentum in the 1750–1850 period, precipitated sub-Saharan Africa into a temporal frame akin to *Neuzeit*. Albeit concerned with Germany, I am of the view, like other scholars operating in the field of postcolonial and decolonial studies (see Lorenz & Berber 2013; Scott 2004; Wilder 2015), that *Futures Past* can be called upon to shed light on the temporal premises informing the colonisation of Africa. As illustrated by the "paradigmatic oppositions" listed in the above quote by Mudimbe, colonial and neocolonial Africa (have) remained haunted by the modern. In an essay on Koselleck, Peter Osborne argues that this notion—the modern—"designates the valorisation of the present *as new* over the past, thereby splitting the present itself from within, and *antiquating* those aspects of the present that are not new" (Osborne in Lorenz & Berber 2013, 73).

The new context generated by *Neuzeit* is captured by two notions, two "anthropological givens" of "possible histories" (Koselleck 2004, 259): the "space of experience" and the "horizon of expectation." The German historian argues that the respective significance accorded throughout history to past, present and future can be examined via these categories which are neither "symmetrical," nor "to be statically related to each other" for "the previously existing space of experience is not sufficient for the determination of the horizon of expectation" (Koselleck 2004, 259). He suggests however that with *Neuzeit* the gap between "experience" and "expectation" became greater. This increased discrepancy mirrors the gradual secularisation of time and the decline of sacred time: "As long as the Christian doctrine of the Final Days set an immovable limit to the horizon of expectation (roughly speaking until the mid-17th century), the future remained bound to the past" (Koselleck 2004, 264). Progress, or the assumption that improvement would take place on earth rather than in the hereafter, gained momentum:

"Henceforth history could be regarded as a long-term process of growing fulfilment which, despite setbacks and deviations, was ultimately planned and carried out by men themselves. The objectives were then transferred from one generation to the next, and the effects anticipated by plan and prognosis became the titles of legitimation of political action. In sum, from that time on, the horizon of expectation was endowed with a coefficient of change that advanced in step with time. [...] progress was directed toward an active transformation of this world [...]." (Koselleck 2004, 266)

This loose theoretical framework being established, I would like now to determine how time, historicity, space, the relation between "experience" and "expectation" and the idea of temporalisation are appraised by Mudimbe. Thus, this chapter will, above all, focus on (neo)colonial temporal politics and on the way in which this historical context engendered the spatialisation of time. Naturally, I will only be able to refer to a limited number of texts, but I will attempt to argue here that Mudimbe's work, whilst providing a diagnostic of colonialism and neocolonialism over the *longue durée*, can also be interpreted as an outright rejection of historical and ontological determinism. In the first part of this chapter, I shall examine, by means of Michel de Certeau's "walking rhetoric" from *The Practice of Everyday Life*, how Mudimbe appraises the spatio-temporal implications of the missionary evangelisation of the former Belgian Congo; the second part will focus on Mudimbe's attempts to come to terms with the legacies of Western modernity, challenge the epistemological violence of the Enlightenment, and question the basis of African neocolonialism; in the final part of this chapter, I shall briefly examine the role ascribed to African intellectual resources in Mudimbe's ongoing critique of Western extroversion.

1. Evangelisation and worldly progress

In *The Idea of Africa*, Mudimbe reflects on the strategy adopted by the church—in fact the regular clergy and some of its orders such as the White Fathers, the Benedictines, and the Dominicans—to "domesticate" the Congolese space through a *temporalisation* of daily existence. The paradox that needs highlighting here is that this process of temporalisation, that is, the management of worldly affairs, was partly implemented by religious orders which, in Europe, had always been reticent to embrace modernity and its temporal regime (see Pirotte 1973). Thus, as argued by Mudimbe in *The Idea of Africa*, sacred and secular times remained interdependent in the Belgian Congo. Indeed, secular progress and Christian salvation were often conflated and simultaneously called upon to service the civilising mission: "conversion to the West is isomorphic with a conversion to Christianity"

(Mudimbe 1994a, 118).[1] This unlikely but *real* and factually attested coalition had the effect of undermining Congolese history and reduced the Congolese present to a not-yet (not yet modern, not yet Christian). Colonial ventures in Africa—whether British, French, Portuguese or Belgian—were worldly enterprises and, as such, predicated on a capitalist logic. However, it is well known that the day-to-day implementation of this resource-hungry system heavily relied on ecclesiastic agents sent over the whole continent by Christian churches and their suborders (see White and Daughton 2012). In the Congo Free State (CFS), for example, the lack of white personnel on the ground had generated pragmatic alliances between state administrators and Catholic priests. Reciprocal deals were struck as in the case of the missionary settlement of Kimuenza where the local school for Congolese pupils was run by Jesuits but funded by the state. Once they completed their education, it was expected that these pupils would enroll in the *Force Publique*, the CFS army responsible for turning Leopold's Congo into a free trade zone. Commenting on this arrangement, David Van Reybrouck concludes: "This much was clear: the Jesuits fought for Jesus, but also for Leopold. The school was run like a Belgian military academy" (Van Reybrouck 2014, 73).

Realpolitik aside, it is however equally important to signal that the Catholic Church and its orders *also* opposed the *modern* logic of the colonial enterprise and its underpinning regime of historicity. François Hartog—like Koselleck—is of the view that Christian time favours the present, that is, "the already fulfilled" by the history of salvation over the future ("the not yet completed"). Indeed, "the already carries more weight, since that 'decisive point' has irreversibly changed the course of history. The world has already been saved. The present ushered in by this 'already' is consequently a privileged time" (Hartog 2015, 61). In colonial sub-Saharan Africa, and in the Belgian Congo as discussed by Mudimbe in *The Idea of Africa*, this model could not operate in the absence of comprehensive evangelisation and of a Christian "already." In this context, the indigenous (pagan) present was always read as a "figure of lack"[2] and for this reason, the future—a future in which modernity, progress *and* Christianity would coalesce—was the only possible "privileged time" to be had. With regard to the history of missionary action in Africa (South Africa in this case), Jean and John Comaroff refer to "two contrapuntal narratives": "One speaks of a specific Christian mission and its consequences; the second, of a more

1. Walter D. Mignolo (2011, 13) aptly speaks of the secular and theological structure of "coloniality."

2. This "sad figure of lack and failure" is also the focus of Dipesh Chakrabarty, but in an Indian context (Chakrabarty 2007, 40-41).

general postenlightenment process of colonization in which Europe set out to grasp and subdue the forces of savagery, otherness and unreason" (Comaroff and Comaroff, 11).

In his examination of missionary time, Mudimbe (Mudimbe 1994a, 121) builds on the biopolitical potential of what Foucault called "historicité évolutive" (Foucault 1975, 188). With regard to "the progress of societies and the geneses of individuals," Michel Foucault argues that:

> "These two great 'discoveries' of the eighteenth century [...] were perhaps correlative with the new techniques of power, and more specifically with a new way of administering time and making it useful [...]. A macro- and micro-physics of power made possible not the invention of history (it had long had no need of that), but the integration of a temporal, unitary, continuous, cumulative dimension in the exercise of controls and the practice of dominations. 'Evolutive' historicity, as it was then constituted—and so profoundly that it is still self-evident for many today—is bound up with a mode of functioning of power." (Foucault 1991, 160–61)

Mudimbe argues that an "idea," that is, a "normalizing project" and "panoptic organization," had to be implemented to follow through this programme whereby space, time, traditions and memories were reordered to fit the exigencies of colonial *and* missionary progress (1994a, 125). This idea—"dreams, models, [and] politics fuse[d]" (Mudimbe 1994a, 112)—resulted from a fallacy of misplaced concreteness whereby arbitrary temporal criteria dreamed up by the Flemish White Fathers shortly after the conquest of the Congo (and the foundation of the CFS in 1885) were introduced to restructure the locals' horizon of expectation:

> "Village life was now subordinated to the missionaries' schedule. After the space, which they reorganized according to a new memory exemplified by the Church, missionaries rapidly command[ed] time and its categories. There will be a religious economy of days, weeks, months, years, espousing a liturgical calendar, and also specific new daily ritual arrangements." (Mudimbe 1994a, 111)

The temporal expropriation of the Congolese present brought about by the regular clergy was also inscribed in the landscape and in the geography. Like Michel de Certeau, Mudimbe uses rhetorical figures, the synecdoche and the asyndeton, to assess various ways in which the Congolese space could be interpreted (walked and, hence, read) and linked to antagonistic memories and the advent of a new regime of historicity. In his "walking rhetorics" (de Certeau 1984, 100), de Certeau contends that the two figures of speech are comparable to "pedestrian speech acts," (ibid., 97) and strategies whereby the (urban) walker creates, reappropriates and gives sense to space: "There is a rhetoric of walking. The art of 'turning' phrases finds an equivalent in an art of composing a path [...]. Like ordinary language, this art implies and combines styles and uses" (De Certeau 1984, 100). Despite their differences, De Certeau posits that these "two pedestrian figures" are in fact "related":

> "Synecdoche expands a spatial element in order to make it play the role of a 'more' (a totality) and take its place (the bicycle or a piece of furniture in a store window stands for a whole street or neighborhood). Asyndeton, by elision, creates a 'less,' opens gaps in the spatial continuum, and retains only selected parts of it that amount almost to relics." (de Certeau 1984, 101)

In his own rhetoric of walking, Mudimbe focuses on a real place, Mpala, located on the Western shores of Lake Tanganyika, in the Belgian Congo (now the Democratic Republic of the Congo, DRC), to ascertain the respective implications of these two rhetorical figures and assess colonial temporal politics (see Mudimbe 1994a, 105–53; Mudimbe 1994b, 45–46). Mpala is hugely significant from a geographical and historical perspective as it is remembered as the site where the first Catholic mission was created during the evangelisation of Eastern Congo. The mission is therefore associated with colonial mythology and the joint effort on part of the crown and the cross—the collaboration between Leopold II and Cardinal Lavigerie (see Ndaywel è Nziem 1998, 292–98)—to bring civilisation and eradicate slavery in this part of the world (see Bennett 1986; Marechal 1992). This site (of memory) also resonates with the action of soldiers—Alphonse Jacques, Louis Joubert, Émile Storms, and Alexis Vrithoff who fought against the Afro-Arab slave traders from Zanzibar—and clerics such as Victor Roelens and Stefano Kaoze, the first-ever Congolese Catholic priest (Cheza 2005). Mudimbe incorporates these historical details and insists on the fact that the Mission of Mpala ought to be regarded "as a political and religious sign" and "a spatial project" embodying the "new memory" engendered by "processes of conversion" (Mudimbe 1994a, 136). Although only one element of the whole edifice, he argues that the fortress erected under the auspices of Émile Storms on the mission site is a synecdoche for it captures the project in its totality: the conquest and the overthrow of the Afro-Arab slavers, but also the gradual consolidation of the evangelising process throughout the colonial period (Mudimbe 1994a, 136).

Thus, the "syn" in "synecdoche" renders the idea of a historical continuum and implies a conjunction between the different stages of this process (the past and the present of the mission). Ultimately, this synecdochic reading of Mpala demonstrates how colonial propagandists were able to engineer positive and *progressive* assessments of the memorial and spatial operations underpinning the transformation of the Congo since 1885.

Indeed, as a site of memory crystalising the conquest and the consolidation of its main political and religious values, Mpala is a space through which one can grasp the strategies adopted by the advocates of imperialism to spatialise time. As argued by Anne McClintock, in a piece focusing on the nation and its gendered invention, 19th-century social evolutionists "secularized time and placed it at the disposal of the national, imperial project. The axis of *time* was projected onto the axis of *space*, and history became global" (McClintock 1997, 92). Mpala symbolises progress and is, in turn, the concrete embodiment of the teleological process elicited by colonial modernity—the process of wholesale conversion captured by Mudimbe's "dichotomizing system" (see the first quote from *The Invention of Africa* in this chapter)—and its new temporal regime.

The adoption of GMT—which was "rather aptly named 'mean time'" (Nanni 2013, 2)—and, more generally, the various attempts on the part of capitalists, colonisers and missionaries to impose this new temporal regime of progress, was predicated on (but also further exacerbated by) the idea of "the synchrony of a-synchronic events" (Hölscher 2013, 144). The emergence of modernity coincides with the awareness among ordinary people that the present is made up of mixed and often diverging temporalities or what Koselleck named (after Ernst Bloch), "the contemporaneity of the noncontemporaneous" (Koselleck 2004). Although Koselleck paid no attention to colonialism in his examination of historical time and was unable to "see further than the frontiers of European society," (Harootunian 2007, 476) he nonetheless acknowledged the significance of early globalisation in the process that led to the emergence of progress as a conquering concept and metaphor: examples of the "Copernican Revolution, the slowly developing new technology, the discovery of the globe and its people living at various levels of advancement [...] are indicative of the contemporaneity of the noncontemporaneous" (Koselleck 2004, 266). The realisation that human development manifested itself unevenly became the very basis of modernisation and the horizon against which some notions originally employed to refer to movement—e.g. progress, advancement and revolution—acquired a temporal meaning. This spatialisation of time was also contingent on a newly recast geography where it was established that the least progressive peoples were to be found in the distant colonies.

This conflation of time and space—Stefan Tanaka (2016, 166) links this operation to what Foucault called the "'irruptive violence of time'" in *The Order of Things* (1970)—is a process, which became part and parcel of the colonial imaginary (and discourse). As such it has up to this day left powerful traces in representations of non-Western locales and whether these are driven by Baudelairean poetry—the timelessness of *L'Invitation au voyage*—or by the Conradian motif of the upstream journey to the *Heart of Darkness*, this imaginary has continued to entertain the fiction of a temporally split humanity. And, in fact, it has persisted "in the contemporary political economic discourses of modernization and development" (Cheah 2016, 200). This "denial of coevalness" or, as demonstrated by Johannes Fabian (2002), this inability to include the "Other" in a Western present, has its roots in a tripartite chronological system in which past, present, and future were ascribed distinct slots on an abstract (but increasingly influential) evolutionary line of progress: "Here time is a metric external to life and events to which they are adjusted, recorded, and arranged. It is a mechanistic and regular temporality that serves as the foundation for the conceptualization of modern history" (Tanaka 2016, 162). This metric was above all servicing imperialistic nation-states and their expansionist agenda. In this context, this reconfigured progress-driven linear history became a knowledge system deployed to domesticate and accumulate data on the colonised territories: "This spatialized time consists of the new units—places and taxonomies—that are formulated to give order and contain the complexity of life" (ibid., 167). The metric informing historical time functions in the same way as a metonymy or a synecdoche. In this regard, Stefan Tanaka, in another contribution, argues that history "has been a technology that facilitates [a] fallacy of misplaced concreteness" (Tanaka 2013, 218), a process whereby an abstraction (modern history) is confused for reality—e.g. "life and events" whose order needs rearranging to fit a theoretical model and its structuring criteria.

Mudimbe is also eager to analyse the way in which this "denial of coevalness" was spatially ordered and he approaches Mpala as an area extending along a south–north axis, with the forest next to the original village at the southern end, and the mission in the north. This other spatial perspective also lends itself to the "walking rhetoric" developed by Michel de Certeau. Mudimbe imagines himself strolling from north to south and decides to interpret this movement by means of the asyndeton and the discontinuities that this figure evokes (the "a" of asyndeton negates the "syn"):

> "The inhabitants of Mpala, being Christian converts, officially abandoned the spirit of the earth, which lives in [Mount] Nzawa. After one century of gradual transformation, the north, with its chimes, which organize life, work, and prayer, and with its stone walls becomes the veritable exemplary body. This north, with its new economic, cultural, and spiritual values, took the place of the old system of values that had previously coordinated activity in the south." (Mudimbe 1994a, 138)

The synecdoche helps to approach the colonial and missionary project as a coherent whole uniting past, present and future along a teleological line of progress; the asyndeton, on the other hand, "burst the bonds that hold together the diachronic continuity of events and erases that which brings together" (Mudimbe 1994a, 136). However, Mudimbe is mindful of the fact that, to return to de Certeau's point, these two figures are "related." The set of oppositions highlighted in this analysis—"the north versus the south, the future versus the past, modernity versus tradition" (Mudimbe 1994a, 139)—demonstrates, ultimately, that the asyndeton also reinforces the historical logic (and ideology) of the colonial and missionary project and, as such, "marks a positive rupture in a progressive plan" (Mudimbe 1994a, 139). In this examination of Mpala, Mudimbe, like Michel de Certeau, acknowledges this existing interface between these two rhetorical figures: "The 'more' of the whole presented by the synecdoche, mobilizing ties, conjunctions, and expansion, corresponds to the 'lesser' of the asyndeton and its games of separation and fragmentation" strategies—indeed, Mudimbe refers here to "Tactics and Strategies of Domestication"[3]—behind the imperialisation of time for Mpala both symbolises the grandeur of the colonial and missionary project and the radical rupture between the Europeans and the locals. Like Koselleck, he holds the view that the separation between sacred and secular time politics is not absolute. However, and this is where Mudimbe's contribution to this debate is so illuminating, Koselleck's analyses of temporalisation never ventured into the colonial domain and remained, as already signalled, largely Eurocentric.

In this discussion on the respective significance of the synecdoche and asyndeton as means to measure the effects of colonisation on indigenous cultures, Mudimbe singles out two main temporal processes. Firstly, the operation consisting in positioning sub-Saharan Africans on a geochronocultural grid in which the progressive and ameliorative logic of Christian salvation and colonial capitalism is presented as the only available horizon of expectation. Secondly, the assumption that the African past is ahistorical and can therefore be elided (see the disjunctive and fragmentary power of the asyndeton); and that the material and immaterial traces of this past in the modern (and colonial) present are mere relics of a mythical (rather than historical) time. The term relic needs to be understood literally—*relinquere*—i.e. as that which has been left behind *and* abandoned. At the same time, this idea conjures up notions of cultural dereliction and ruination and of a past which, as a result, requires

3. This is the title of a section from *The Idea of Africa*, p. 114-123.

Western scientific and archival attention and redemptive guardianship (Van Beurden 2015). This assumption—the allochronistic opposition between historical *nations* and primitive *territories*—significantly shaped the new "museumizing imagination," (Anderson 1991, 178) aesthetic agenda, and curatorial practices that would accompany imperialism.

2. Modernity and its (neo)colonial legacies

I have described so far one of the strategies developed by the author to diagnose modernity. Here, like in many other critical accounts undertaken by Mudimbe, modernity is dismissed as a violent process put in place to implement *progress*. It is violent because it negates the African space of experience, submits the relationship between the West and Africa to a strict "historicité évolutive" (see Foucault's quote) and to a biopolitical order in which Africans are reduced to "*docile bodies*" and minds (Mudimbe 1997, 50–56). Here, as in other texts, Mudimbe explores the way in which the resources of the "colonial library"—the large body of Western knowledge and scholarship about Africa whose "pervasive effectiveness during the nineteenth and the twentieth centuries" (Mudimbe 1988, 175) contributed to the colonisation of the African continent—were deployed to stage the invention of Africa; and impose throughout the continent a Western horizon of expectation for the paradox is that modernity, as a project, has continued to shape postcolonial nationalist ventures in Africa (and elsewhere).

Even anti-colonial figures were rarely able to depart from the developmentalist tropes produced by the "mechanistic and regular temporality that serves as the foundation for the conceptualization of modern history" (Tanaka 2016, 162). The Marxian and Marxist discourses of decolonisation—whether by Che Guevara, Amílcar Cabral, Sartre, Nelson Mandela and Kwame Nkrumah—were suffused with dialectics-inflected phrases and schemata in which the "now" was still a "not-yet" (Chakrabarty 2007, 8) to be perfected in the future, for "[p]rogress and revolution march together" (Hartog 2013, 126). Of course, it is not my intention to conflate these figures who, whilst being contemporaries, operated in different contexts. However, it is a fact that they attempted to adapt socialism to African realities and examine the contradictions elicited by colonial capitalism (see Camara 2008, ix-x) and it is in this sense that "activist thinkers participating in decolonization movements were attracted to the materialist dialectical variety of teleological time as a schema for making sense of anticolonial resistance and revolution" (Cheah 2016, 197). Sartre, for instance, embraced the Hegelian dialectic to explain historical change and militate for the eradication of the colonial system. Thus, his thinking was inflected by Marxist and Marxian principles since Marx himself had adapted the Hegelian master–slave dialectic to account for the tensions between conflicting forces (the bourgeoisie and the proletariat) in the capitalist system and argue that a clash between these forces (the thesis and the antithesis) would provide the basis for the emergence of a new socialist synthesis. When adapted to the (neo)colonial question and its racial context, this extroverted framework remains unconvincing as it examined racial discrimination through the exclusive lens of economic and social conflicts. In his reading of "Orphée noir," Fanon famously expressed his unease at being reduced to the deterministic march of the dialectic:

> "Jean-Paul Sartre, in this work, has destroyed black zeal. [...]. The dialectic that brings necessity into the foundation of my freedom drives me out of myself. It shatters my unreflected position. Still in terms of consciousness, black consciousness is immanent in its own eyes. I am not a potentiality of something, I am wholly what I am. I do not have to look for the universal. No probability has any place inside me. My Negro consciousness does not hold itself out as a lack. It *is*." (Fanon 2008 [1967], 103)

Indeed, "Orphée noir" is predicated on the idea that tensions between two main conflicting forces—the white world and negritude—will generate the conditions for a new synthesis (a race-less postcolonial world). Equally, it is important to acknowledge that "historical difference" (Chakrabarty 2007)—the "Other's" time, first dismissed by Western historians as ahistorical, then celebrated as a sign of cultural authenticity—also provided the basis for a "metaphysics of difference" and became the instrument of African identity politics "founded on membership of the black race" (Mbembe 2002, 240–41). Time, in its modern and colonial meaning ("modern" and "colonial" are synonymous here), is a pliable notion that both contributed to the longevity of the colonial system and fulfilled the *évolués'* progressive desires.

One of the main issues is that modernity is a contested notion and that it is of course not completely synonymous with colonialism and its coercive biopolitical techniques. Modernity is also coterminous with the Enlightenment and the emergence of the modern individual as an independent and critical thinking agent and producer of possible futures. However, the Enlightenment, as a concept and a moment, is problematic because the rise of this modern, enlightened and critical individual occurred against the background (and at the expense) of a two-tier conception of humanity. This "allochronistic" (Fabian 2002) vision was notoriously defended by some key Enlightenment philosophers such as Hume and

Kant (see Bernasconi 2003; Eze 1997b; Eze 2008). In this sense, Mudimbe is both a critic *and* a—cautious—advocate of modernity.

Cheminements. Carnets de Berlin, a diary that Mudimbe kept when he was a visiting professor at the Berlin's Freie Universität, offers a telling example of his ambivalent relation to modernity. Incidentally, it is interesting to signal that whilst Koselleck never wrote about Africa, Mudimbe uses Berlin to understand *modern* African history and the context that led to the violent occupation of the Congo Free State. Although Koselleck and Mudimbe never met, it is important to highlight the fact that their works are profoundly autobiographical. At a macrolevel, Mudimbe's writing project is overwhelmingly concerned with understanding the role of Western disciplines in the "invention" of Africa; at a microlevel, however, his production has focused on the significance of these disciplines for his own agency and freedom as an African intellectual who was once colonised by Belgian Benedictines, "francophonized" and submitted to "Greco-Roman values" (Mudimbe 1991a, 94). Koselleck, for his part, dedicated his academic career to German history but here, too, this endeavour is shaded by a very personal trajectory. At the age of eleven (in 1934), he was enrolled in the Hitlerjugend and was later drafted into the German army. After fighting on several fronts in the Soviet Union, France and Germany, he was eventually captured by the Soviets in 1945 (Olsen 2012, 11–12) and was sent to the Auschwitz concentration camp where he worked as a prisoner of war in a debris removal operation supervised by the Red Army (Olsen 2012, 33, note 20). This experience would prove crucial in his career as an academic:

> "[H]e presented his work as personally motivated attempts to grasp the historical background of the modern world, in particular World War II, including how it was experienced, and how it could be understood and coped with. With reference to these experiences, he also explained his fixation on topics such as "crisis," "conflict," and "death," as well as his aversion to pathos-ridden notions such as "nation," "fatherland," and "heroism," including his skepticism regarding all talk of progress in modern society, its politics, and its science." (Olsen 2012, 13)

Mudimbe's work has also been preoccupied by attempts to come to terms with progress and modernity and, of course, by a lifelong ambition to uncover the Eurocentric foundations of the Enlightenment. In *Cheminements*, whilst exploring the real significance of Berlin in the history of Europe and of his native country—the notorious Berlin Conference which sanctioned the partition of sub-Saharan Africa in 1885—he nonetheless describes himself "*intellectuellement soumis à l'héritage des Lumières*" [intellectually submitted to the legacy of the Enlightenment; my translation] and pays tribute to the "*pensée libre, perpétuellement critique*" [perpetually critical free thinking; my translation] generated by the Enlightenment, the French Revolution and modernity (Mudimbe 2006, 130). It seems that Mudimbe decided here to set aside the attested collusion between, on the one hand, the Enlightenment (and modern European philosophy) and, on the other, modern imperialism for, as argued by Emmanuel Chukwudi Eze:

> "[W]hen we study the nature and the dynamic of European modernity, we examine the intellectual and the philosophical productions of the time in order to understand how, in too many cases, they justified imperialism and colonialism. Significant aspects of the philosophies produced by Hume, Kant, Hegel, and Marx have been shown to originate in, and to be intelligible only when understood as an organic development within, larger sociohistorical contexts of European colonialism and the ethnocentric idea: Europe is *the* model of humanity, culture, and history in itself." (Eze 1997b, 6)

Thus, Mudimbe's appeal to the Enlightenment is, in this specific instance, quite reductive for "critical free thinking" is but one of the many features of the Enlightenment. And, what is more, critical thinking is not the exclusive preserve of the Enlightenment as it had been practised well before in ancient Egypt, Greece and Rome. This question of "*héritage*" [legacy] is however an important aspect of Mudimbe's intellectual trajectory. He has always been on the side of "the unhappy 'historian[s] of the same'" (Mudimbe 1988, 34). He used this unusual expression in relation to Foucault and Lévi-Strauss and their own ability to challenge the divides between the normal and the aberrant, the significant and the insignificant. Mudimbe's approach is, indeed, predicated on ideas articulated by Foucault in *The Archaeology of Knowledge*:

> "All his books provide good examples of this exercise, which brings to light the long, difficult, and permanent struggle of the Same and the Other. By promoting a critical archaeology of knowledge, not only does he separate himself from a history but also from its classical presuppositions, which lead to and serve the arrogance of the Same. In his *Discourse on Language*, Foucault delineates this objective: 'to question [the Western] will to truth; to restore to discourse its character as an event; to abolish the sovereignty of the signifier' (1982, 229)." (Mudimbe 1988, 34)

Mudimbe's affiliation to continental thought is wide-ranging and long-standing but is anything but subservient. In "Western Legacy and Negro Consciousness" (2016, first published in French in 1968), he explores this idea of legacy (or heritage) as a means to determine the relation between the West and Africa in the early years of the postcolonial era. In this disquisition, Mudimbe moves away from a genealogical understanding of cultural legacies and from the idea that the world, and world history, is ordered on the basis of a strict concatenation of centres and peripheries. Whilst dealing with African modernity at the end of the 1960s, this article also examines how different conceptions of time have shaped the place, the role and the significance of the individual subject in Europe and Africa. Mudimbe marshals here a rich and complex network of sources predominantly pertaining to the Marxist tradition to examine the factors that have precipitated the westernisation of sub-Saharan Africa. Through an analysis of Endre Sík's *History of Black Africa*, he contends that the continent is more often than not used to expound theses—in this case the principles informing historical materialism—which have the unfortunate effect of effacing African singularity at the expense of a supra-historical framework (Mudimbe 2016, 14–15). Here, as later in *L'Odeur du père* and *The Invention of Africa*, it is however important to highlight that Mudimbe remains sympathetic to the explicatory resources of Marxism to account for the emergence of modernity in Europe *and* in Africa. In the following quote, he is referring to European history:

> "... we are [...] aware of—or perhaps more accurately, we understand—the declaration made by Marx, for whom the history of humanity 'becomes' when accompanied by an increase in productive forces and social relationships. This amounts to a declaration on the recent nature of this 'history,' which is itself a creation both of productive forces that have been developed to a state of totality and of universal relationships whose emergence on the strength of large-scale industry has led to the dissolution of earlier relationships and the birth of new ones." (Mudimbe 2016, 14)

This new context also played a major role in the development of colonial Africa. However, at a time—the late 1960s—when most historical and political transformations were described via Marxist grids, Mudimbe cautions that this process cannot on its own explain African westernisation. He implies, and it is the major premise of this early article, that Europe, like Africa, is an unstable concept which can at best be grasped through its diversity rather than any invented "unity" (Mudimbe 2016, 13–14). Thus, he contends that in the analysis of the many encounters generated by colonialism in Africa, scholars should prioritise certain "imprints" and "legacies":

> "In the diverse conditions which saw the development of the productive forces that each colonising country imposed on its African colonies, Europe, at once unified and diverse, left Africa a series of legacies that in a way constitute perhaps the most visible and most real foundations of the unity of black Africa today. Three main legacies can be identified: the acceleration of the Neolithic revolution, the epistemological revolution, and the thematisation of the alphabetic revolution." (Mudimbe 2016, 16)

For the purpose of this argument, I shall chiefly focus on the "epistemological revolution" as it offers the frame against which modern Africa came into being, was *invented* and perhaps also became a pan-African reality. This issue, as will be briefly developed here, provides another opportunity to explore modernity and its impact on the decolonisation of Africa *and* the emergence of African philosophy. Mudimbe's testimony is in this regard exemplary for he stands at the crossroads of at least three memories. First, his familial bonds as he recalls that, as a young boy, he went through the initiation rituals of his parents' socio-ethnic group in Kasai (Mudimbe 1991a, 94). Then, as a former Benedictine, the religious order that shaped his personal vision and *routine*, "*Ora et Labora*" [pray and work] (Mudimbe 1994b, 15; and Mudimbe 2006, 125), and that of his *alter ego*, Frère Matthieu. Finally, as an academic who witnessed the development of ethnophilosophy, read its main proponents (Placide Tempels, Alexis Kagame, F.M. Lufuluabo and Vincent Mulongo) and avidly threw himself into the study of continental thought (existentialism, structuralism and post-structuralism) when researching in Lovanium, Besançon, Paris, Louvain, Lubumbashi and the US.

Whilst possessing clear autobiographical resonance (Mudimbe's work, as argued earlier, operates at both a micro and macrolevel), this intricate network of texts is mobilised to comment on the political situation in Mobutu's Congo/Zaire and the gradual stifling of critical thinking under that regime. Exactly twenty years after the publication of this early article, Mudimbe would more explicitly take Mobutu to task (but also Houphouët-Boigny, Ahidjo, Senghor and Kenyatta) for preventing philosophy from "questioning the meaning of political power and interrogating all power–knowledge systems" (Mudimbe 1988, 185). By delving into Bantu traditions, Mudimbe the philosopher implicitly foreshadows the predicament experienced by African intellectuals and academics from the 1970s onwards. Bantu authenticity does not easily lend itself to the practice of philosophy for it is grounded in an "empirico-ontological" conception of time in which individuals are what they are rather than what they might become:

> "The ontological status of an individual was based on his place in the eternal hierarchy of [vital] forces. Eternal because, if we take the example of a man's life, we can see that for it to be a 'complete life,' it must meet the expectations of his ancestors. A child born into the name of an ancestor is not and will not be a man unless he finds his place in tradition and reflects that tradition as best he can. And one's existence within a community, with its succession of rites of initiation and the regularity of its rites of passage, is not a path towards the future on the strength of one's assumptions about the present,

but rather a life of permanent tension in which one must embody in the present a past that offers only one reading, a finite, complete and absolute reading—that of one's ancestors." (Mudimbe 2016, 17)

Thus, Mudimbe argues that in the Bantu worldview, the space of experience remained paramount for "the cult of the ancestors seemed like an attempt to make the past present" (N'sougan Ablegmagnon, cited by Mudimbe 2016, 18). The epistemological revolution wrought by colonial modernity remains therefore a complex process:

"The encounter between the West and Africa, while it did not completely upset this 'Weltanschauung,' did rattle it profoundly: negatively by systematically denying traditional heritage, but no doubt positively by introducing a revolutionary idea, that of man as the canonical measure of all values, responsible for producing his own being and all that he is." (Mudimbe 2016, 20)

Beyond its excesses and violence, this encounter is also regarded positively because it offers the opportunity of challenging nativist identity politics at a time when traditions and the cult of the ancestors were weaponised to serve the political ambitions of emerging strongmen in the Congo and beyond. This wide-ranging concern is explored at length in Mudimbe's work and more specifically when he investigates the heuristic possibilities of ethnophilosophy (see Mudimbe 1988, 154–61; Mudimbe 1991a, 32–68). His third novel, *Le Bel immonde* neatly translates the oppressive effects of clannish politics. Members of ethnic communities, because they are "the fingers of a single hand, the limbs of a single body" (Mudimbe 1989, 70),[4] are deprived of this ability to become the producers of their own being. Bantu traditions, argues Mudimbe, should not be invoked to restore the past in the present but to be the conduit of critical interrogations. This idea is an important element of Mudimbe's intellectual project. He is a Bantu who was Christianised and trained in the very disciplines—philology, anthropology, history and philosophy—that have aided and abetted the (neo)colonial enterprise, cemented its allochronism, and fostered what has been referred to in this piece as the spatialisation of time. As demonstrated by Mudimbe from the very outset of his career, this *modern* conception of time and history is the product of stadial theories developed from the 18th century onwards in the natural sciences and in philology and anthropology:

"Le schéma d'évolution des sociétés humaines, ses séquences du développement de la parenté et du mariage révèlent, du point de vue de la méthode, des présupposés théoriques similaires à ceux qui soutiennent les *Lectures on the Science of Language* (1861 et 1864) [*by Friedrich Max Müller*]. Ceux-ci descendent, en droite ligne, de la 'Stammbaumtheorie,' théorie de l'arbre généalogique de Schleicher pour qui les langues naissent, croissent, se

4. *Le Bel immonde* was translated as *Before the Birth of the Moon* (1989).

développent, se ramifient à la manière d'un arbre, puis vieillissent et meurent, obéissant en cela à des lois naturelles rigides." (Mudimbe 1973a, 17)

[The pattern of evolution of human societies, its sequencing of the development of kinship and marriage reveal, from a methodological point of view, theoretical assumptions akin to those supporting the *Lectures on the Science of Language* (1861 and 1864). These originate, in a straight line, from the "Stammbaumtheorie," the genealogical tree as theorised by Schleicher for whom languages are born, grow, develop, branch out like a tree, then grow old and die, obeying in this process rigid natural laws. *My translation.*]

By showing that these traditions and worldviews are coeval and can cohabit in one individual, but that this individual, in turn, does not have to adhere to their logic and that this logic constitutes the basis from which one can interrogate Africannesss, its pastness but also futurity, Mudimbe invalidates the tripartite and developmental conception of time (pre-colonial, colonial, and postcolonial) with which modern Africa has been invented. Equally, the reflection on Bantu authenticity generated by Placide Tempels, his epigones and their critics (Fabien Eboussi Boulaga, for example) can provide an analogous critical framework:

"[i]t is on this very notion of authenticity that Eboussi Boulaga established his *La Crise du Muntu: Authenticité africaine et philosophie* (1977), unfolding a problem of origin: what is an African and how does one speak of him or her and for what purpose? Where and how can one gain the knowledge of his or her being? How does one define this very being, and to what authority does one turn for possible answers? It is obvious that the significance of these questions has nothing to do with ethnophilosophy, nor with a cheap, easy exploitation of the notion of authenticity in the sense in which the Zairian government used it in the early 1970s. In effect, these questions originate elsewhere. They are ones I consider marked by the demands of a critical philosophy." (Mudimbe 1988, 153)

3. Endogenous resources and extroversion

Thus, modernity, as a concept describing a rupture with the ancientness of traditions, is complex because the modern, however new it might be, is never completely divorced from traditions. Aleida Assmann explains this tension between past, present and future by means of Odo Marquard's *Zukunft braucht Herkunft* (*The Future Needs Origin*) and the "compensation theory" developed in this book. In this logic, progress and the core principles of the modern regime of historicity are not challenged but accommodated through the development of "a culture of preservation and memory." For the compensation theorists, "the *homo conservator* is the *Doppelgänger* of the *homo faber*: Both coevolve within the modern time regime, and it is the dialectical function of one to temper the painful and radical effects of the other" (Assmann 2013, 51). By the same token, it would be erroneous to reduce Mudimbe's modernities to two figures—modernity as colonialism and modernity as Enlightenment—for there is another dimension to which he has returned and, again, from the very beginning of his career as a scholar and creative writer: modernity and its African reappropriations.

On balance, however, it must be said that this future-orientated modernity features less prominently in his work and that he has overwhelmingly explored Africa's "gnostic malady" (Masolo 1994, 188). The fact that he was born during the colonial period plays here a significant role and explains why he has prioritised the links between alienation and knowledge. Mudimbe is a product of the Belgian developmentalist programme and, through his education, he became a *de facto* member of the *évolué* class. This membership is, however, problematic: it has shaped his career and is at the heart of the epistemological debates that his work has generated. Furthermore, it reflects some of his fictional characters' bad faith (in the Sartrean sense of the phrase). Indeed, Landu (*Entre les eaux*) and Nara (*L'Écart*)[5] are the victims of their own erudition and inability to extricate themselves from thought procedures created for and by the (neo)colonisers (see Mudimbe 1973a, 102–3): as the West's "being-for-others," these figures are condemned to reproduce the style, paradigms and categories employed and established elsewhere. Interestingly, Landu, the priest-cum-revolutionary of *Entre les eaux* is unable to see God "except through the stained glass of European cathedrals" (Mudimbe 1991b, 82).

Despite this general tendency, Mudimbe has, as suggested above, also reflected on the endogenous resources offered by African vernacular cultures to mitigate the effects of extroversion and develop a "*science du dedans*" [science from within] (Mudimbe 1982, 57). His examination of contemporary African art is undoubtedly his most concrete contribution to this debate. In "Reprendre" (Mudimbe 1991c), he shows that his examination of African aesthetic traditions is not conducted to pay tribute to the "purity" of some "dead ancestors" but to highlight the multifaceted dimensions of traditional techniques and motives (Mudimbe 2016, 200).[6] He suggests that traditions were never set in stone and that wherever they were interrupted (or disrupted)—for instance by colonial modernity and the latter's aesthetic priorities and prejudices—they could be taken up again (*reprendre* in French). And that this process of *reprendre* is the basis from which African

5. These two novels were respectively translated into English as *Between Tides* (1991) and *The Rift* (1993).

6. It was also one of the chapters of Mudimbe's *The Idea of Africa*. Here, I shall use the version included in *The Mudimbe Reader* (2016), 200–16.

artists contribute to an African modernity, not as passive recipients of imported techniques or immutable traditions but as genuine producers whose practice, whilst rooted in Africa, remains attentive to contemporary trends, local transformations, and global aesthetic evolutions.

African systems of thought, sorcery, divination, religions, and myths are the other cultural signs taken on board by Mudimbe to examine this issue of the possible reappropriation of a deep-seated African gnosis which, he intimates, *could* be called upon to cure sub-Saharan Africa of its "gnostic malady" and allow the continent to embrace modernity with endogenous tools. Like Gérard Buakasa Tulu kia Mpansu, the author of a voluminous thesis on fetishism in BaKongo communities, Mudimbe believes that the study of *kindoki* (witchcraft) is essential for, as a "*premier discours*," (Mudimbe 1982, 146) it enables one to understand the hidden mechanisms on which Kongo culture and society are ordered. His exploration of BaLuba myths in *Parables and Fables* is predicated on an analogous ambition (see Fraiture 2013, 36–39). However, this aspect of Mudimbe's work, albeit intriguing and erudite, remains a little tentative. And this inconclusiveness owes a great deal to the fact that this exegetic enterprise—the salvaging of this hidden gnosis—is too formidable a task:

> "Could not one hypothesize that, despite the cleverness of discourses and the competency of authors, they do not necessarily reveal *la chose du texte*, that which is out there in the African traditions, insistent and discrete, determining the traditions yet independent from them? Colonialism and its trappings, particularly applied anthropology and Christianity, tried to silence this. African discourses today, by the very epistemological distance which makes them possible, explicit, and credible as scientific or philosophical utterances, might just be commenting upon rather than unveiling *la chose du texte*." (Mudimbe 1988, 183)

The excavation of this gnosis, then, remains an elusive exercise for the methodology to retrieve it and translate it in terms that are not already contaminated by "colonialism and its trappings," lacks scientific reliability, a point that Mudimbe would reiterate in *Parables and Fables*. It is interesting that already in "Western Legacy and Negro Consciousness," twenty years before the publication of *The Invention of Africa*, he was casting doubt on the success of this undertaking:

> "The weight of our Western legacy today is such that it would be untrue to say that Africa can construct itself with no regard for this legacy. And the processes initiated by it can but evolve. It is true that Africa also carries the weight of its own past, which means that in answering the questions that are being asked and will be asked of it, the otherness of its own genius can shine through. Nonetheless, any attempt to privilege this legacy via sentimental

> choices would be to lack a sense of history. We cannot assume our tradition by insisting on its originality, but by a will to unleash our creative potential, and by recognising that the obstacle we are contesting has its origins in a situation that has been alienated." (Mudimbe 2016, 23)

Conclusion

This chapter has focused on the notion of modernity and has demonstrated that for the Congolese author Valentin-Yves Mudimbe the term remains shrouded in ambiguity. Modernity's complexity can be partly captured through the dialectical relationship between "experience" and "expectation," the two temporal concepts forged by Reinhart Koselleck to comment on the secularisation of time and the advent of modern history. This discipline, as argued by Koselleck, François Hartog but also Michel Foucault, was transformed during the Enlightenment. Indeed, it became a vehicle to reflect on the developmentalist and progress-driven nature of post-revolutionary societies. This *modern* "evolutive historicity" (Foucault) coincided with the spatialisation of time, a process facilitated by imperial geography and its division of the earth into time zones. Henceforth, time's duration was discarded in favour of a tripartite periodisation whereby the present is tasked with planning the new and discarding the ancient. This method had the tendency of radicalising the distance between Europe's remote *and* "allochronistic" others. Via Michel de Certeau, Mudimbe sets out to analyse the consequences of this spatialisation on Mpala, a famous colonial site of memory located in eastern Congo. Certeau's "walking rhetoric"—and his use of the synecdoche/asyndeton—is called upon to reveal the spatio-temporal and ethnocentric implications of the (neo)colonial project. Modernity is denounced as a violent process which, whilst "domesticating" and "'regenerating' the African space and its inhabitants" (Mudimbe 1988, 2), excludes the Congolese and their own memory. Modernity, however, offers also the opportunity to escape communitarianism and this praise of modernity—modernity *qua* Enlightenment—needs to be read against the backdrop of African postcolonial politics, the rise of nativist discourses and the "ontologizing of Eurocentric ideas projected and presented as the African's own self-conception" (Serequeberhan 1994, 47). In this sense, modernity is a terrain allowing the development of individual agency and critical thinking, even though, of course, the advent of critical thinking predates European modernity. This context *could* also lend itself to the emergence of "*une pensée africaine authentique*" [authentically African thought; my translation] (Mudimbe 1982, 43). There is, however, no happy ending here for Mudimbe was conscious of the fact that the Africanisation of the human and social sciences, in addition to the practice of African philosophy, remained, in the last two decades of the 20th century, still contingent on the gnostic "smell" of "an abusive father" (Mudimbe 1982, 35; my translation).[7]

I would like to thank the editors for their very useful comments on the first drafts of this chapter.

References

Anderson, Benedict R. 1991. *Imagined Communities: Reflections on the Origin and Spread of Nationalism*. London and New York: Verso.

Assmann, Aleida. 2013. "Transformations of the Modern Time Regime." In *Breaking Up Time*, edited by Berber Bevernage and Chris Lorenz, 39–56. Göttingen: Vandenhoeck & Ruprecht.

Balandier, Georges. 1970. *The Sociology of Black Africa: Social Dynamics in Central Africa*. Translated by Douglas Garman. New York and Washington: Praeger Publishers.

Bennett, Norman R. 1986. *Arab versus European. Diplomacy and War in Nineteenth-century East Central Africa*. New-York, NY: Africana Pub. Co.

Bevernage, Berber and Chris Lorenz, eds. 2013. *Breaking Up Time: Negotiating the Borders Between Present, Past, and Future*. Göttingen: Vandenhoeck & Ruprecht.

Bernasconi, Robert, and Sybol Cook Anderson, eds. 2003. *Race and Racism in Continental Philosophy*. Bloomington; Indianapolis, IN: Indiana University Press.

Buakasa Tulu kia Mpansu, Gérard. 1973. *L'Impensé du discours: "kindoki" et "nkisi" en pays kongo du Zaïre*. Kinshasa: Presses universitaires du Zaïre; Brussels: Centre d'Étude et de Documentation Africaines.

Camara, Babacar. 2008. *Marxist Theory, Black/African Specificities, and Racism*. Lanham, MD, and Plymouth: Lexington Books.

Chakrabarty, Dipesh. 2007 [2000]. *Provincializing Europe: Postcolonial Thought and Historical Difference*, with a new preface by the author. Princeton, NJ, and Oxford: Princeton University Press.

Cheah, Pheng. 2016. *What is a World? On Postcolonial Literature as World Literature*. Durham, NC, and London: Duke University Press.

Cheza, Maurice. 2005. "L'Accompagnement armé des missionnaires dans l'Afrique des Grands Lacs." In *Les Conditions matérielles de la mission. Contraintes, dépassements et imaginaires, XVIIe-XXe siècles*, edited by Jean Pirotte, 93–103. Paris: Khartala.

7. This chapter draws on ideas developed in my monograph: *Past Imperfect: Time and African Decolonization* (Fraiture 2021).

Comaroff, Jean and John L. Comaroff. 1991. *Of Revelation and Revolution: Christianity, Colonialism, and Consciousness,* vol. 1. Chicago, IL: University of Chicago Press.

de Certeau, Michel. 1984. *The Practice of Everyday Life.* Translated by Steven Rendall. Berkeley, CA: University of California Press.

Eboussi Boulaga, Fabien. 1977. *La Crise du Muntu. Authenticité africaine et philosophie.* Paris : Présence africaine.

Eze, Emmanuel Chukwudi, ed. 1997a. *Race and the Enlightenment: A Reader.* Malden, MA: Blackwell Publishers.

Eze, Emmanuel Chukwudi, ed. 1997b. *Postcolonial African Philosophy. A Critical Reader.* Cambridge, MA: Blackwell Publishers.

Eze, Emmanuel Chukwudi. 2008. *On Reason: Rationality in a World of Cultural Conflict and Racism.* Durham, NC, and London: Duke University Press.

Fabian, Johannes. 2002 [1983]. *Time and its Other: How Anthropology Makes its Objects.* New York: Columbia University Press.

Fanon, Frantz. 2008 [1967]. *Black Skin, White Masks.* Forewords to the 2008 edition by Ziauddin Sardar and Homi K. Bhabha; translated by Charles Lam Markmann. London: Pluto Press.

Foucault, Michel. 1970 [1966]. *The Order of Things: An Archaeology of the Human Sciences.* London: Tavistock Publications. https://monoskop.org/images/a/a2/Foucault_Michel_The_Order_of_Things_1994.pdf.

Foucault, Michel. 1975. *Surveiller et punir : Naissance de la prison.* Paris: Gallimard.

Foucault, Michel. 1991 [1975]. *Discipline and Punish: the Birth of the Prison.* Translated by Alan Sheridan. Harmondsworth: Penguin Books.

Foucault, Michel. 2002. *The Archaeology of Knowledge.* Translated by Alan M. Sheridan Smith. London: Routledge.

Fraiture, Pierre-Philippe. 2013. *V.Y. Mudimbe: Undisciplined Africanism.* Liverpool: Liverpool University Press.

Fraiture, Pierre-Philippe. 2021. *Past Imperfect: Time and African Decolonization.* Liverpool: Liverpool University Press. https://doi.org/10.2307/j.ctv1kwxfhx.

Geschiere, Peter, Birgit Meyer, and Peter Pels, eds. 2008. *Reading in Modernity in Africa.* Bloomington, IN: Indiana University Press.

Harootunian, Harry. 2007. "Remembering the Historical Present." *Critical Inquiry* 33, no. 3: 471–94. https://doi.org/10.1086/513523.

Hartog, François. 2013. "The Modern *Régime* of Historicity in the Face of Two World Wars." In *Breaking Up Time*, edited by Berber Bevernage and Chris Lorenz, 124–33. Göttingen: Vandenhoeck & Ruprecht.

Hartog, François. 2015. *Regimes of Historicity: Presentism and Experiences of Time.* Translated by Saskia Brown. New York: Columbia University Press.

Hölscher, Lucian. 2013. "Mysteries of Historical Order: Ruptures, Simultaneity and the Relationship of the Past, the Present and the

Future." In *Breaking Up Time*, edited by Berber Bevernage and Chris Lorenz, 134–51. Göttingen: Vandenhoeck & Ruprecht.

Koselleck, Reinhart. 1979. *Historische Semantik und Begriffsgeschichte.* Stuttgart: Klett-Cotta.

Koselleck, Reinhart. 2004. *Futures Past: on the Semantics of Historical Time.* Translated with an Introduction by Keith Tribe. New York: Columbia University Press.

Koselleck, Reinhart. 2010 [1979]. "'Erfahrungsraum' und 'Erwartungs-horizont': zwei historische Kategorien." In *Vergangene Zukunft: Zur Semantik geschichtlicher Zeiten.* Frankfurt am Main: Suhrkamp Verlag.

Marechal, Philippe. 1992. *De «Arabische» campagne in het maniema-gebied (1892–1894). Situering binnen het kolonisatieproces in de onafhankelijke Kongostaat.* Tervuren: Musée Royal de l'Afrique centrale.

Marquard, Odo. 2003. *Zukunft braucht Herkunft. Philosophische Essays.* Stuttgart: Reclam.

Masolo, A.D. 1994. *African Philosophy in Search of Identity.* Bloomington and Indianapolis, IN: Indiana University Press; Edinburgh: Edinburgh University Press.

Mbembe, Achille. 2002. "African Modes of Self-Writing." Translated by Steven Rendall. *Public Culture* 14, no. 1: 239–73. https://doi.org/10.1215/08992363-14-1-239 [archive].

McClintock, Anne. 1997. "'No Longer in a Future Heaven': Gender, Race and Nationalism." In *Dangerous Liaisons: Gender, Nation, and Postcolonial Perspectives*, edited by Anne McClintock, Aamir Mufti, and Ella Shohat, 89–112. Minneapolis, MN: University of Minnesota Press.

Mignolo, Walter D. 2011. *The Darker Side of Western Modernity: Global Futures, Decolonial Options.* Durham, NC, and London: Duke University Press.

Mudimbe, Valentin Yves. 1968. "Héritage occidental et conscience nègre." *Congo-Afrique*, 26: 2–14.

Mudimbe, Valentin Yves. 1973a. *L'Autre Face du royaume. Une introduction à la critique des langages en folie.* Lausanne: L'Âge d'homme.

Mudimbe, Valentin Yves. 1973b. *Entre les eaux.* Paris: Présence africaine.

Mudimbe, Valentin Yves. 1979. *L'Écart.* Paris: Présence africaine.

Mudimbe, Valentin Yves. 1982. *L'Odeur du père: essai sur des limites de la science et de la vie en Afrique noire.* Paris: Présence africaine.

Mudimbe, Valentin Yves. 1988. *The Invention of Africa: Gnosis, Philosophy, and the Order of Knowledge.* Bloomington and Indianapolis, IN: Indiana University Press; London: James Currey.

Mudimbe, Valentin Yves. 1989. *Before the Birth of the Moon.* Translated by Marjolijn De Jager. New York: Simon & Schusters Books.

Mudimbe, Valentin Yves. 1991a. *Parables and Fables: Exegesis, Textuality and Politics in Central Africa.* Madison, WI: University of Wisconsin Press.

Mudimbe, Valentin Yves. 1991b. *Between Tides*. Translated by Stephen Becker. New York: Simon & Schuster.

Mudimbe, Valentin-Yves. 1991c. "'Reprendre': Enunciations and Strategies in Contemporary African Art." In *Africa Explores. 20th Century African Art,* edited by Susan Vogel, 276–87. Munich: The Center for African Art and Prestel.

Mudimbe, Valentin Yves. 1993. *The Rift*. Translated by Marjolijn De Jager. Minneapolis, MN: University of Minnesota Press.

Mudimbe, Valentin Yves. 1994a. *The Idea of Africa*. Bloomington, IN: Indiana University Press.

Mudimbe, Valentin Yves. 1994b. *Les Corps glorieux des mots et des êtres. Esquisse d'un jardin africain à la bénédictine*. Paris: Présence africaine; Montréal: Humanitas.

Mudimbe. Valentin Yves. 1997. *Tales of Faith: Religion and Political Performance in Central Africa*. London and Atlantic Highlands, NJ: The Athlone Press.

Mudimbe, Valentin Yves. 2006. *Cheminements. Carnets de Berlin (avril-juin 1999)*. Québec: Humanitas.

Mudimbe, Valentin Yves. 2016. "Western Legacy and Negro Consciousness: an Introductory Study of the Sources of African Ideology." Translated by Myles O'Byrne. In *The Mudimbe Reader*, edited by Pierre-Philippe Fraiture and Daniel Orrells, 13–24. Charlottesville, VA, and London: University of Virginia Press.

Mudimbe, Valentin Yves. 2016 [1991]. "'Reprendre': Enunciations and Strategies in Contemporary African Art." In *The Mudimbe Reader*, edited by Pierre-Philippe Fraiture and Daniel Orrells, 200–16. Charlottesville, VA, and London: University of Virginia Press.

Müller, F. Max. 2013. *Lectures on the Science of Language: Delivered at the Royal Institution of Great Britain in 1863*. Cambridge: Cambridge University Press.

Nanni, Giordano. 2013. *The Colonisation of Time: Ritual, Routine and Resistance in the British Empire*. Manchester: Manchester University Press.

Ndaywel è Nziem, Isidore. 1998. *Histoire générale du Congo. De l'héritage ancien à la République Démocratique*. Paris-Bruxelles: Duculot.

Olsen, Niklas. 2012. *History in the Plural. An Introduction to the Work of Reinhart Koselleck*. New York: Berghahn Books.

Osborne, Peter. 2013. "Global Modernity and the Contemporary: Two Categories of the Philosophy of Historical Time." In *Breaking Up Time*, edited by Berber Bevernage and Chris Lorenz, 69–84. Göttingen: Vandenhoeck & Ruprecht.

Pirotte, Jean. 1973. *Périodiques missionnaires belges d'expression française. Reflets de cinquante années d'évolution d'une mentalité 1889–1940*. Louvain: Publications Universitaires de Louvain.

Probst, Peter, Jan-Georg Deutsch, and Heike Schmidt, eds. 2002. *African Modernities*. Oxford: James Currey.
Sartre, Jean-Paul. 1948. "Orphée noir." In *Anthologie de la nouvelle poésie nègre et malgache de langue française*, edited by Léopold Sédar Senghor, ix-xliv. Paris: Presses universitaires de France.
Scott, David, *Conscripts of Modernity: the Tragedy of Colonial Enlightenment*. 2004. Durham, NC, and London: Duke University Press.
Serequeberhan, Tsenay. 1994. *The Hermeneutics of African Philosophy: Horizon and Discourse*. New York and London: Routledge.
Sík, Endre. 1966. *History of Black Africa*. Budapest: Akadémiai Kiadó.
Táíwò, Olúfémi. 2010. *How Colonialism Preempted Modernity in Africa*. Bloomington, IN: Indiana University Press.
Tanaka, Stefan. 2013. "Unification of Time and the Fragmentation of Pasts in Meiji Japan." In *Breaking Up Time*, edited by Berber Bevernage and Chris Lorenz, 216–35. Göttingen: Vandenhoeck & Ruprecht.
Tanaka, Stefan. 2016. "History without Chronology." *Public Culture* 28, no. 1: 161–86. https://doi.org/10.1215/08992363-3325064.
Van Beurden, Sarah. 2015. *Authentically African: Arts and the Transnational Politics of Congolese Culture*. Athens: Ohio University Press.
Van Reybrouck, David. 2014. *Congo: the Epic History of a People*. Translated from Dutch by Sam Garrett. London: Fourth Estate.
White, Owen and James Patrick Daughton, eds. 2012. *In God's Empire: French Missionaries and the Modern World*. New York, and Oxford: Oxford University Press.
Wilder, Gary. 2015. *Freedom Time: Negritude, Decolonization and the Future of the World*. Durham, NC, and London: Duke University Press.
Williams, Raymond. 1985. *Keywords: A Vocabulary of Culture and Society*. Oxford: Oxford University Press. [Archive]

Les Corps glorieux des mots et des êtres, extrait

An Excerpt from *Les Corps glorieux des mots et des êtres*

V.Y. Mudimbe

Extrait de : Mudimbe, V.Y., *Les Corps glorieux des mots et des êtres : esquisse d'un jardin africain à la bénédictine*

Paris : Présence africaine ; Montréal : Humanitas, 1994, pp. 41-47.[1]

Version originale française

Entre 1885 et 1935, il y a, et très efficacement, une politique coloniale du toponyme. Elle opère à l'instar d'autres modes de domestication. Ainsi, par exemple, de nouveaux noms transforment des lieux africains en signes d'une dévotion monarchique : Albertville nomme ce qui deviendra Kalemie ; Baudouinville, Moba ; Léopoldville, Kinshasa. Ou encore, des signes africains récitent la mémoire vivante de l'épopée de l'exploration, comme ce fut le cas pour Banningville (Bandundu), Coquilhatville (Mbandaka), Stanleyville (Kisangani) ; ou, enfin, répondent, comme duplication, à des lieux lointains : tel le poste de Kwilu-Ngongo qui devint Moerbeke. En ces noms, c'est notre échec qui se célébrait. La critique de cet exercice et la débaptisation qui, au Zaïre, eurent lieu entre 1965 et 1970 au nom de l'authenticité de l'histoire et de l'espace, n'ont jamais - et d'ailleurs, le pouvaient-ils réellement ? - prétendu, dans la reprise d'anciens noms, retrouver et ramener la mémoire à un ordre primordial réel. C'est que la toponymie coloniale disait, non seulement une réorganisation radicale d'un ancien site et son quadrillage comme lieu administratif, mais, mieux encore et de manière générale, elle marquait *l'invention* de ce lieu et de son corps. Ses circuits et ses pulsions devaient réfléchir une nouvelle économie. Les missionnaires catholiques le signifiaient bien, dès le dernier quart du dix-neuvième siècle, en remplissant la carte géographique de tropismes sémantiques. Ceux-ci indiquaient l'avancée de leur action et l'évidence d'un nouvel ordre des choses. Ainsi, pour nous en tenir seulement à quelques postes fondés par les missionnaires de Scheut au Kasaï : Hemptine-Saint-Benoît, Kabwe-Christ Roi, Katende-Saint-Trudon, Mikalayi-Saint-Joseph etc. Le terme ou nom africain, d'emblée, se fléchit ici à la grâce et au pouvoir d'une conversion. Joint à un nom de saint, il cesse, immédiatement, d'être un nom propre pour devenir adjectif. De cette manière, il autorise aussi une différence entre, par exemple, Panda-Saint-Joseph dans le Sud du Katanga (à Likasi), où je fus baptisé, et Mikalayi-Saint-Joseph au Kasaï.

Le nom propre, écrivait feu mon ami Michel de Certeau, creuse des poches de valeurs familières ou cachées. Il peut avoir signification parce

1. Les directeur·ices d'ouvrage tiennent à remercier sincèrement les proches de V.Y. Mudimbe pour leur avoir accordé l'autorisation de reproduire cet extrait.

Excerpt from: Mudimbe, V.Y., *Les Corps glorieux des mots et des êtres : esquisse d'un jardin africain à la bénédictine*

Paris : Présence africaine ; Montréal : Humanitas, 1994, pp. 41-47.
Translation by Emelyn Lih.[1]

English translation

Between 1885 and 1935, there was a colonial policy of the toponym—a very effective one. It operated along the same lines as other modes of domestication. Thus, for example, new names transformed African places into symbols of monarchical devotion: Albertville was the name of what was to become Kalemie; Moba became Baudouinville; Kinshasa, Léopoldville. Or, further, African signs recited the living memory of the epic of exploration, as in the cases of Banningville (Bandundu), Coquilhatville (Mbandaka), Stanleyville (Kisangani); finally, they even answered, in a kind of reduplication, other, distant places: hence the Kwilu-Ngongo outpost became Moerbeke. In these names, our defeat was being celebrated. The critique of this exercise, and the name-changing process which took place in Zaïre between 1965 and 1970 in the name of history and authenticity, never claimed—and indeed, was making such a claim really possible?—to locate and return memory to a primordial, true order by reviving old place names. For not only did colonial toponymy bespeak a radical reorganisation of an existing site and its surveillance as an administrative locale: better yet and more broadly, renaming marked the *invention* of that new place and of its body. The site's circuits and drives had to reflect a new economy. Catholic missionaries made this clear, as early as the last quarter of the nineteenth century, by filling the geographical map with semantic tropisms. These indicated the advance of their actions and the proof of a new order of things. Limiting ourselves to the posts founded by the Scheut missionaries in the Kasaï region, we have Hemptine-Saint Benoît, Kabwe-Christ Roi, Katende-Saint Trudon, Mikalayi-Saint Joseph, and more. The African name or term, from the outset, bent before the grace and force of conversion. Twinned with a saint's name, it immediately ceased to be a proper noun and turned into an adjective. In this way it also served to mark differences between, say,

1. The editors are very thankful to Mudimbe's relatives for granting them the permission to reproduce this extract.

que, à l'instar d'une vocation ou d'un appel qui marque une psychologie et oriente un cheminement, il donne sens à un espace. La meilleure manière d'illustrer ce fait serait d'user *la marche*. Pour reprendre Michel de Certeau, la marche est fondamentalement paradoxale. Marcher, c'est en effet, en raison d'exigences externes qui s'imposent à celui qui s'avance (je dois aller là, il me faut ceci ou cela etc.), aller au dehors de soi, hors de chez soi. Mais marcher est aussi reconduire et étendre un espace intérieur : ceci est mon jardin, ma rue, mon village, ma région etc., et je peux les nommer.

Voilà un nom propre : Kapolowe. J'ai, autrefois, rêvé d'en écrire l'histoire. Je n'ai pas pu le faire et ne pourrai jamais le faire. J'ai orienté une de mes étudiantes vers le sujet. En vain. Kapolowe est une *localité* entre Likasi et Lubumbashi. Une petite gare sur le chemin de fer qui relie Ndola à Port-Francqui (Ilebo). Le 30 juin 1969, alors que le Congo Belge célèbre la fin d'une ère, c'est-à-dire au total et seulement, la rature d'un adjectif. Dom Théophanes me dépose en voiture à la porte sud de Jadotville. D'instinct, j'ai décidé de *marcher* jusqu'à Kapolowe. J'avais, patiemment, repris avec lui mon enfance : me remettre à moi-même une vue d'un passé. En réalité, je m'étais employé à me justifier. Solitaire, je me cherchais un oasis. Dom Théophanes m'avait opposé son regard et un silence. J'étais un bénédictin face à un bénédictin. Il ne doutait pas de moi et n'avait aucune raison de mettre en doute mes origines. Il les connaissait, m'avait élu à neuf ans, et était directement responsable de mon désir. Mais il était devenu sceptique, lointain. Je lui avais opposé, une journée durant, ma Foi. Un nœud nous réunissait : la *Règle* de Saint-Benoît. Mais tout nous séparait en ce moment précis de l'histoire : l'âge, la race, la vocation, et peut-être même notre impuissance commune face aux exigences et à l'appel de Saint-Benoît. Je m'étais découvert. Ma confession, libre et sincère, ne relevait ni de jeux ni des coutumes d'usage. Immonde, parce qu'agnostique, j'aurais voulu connaître les politesses à accomplir pour mériter un statut probablement impossible. Dom Théophanes m'a écouté. Toute une journée. En fin d'après-midi, il m'a conduit à la sortie de Jadotville. Rien de fixe dans ma tête. J'ai voulu reprendre, point par point, notre conversation : est-ce que le montage de ma confession trahissait ma névrose culturelle et, si oui, pour quelles raisons ?

Je marche donc vers Kapolowe. J'arriverai à la gare de Kapolowe aux environs de minuit. Je marche lentement. Je suis *in situ* et avance, heureux de pouvoir nommer des liens concrets. Ils unissent l'ordre d'une conquête et la métamorphose de l'espace que je traverse. D'autre part, les marques ou signes d'un passé (*un avant*) en cette nuit, devraient pouvoir répéter, et redire leurs propres différences comme expériences violentées. Dans

Panda-Saint Joseph, in the south of Katanga province (in Likasi), where I was baptised, and Mikalayi-Saint Joseph, in Kasaï.

The proper name, wrote my late friend Michel de Certeau, digs spaces for familiar or hidden values. It signifies because, like a vocation or a call which influences one's psyche and orients one's path, it gives meaning and direction to a space. The best way to illustrate this would be to use walking. Still following Michel de Certeau, walking is fundamentally paradoxical. Indeed, walking—because of external demands that impose themselves on the person advancing in space (I have to go there, I need this or that, etc.)—is the act of going outside oneself, outside one's home. But walking is also—according to inner convictions that the act can make visible—to maintain and extend an inner space: this is my garden, my street, my village, my region, etc., and I can name them.

Take a proper name: Kapolowe. Once I dreamed of writing its history. I was not able to, and I never will be able to. I advised one of my students to do so. In vain. Kapolowe is a *locality* between Likasi and Lubumbashi. A little stop along the railroad that links Ndola to Port-Francqui (now Ilebo). On June 30, 1960, as the Belgian Congo celebrated the end of an era, that is, all in all and only, the crossing-out of an adjective, Dom Théophanes dropped me off by car at the south gate of Jadotville. Instinctively, I chose to *walk* to Kapolowe. Dom Théophanes and I had patiently reviewed my childhood, giving myself the gift of a view of the past. In truth, I had been at pains to justify myself. A man alone, I was searching for an oasis. Dom Théophanes' answer had been his gaze and his silence. I was a Benedictine facing a Benedictine. He did not doubt me and had no reason to doubt my origins. They were known to him: he had chosen me when I was nine, and he was directly responsible for my desire [to join the order]. But now he had become sceptical, distant. For a whole day I had argued my faith to him. We were tied together by a knot: the Rule of Saint Benedict. But in this historical moment, everything separated us: age, race, vocation, and even, perhaps, our shared powerlessness before the demands and the call of Saint Benedict. I had been frank. My confession, free and sincere, bore no relation to the standard games and customs. I was vile because of the agnosticism I expressed, yet I would have liked to know what protocol to follow to be worthy of a better—but no doubt impossible—status. Dom Théophanes listened to me. All day long. As the afternoon came to a close, he brought me to the edge of Jadotville. Nothing was stable in my mind. I wanted to go over our conversation, point by point: did the way I'd put together my confession betray my cultural neuroses? If so, why?

le nom Congo-Belge par exemple, l'adjectif qui disparaît ce 30 juin 1960 est un objet parfait. Le vide qu'il laisse est, dès ce moment, inscrit dans l'histoire qui s'ouvre. Toutefois, il est un fait clair que l'évidence de la rupture, si elle est un fait, n'est nullement dans la rature de l'adjectif, ni même dans les signes nouveaux que cette suppression pourrait autoriser, mais dans le corps qui (sur-)vit comme terme et lettre de la métamorphose.

Kapolowe est un trait qui me rappelle et, effectivement, un autre lieu : Mpala. Non seulement parce que les deux bourgs se confondent avec une mission catholique et, économiquement, vivent principalement de la pêche. Mais l'espace y a été arrangé de la même manière. À une extrémité, la « mission » avec ses édifices (la résidence des ecclésiastiques, l'église, la maison des Sœurs, l'École etc.). À l'autre extrémité, le village avec de part et d'autre d'une unique rue centrale, des cases et quelques boutiques. Entre ces deux aires, il y a un espace vide, un espace vague d'un intérêt réel. Il n'est ni jardin, ni forêt. En somme, il n'est ni conjugaison de parterres, ni désordre absolu. Il irrite dans ce qu'il dévoile : la séparation. Il est tactique. Il répète et illustre un énoncé classique en damiers qu'à Élisabethville le pouvoir a nommé en un effet transparent : l'Avenue Limite Sud. La symbolique établie par cette distance et cette séparation en blanc et noir semble, paradoxalement, invoquer le mariage des deux extrémités. En somme, le Sud pourrait, un jour, devenir le Nord. On le sait cependant, cela est, géographiquement impossible. Du coup, la séparation raciale comme géographique trouverait sens en la métaphore truquée que dit une conjonction symbolique : Kapolowe-Saint-Gérard, comme on désignait le lieu dans les années 1920.

Toutefois, Kapolowe-Saint-Gérard, comme nom et comme symbole, nomme le croyable et le crédible. Le nom désigne, en effet, comme aurait dit Michel de Certeau, ce qui autorise une appropriation à partir d'une mémoire silencieuse : un projet, une légende, une histoire. Dans la nuit du 30 juin 1960, sur la route déserte où je marche solitaire, ce que le toponyme active, c'est l'ambiguïté essentielle des lieux. Le premier missionnaire qui vint dans la région apprit le bemba afin de communiquer. À l'époque du projet d'organiser une abbaye bénédictine à Kapolowe, dans les années 1920, le sanga est la langue véhiculaire. En 1958, lorsque j'y passe une semaine, il me faut demander au curé, un Bénédictin, Dom Barnabé Poilvache qui fut mon aumônier lorsque j'étais louveteau dans les années 1950 à Jadotville, s'il lui arrive de prêcher en swahili qui est, alors, la *linga franca*. J'ai été à Kapolowe la dernière fois en 1972. J'y conduisais une jeune étudiante française qui voulait y vivre comme une ethnologue.

So I walk toward Kapolowe. I would arrive at the Kapolowe train station around midnight. I walk slowly. I am *in situ* and I advance, happy to be able to name concrete connections. They bring together the order of a conquest and the metamorphosis of the space I move through. On another level, the marks or traces of a past (a *before*) in this night ought to be able to repeat and give new voice to their own differences as brutalized experiences. In the name 'Belgian Congo,' for instance, the adjective that disappeared on this thirtieth of June 1960 is a perfect artifact. The space it leaves is, from this moment on, inscribed in the new history opening its doors. Yet the fact is clear that the proof of the rupture, if the rupture is indeed fact, is in no way in the crossing-out of the adjective, nor even in the new signs that this erasure might authorise, but rather in the body that lives (and survives) as term and letter of the metamorphosis.

Kapolowe is a line of erasure that calls me back, and is also, indeed, another place: Mpala. Not only because both towns are intertwined with their own Catholic mission and depend primarily on fishing to subsist economically. But also because their space is organised in the same way. At one end, the 'mission' with its outbuildings—the residence of the clergy, the church, the nuns' house, the school, etc. At the other end, the village, with houses and a few shops lining a single main street. Between these two zones, there is an empty space, a vacant space of definite interest. It is neither garden nor forest. In other words, it is neither an arrangement of flowerbeds, nor total chaos. It irritates by what it reveals: separation. Its purpose is tactical. It repeats and illustrates a classic chequered disposition of space which, in Elisabethville, was given a transparent name by the powers in place: Southern Limit Avenue. The symbolism established by this distance and this separation into black and white seems paradoxically to invoke the marriage of the two extremes. In a sense, then, the South might, someday, become the North. And yet we know that, geographically, such a thing is impossible. So racial separation as geography finds expression in the rigged metaphor which a symbolic conjunction expresses: Kapolowe-Saint Gérard, as the place was called in the 1920s.

Nonetheless, the name and the symbol 'Kapolowe-Saint-Gérard' circumscribe what is believable and what is plausible. The name designates, as Michel de Certeau would have said, that which authorizes an appropriation emerging from an unspoken memory: a project, a legend, a history. In the night of June 30, 1960, along the empty road where I walk, alone, what the toponym activates is the essential ambiguity of places. The first missionary who arrived in the region learned Bemba in order to communicate. In the 1920s, when the project to set up a Benedictine abbey in Kapolowe

À ma surprise, j'ai découvert que les voix fortes dans les bars et les lieux publics parlaient lingala.

Considérons à présent le village de Mpala comme autre illustration. Il y a quelque chose d'absolu dans ce qu'il représente. Historiquement, Mpala est un *plus* : il prend vie dans la forteresse d'Émile Storms dont hérite la mission des Pères Blancs en 1885. Le bâtiment de la mission est massif. Il se présente d'emblée comme murailles, et celles-ci sont solides, immenses, fermées sur elles-mêmes. Des tourelles rappellent l'ordre des gardes et des rainures pour fusils manifestent encore la signification originelle du fort. Ce bâtiment est une *synecdoque* : il dit sa propre spatialité et le projet qui l'a rendu possible. Je peux noter les figures suivantes : l'exercice esclavagiste des Arabisés du dix-neuvième siècle qui exploitent la région, le projet missionnaire qui lui succède comme étape dans la constitution d'un royaume chrétien dont rêve alors le Cardinal de Lavigerie ; et enfin la mission catholique qui, les dix premières années de ce siècle, s'aménage comme un « fort » politique battant monnaie et organisant militairement sa propre protection. Elle s'illustre dans le rôle qu'elle incarne au début de la première guerre mondiale. Elle accueille des « protégés » de l'Église et de la Belgique (alors symboliquement nommée la Mère-Patrie), résiste durant la première guerre contre l'attaque et les coups de canon allemands qui proviennent de l'autre côté du lac séparant le Congo-Belge du Tanganyika ; et en 1918, célèbre en un *Te Deum* historique, la fin d'une guerre européenne à laquelle elle s'est charnellement identifiée.

Comme signe politique et religieux, la Mission de Mpala est ainsi une *synecdoque.* Elle étend, en une expansion sémantique, le territoire limité d'une « paroisse » catholique. Une église et ses dépendances deviennent des fragments d'un *plus* spatial se déroulant comme nouvelle mémoire ou, plus exactement, comme mémoire de l'histoire de la conversion de la région. Cette nouvelle mémoire collective s'identifie à un espace mais aussi à une tradition. Elle s'impose, en effet, comme opération et processus d'une causalité double, l'une *ad extram,* et l'autre, *ad intram.* De ce fait, quelle que soit la richesse ou la pauvreté des souvenirs, cette mémoire est un lieu de rencontre, d'influences réciproques et, à ce titre, de tensions. À Mpala, la causalité externe est déterminante : elle explique le pouvoir ecclésiastique et la pertinence de la raison coloniale.

En paradoxe, l'espace géographique de la mission de Mpala fait surgir une autre figure : *l'asyndète.* Celle-ci brise des liens, défait la continuité historique des événements et efface ce qui, comme conjonction, affermit la cohérence de la nouvelle mémoire ou les nœuds reliant logiquement des fragments. Par exemple, la rivière Lukufo, le village et l'école de la

was formed, Sanga was the vehicular language. In 1958, when I spent a week there, I had to ask the priest—a Benedictine named Dom Barnabé Poilvache, who was my chaplain when I was a tyro member of the order, in the 1950s in Jadotville—whether he ever preached in Swahili, which was the lingua franca at that time. The last time I found myself in Kapolowe was in 1972. I was accompanying a young French student who wanted to live there as an ethnologist. To my surprise, I discovered that the loudest voices in the bars and public spaces were speaking Lingala.

Let us now consider the village of Mpala as another illustration. There is a touch of the absolute in what it represents. Historically, Mpala is *more*: it took shape around the fort constructed by Émile Storms, which the White Fathers missionaries inherited in 1885. The mission building is massive. It appears initially as a forest of walls, and those walls are solid, immense, closed in on themselves. Turrets remind one of the watchmen's rounds, and the grooves for resting guns indicate the fort's original purpose. The edifice is a *synecdoche*: it expresses its own spatiality and the project that made it possible. I can identify the following aspects of its style: the enslaving activity of the Arabised nineteenth-century individuals that exploited the region; the missionary project that was one step toward constituting the Christian realm that Cardinal Lavigerie dreamed of; and finally, the Catholic mission which, over the first ten years of the twentieth century, set itself up as a political 'fort,' coining money and organising its own military protection. The Catholic mission drew praise for the role it took on at the beginning of the First World War. The mission welcomed 'protégés' of the Church and of Belgium (then symbolically known as the Motherland); resisted, during the First World War, the German attacks and cannon fire coming from the other side of the lake separating Belgian Congo from Tanganyika; and in 1918, celebrated with a historic *Te Deum* the end of a European war with which it had fully, corporeally identified itself.

As a political and religious sign, the Mpala Mission is thus a *synecdoche*. It extends, in a kind of semantic expansion, the limited territory of a Catholic 'parish.' A church and its outbuildings become the fragments of a spatial *more* that unfolds as a new form of memory, or more precisely as the memory of the region's history of conversion. This new collective memory identifies with a space but also with a tradition. Indeed, it acts as operation and process of a dual causality, one *ad extram*, the other *ad intram*. For this reason, regardless of how rich or poor the stock of remembrances may be, this memory is a meeting place, a site of reciprocal influences—and thus of tensions. In Mpala, the external causality dominates, explaining ecclesiastical power and the relevance of colonial reason.

mission avant l'indépendance se défont. Le sol-même de la mission se fissure comme s'il lui fallait témoigner aussi. Les missionnaires européens ont d'ailleurs abandonné cette forteresse dans les années 1970, la confiant à la garde et aux soins d'un catéchiste zaïrois qui, ainsi actualise l'envers du désir des fondateurs de Mpala-la-forteresse : le lieutenant Storms, les Pères Blancs Moinet et Moncet, le capitaine Joubert. D'un côté donc, le signe de l'Empire et de la conquête s'instaura comme générosité contre l'esclavage et le paganisme et, en un même mouvement, s'érigea comme lieu de mythomanie. De l'autre côté du temps, dérisoire, un catéchiste veille, à présent, sur des bâtiments immenses mais désertés. Il ne semble préoccupé que par l'espérance absurde de sa propre conversion à la loi d'une conquête et d'une mémoire récentes. Elles se sont imposées à lui, comme dans le cas de mon père, j'imagine, comme nécessité de son intégration dans le royaume d'une nouvelle organisation du pouvoir. Et il se doit de les protéger contre son propre passé.

Un inventaire plus approprié du sens de *l'asyndète* pourrait s'établir, plus aisément, à partir de ce que l'espace de Mpala lui-même propose. Ré-imaginons, comme je l'ai fait, que je suis en train de descendre de la « mission » et m'avance vers le « village » de Mpala. Je vais du Nord au Sud. Derrière moi : la mission, le cap Tembwe et le Delta de la Lukufu.

Devant : le village et, au loin, le mont Nzawa domine tout l'horizon au Sud et s'esquisse de la galerie forestière qui s'étale jusqu'à l'Ouest. Convertis au christianisme, les habitants de Mpala abandonnèrent officiellement, au début de ce siècle, le génie de la terre qui habite le Nzawa. En moins d'un siècle de transformations progressives, le Nord, avec sa cloche organisant le temps de la vie, du travail et de la prière, et ses murailles de pierre, est devenu livre et corps exemplaires. Ce Nord s'est substitué, avec ses nouvelles grilles (économiques, culturelles et spirituelles), à l'ensemble ancien qu'activait le Sud. Cette modification fut et se trouve être encore brisure dont témoignent des propositions qui rendent compte de la fonction du manque. En effet, mon commentaire sur la modification de l'espace de Mpala se conçoit et s'indique en négatif : *à la place de*, ou, en référence silencieuse, à un champ ou ordre dit traditionnel dont témoignerait, par exemple, la divinité du Nzawa.

La coupure ou le déplacement que signifie l'opposition entre le Nord et le Sud de Mpala (ce à quoi ouvrent les promesses de l'école au Nord comme distance par rapport aux mœurs et agencements symboliques enseignés à ceux que l'on initie dans la forêt du Sud) montre, en réalité, que l'*asyndète* marque, pour ainsi dire, une rupture positive en un schéma évolutif. La fragmentation du temps répond, comme image et comme

Paradoxically, the Mpala mission's geographical space brings out another stylistic analogy: the *asyndeton*. An asyndetic space breaks links, undoes the historical continuity of events and erases that which, as conjunction, bolsters the new memory's coherence or the knots of meaning creating logical connections between fragments. For example: the Lufuko River, the village and the mission school from before independence are disconnected. The very earth on which the mission is built develops cracks as if it too were compelled to bear witness. Other European missionaries would abandon the fortress in the 1970s, entrusting it to the keeping and the care of a Zairean catechist who thus actualises the underside of the wishes of Mpala-the-fortress's founders: Lieutenant Storms, the White Fathers Moinet and Moncet, Captain Joubert. On one side, then, the sign of Empire and conquest set itself up as generosity against slavery and paganism, while in the same gesture it became a hotbed of mythomania. Today, at the other end of the time spectrum, a lone, ludicrous catechist watches over immense but deserted buildings. The catechist himself seems preoccupied solely by an absurd hope for his own conversion to the law of a recent conquest and shared memory. Conquest and memory imposed themselves on him, as they did on my father, I imagine: they are the price of his integration into the realm of a new organisation of power. And he has taken on the role of protecting them against his own past.

A more appropriate inventory of the meaning of the *asyndeton* could set itself up yet more easily based on what the space of Mpala itself proposes. Let us reimagine, as I have done, that I am walking down from the 'mission' and heading toward the 'village' of Mpala. I am traveling from North to South. Behind me are the mission, the Tengwe headland and the Lufuku Delta. Ahead of me lie the village and, in the distance, the Nzawa peak, dominating the entire southern horizon and emerging from the riverbank woods spreading out to the west. Once they had converted to Christianity, Mpala's inhabitants abandoned, officially, at the beginning of the century, the earth spirit that lived in Mount Nzawa. In less than a century's worth of gradual transformation, the North, with its bell organising the times devoted to life, work, and prayer—and its high stone walls—became an exemplary book and body. By a process of substitution, this North and its new grids (economic, cultural, spiritual) replaced the old ensemble animated by the South. Such a modification was and still is a fracture to which propositions that give an account of this absence's function bear witness. My own remark on the modification of Mpala's space was conceived and expressed negatively: *in the place of*, or in silent reference to, a field or

réalité, à l'écart qui, dans l'espace réel de Mpala, opposa très concrètement, jusque dans les années 1960, deux jeux de formes et symboles : le Nord contre le Sud, le futur contre le passé, la modernité contre la tradition. Analysée rigoureusement, cette opposition pourrait être conçue comme lieu de rencontre de *l'asyndète* et de *la synecdoque*. Au *moins* de *l'asyndète* et à ses jeux d'écart et de brisures, répond *le plus* de la totalité invoquée par *la synecdoque* qui mobilise liens, conjonctions et expansions.

L'acculturation promue par ce lieu n'a été au service du colonisé et de sa société, malheureusement, que comme l'envers d'un autre projet. Son objectif était, avant tout, de servir le pouvoir colonial. Afin de s'établir, celui-ci inventa une nouvelle société. À Mpala, comme ailleurs au Congo, le renouvellement de l'espace s'élabore au départ de trois principaux paradigmes : la religion et le code éthique chrétiens (croyances et pratiques) ; et, au début, un enseignement strictement élémentaire (lire, écrire, calculer) auquel l'on joint, exceptionnellement, l'étude de la langue française ; enfin, la promotion du travail manuel et de son utilité pour le Congolais. Ce programme officiellement promulgué donne ses preuves dès les années 1930. Monsieur E. De Jonghe, dans *L'Enseignement des Indigènes au Congo-Belge* (1931), se plaint du Noir devenu *déraciné* qui « se croit l'égal du blanc et même supérieur ». Dois-je penser à mon père ou à moi-même aujourd'hui ? Un de mes amis belges, Jean-Louis Litt, un sociologue, commentait ce fait, notait qu'il était « normal qu'un enseignement soigneusement programmé pour inculquer aux Noirs un nouveau code (...) ait abouti à les déraciner : le contraire eût été étonnant. Par ailleurs, les Blancs se sont imposés comme "groupe de référence" aux Noirs et ce genre de relations inter-groupes soulève toujours des problèmes entre les signes d'intégration Culturelle ».

Ainsi, c'est dans le village, à mi-chemin entre les signes totalitaires de la « Mission » de Kapolowe ou de Mpala et ceux de «la forêt» que se donne à voir et à penser l'union possible des symboles de ma modernité et de ma tradition. Par exemple, les cases en terre battue ou, parfois, en blocs de ciment, y ont une forme rectangulaire. Cette forme géométrique est *un texte récent*. Certes, elle intègre encore, dans la forme qui constitue le toit, comme dans la glaise et le bois soumis au moule pour former les murs, l'ancienne manière de construire et les matériaux d'usage qu'observèrent E. Storms et les premiers Pères Blancs. Mais cette forme rectangulaire, aujourd'hui générale, provient de l'extension d'un modèle architectural swahili que la Mission et l'autorité coloniale promeuvent au début du siècle. Il se substitue à la hutte ronde au toit conique des Tabwa, que Léon Dardenne (1865-1912) semble avoir bien reproduire dans les esquisses

order one could call traditional, of which the divinity inhabiting Nzawa would be a manifestation.

What the break or displacement signified by the opposition between Mpala's North and South truly shows—an opposition opened by the Northern school's promises of distance from the customs and symbolic arrangements taught to those who are initiated in the Southern forest—is that the *asyndeton* marks what we might call a positive breach in an evolving pattern. The fragmentation of time responds, as image and reality, to the gap in the actual space of Mpala, which until the 1960s separated two sets of forms and symbols: North against South, future against past, modernity against tradition. Rigorously analysed, this opposition could be conceived as the juncture of *asyndeton* and *synecdoche.* As answer to the *asyndeton*'s *less*, to its games of gaps and cracks, we have the *more* of the totality invoked by the *synecdoche*, one that mobilises connections, conjunctions, and expansions.

The acculturation promoted by this place only served the colonized and their society, alas, as the underside of another project, whose objective was above all to serve the colonizer's power. In order to establish itself, the colonizer invented a new society. In Mpala, and moreover in the Congo as a whole, spatial renewal builds on three principal paradigms: Christian religion and ethical codes (beliefs and practices); an early education with a limited mandate (reading, writing, basic math) to which is added the study of the French language as an exceptional complement; lastly, the promotion of manual labour and its usefulness for the Congolese. This officially announced programme began to show results as early as the 1930s. Mr. E. De Jonghe, in his *L'Enseignement des Indigènes au Congo-Belge* [Teaching the Natives of the Belgian Congo] (1931), deplores the now *uprooted* Black man who 'fancies himself the white man's equal and even superior.' Should I think of my father? Of myself, today? One of my Belgian friends, the sociologist Jean-Louis Litt, discussing this phenomenon, noted that it is 'normal that a curriculum carefully planned to inculcate a new code to Black people [...] should have resulted in their finding themselves rootless: anything else would have been astonishing. What is more, the White people presented themselves as a kind of "group of reference" to the Black people, and this type of relationship between groups always raises issues regarding the signs of cultural integration.'

It is thus in the village, halfway between the totalitarian signs of the 'Mission' in Kapolowe or Mpala and those of the 'forest,' that the possible union between the symbols of my modernity and my tradition lets itself be thought and seen. The huts, for example, made of beaten earth or

qu'il dessine lors de la mission scientifique Charles Lemaire au Katanga (1889-1900).

C'est dans ce contexte que, protégé à l'extrême, il me faut grandir, il me faut croître. Bien-sûr, Dom Théophanes n'est pas mon père. Mais il incarne un style, signifie et me suggère un avenir. Tout, alentour, lui donne raison et m'invite à me plier. Je le fais, et sans regrets. Au fait, ai-je un autre choix réellement ? Mes parents naturels n'existent pas. Plus exactement, ils constituent une absence obligée pour ma conversion et ma promotion. Leur annulation me brise dans le sens du pouvoir. Un motif ambigu peut accorder mes angoisses d'adolescent à l'ordre d'un orgueil magistral : *Multi sunt vocati, pauci sunt electi* : beaucoup sont appelés, mais peu sont élus. J'appartenais, pensai-je, au monde des élus.

sometimes blocks of cement, have a rectangular shape in these towns. That geometrical choice is *a recent text*. To be sure, it still incorporates, in the straw that makes up the roof, as in the clay and wood laid in moulds to shape the walls, the old ways of building, and the same materials observed by E. Storms and the first White Fathers. But this rectangular shape, which today is widespread, comes from the extension of a Swahili architectural model that the Mission and the colonial authorities promoted at the beginning of the century. It replaced the round huts with a conical roof built by the Tabwa, which Léon Dardenne (1865–1912) seems to have accurately reproduced in the sketches he made during Charles Lemaire's scientific expedition to the Katanga region in 1899–1900.

This is the context in which, protected to an extreme extent, I must grow, I must develop. Dom Théophanes is not my father, of course. But he incarnates a style, signifies and suggests to me a future. Everything around us pleads in his favour, prevails upon me to yield. I do so, and without regret. In truth, do I have any other choice? My biological parents do not exist; or more precisely, they constitute an absence necessary for my conversion and my advancement. Their cancelling-out breaks me, sending me in the direction of power. An ambiguous refrain allows me to harmonize my adolescent angst with the order's haughty pride: *Multi sunt vocati, pauci sunt electi*. Many are called but few are chosen. I belonged, thought I, to the world of the chosen.

Sammy Baloji, figurer la mémoire stratifiée d'un territoire forgé par la politique coloniale

Une conversation avec Maëline Le Lay, au prisme des écrits de V.Y. Mudimbe

---

Sammy Baloji: Depicting the Stratified Memory of a Territory Forged by Colonial Policy

A Conversation with Maëline Le Lay, through the Prism of the Writings of V.Y. Mudimbe

---

Version française

Kasala pour moi-même
Fiston Mwanza Mujila

j'ai décidé d'être heureux
de danser la rumba jusqu'à l'usure
de reprendre tous mes noms, bricoles d'antan
de demeurer l'enfant de la mine
et du chemin de fer
la mémoire familiale épousant la locomotive
l'exil dans l'œuf, l'éternelle solitude
(Mwanza Mujila 2021)

Bruxelles, décembre 2020.

Sammy Baloji, plasticien et artiste visuel reconnu dans le champ de l'art contemporain, est un artiste né en 1978 et grandi à Lubumbashi, au Katanga, République démocratique du Congo, dans un pays qui s'appelait encore le Zaïre. Sammy Baloji était encore enfant lorsque V.Y. Mudimbe quitta le pays mais c'est de cette époque et de la période coloniale dont traite majoritairement l'artiste dans son œuvre, à l'instar de Mudimbe. Ils ont donc en commun de proposer une réflexion stimulante sur la mémoire et l'épistémologie de l'Afrique (notoirement du Congo).

Au vu de l'influence évidente de l'œuvre de Mudimbe sur celle de Sammy Baloji – notamment *A Blueprint for Toads and Snakes*[1] et le film complémentaire *Tales of the Copper Cross Garden* (2018), c'est tout naturellement que nous avions invité l'artiste à participer aux manifestations autour de la pensée de V.-Y. Mudimbe organisées à Nairobi en décembre 2019.

Dans cette conversation informelle s'entrelacent des réflexions autour de la politique de bâti et d'aménagement de la ville coloniale – ici la capitale du cuivre, Élisabethville (qui deviendra Lubumbashi, au Katanga minier) –, sur sa manière de figurer la mémoire de ce lieu et d'interroger les liens de continuité ou de rupture d'une époque à l'autre, et sur la façon dont sa lecture de Mudimbe fait écho à sa recherche-création.

Cet échange vivant résulte d'une forme de compagnonnage entre Sammy Baloji et moi-même, depuis une dizaine d'années, de Lubumbashi à Paris et Bruxelles, puisque nous avons travaillé à plusieurs projets communs[2].

1. Le site de la galerie Framer Framed, à Amsterdam, où fut réalisée l'exposition, offre de nombreuses vues sur l'installation, ainsi qu'une documentation abondante, notamment le livret d'exposition (Velsen 2018 ; "Exhibition: A Blueprint for Toads and Snakes" 2018).

2. Après avoir participé à l'édition 2008 de la biennale d'art contemporain Picha à Lubumbashi, dirigée par Sammy Baloji, dans le cadre d'une collaboration entre

English Version

Translation by Michael Paul.

Kasala for myself
Fiston Mwanza Mujila

I decided to be happy
to dance the rumba till worn out
to take back all my names, yesterday's odds an ends
to stay a child of the mine
and the railroad
the family memory married to the engine
the exile in the bud, eternal solitude
(Mwanza Mujila 2021)

Brussels, December 2020.

Sammy Baloji, a recognised visual plastic artist in the field of contemporary art, was born in 1978 and grew up in Lubumbashi, in Katanga, the Democratic Republic of Congo—a country then called Zaire. Sammy Baloji was still a child when V.Y. Mudimbe left the country, but it is from this time and the colonial period that the artist takes inspiration in his work, as did Mudimbe. So, what they have in common is that they both provide a stimulating reflection on the memory and the epistemology of Africa (and notably of the Congo).

Given the obvious influence of the work of Mudimbe on Sammy Baloji's own work—in particular *A Blueprint for Toads and Snakes*[1] and the film associated with it, *Tales of a Copper Grass Garden* (2018)—it was altogether natural to invite the artist to take part in the events focused on the thinking of V.Y. Mudimbe held in Nairobi in December 2019.

In this informal conversation are interwoven reflections on the built environment and urban planning policy of the colonial city—here the copper capital, Élisabethville (which became Lubumbashi) in the mining region Katanga)—on his way of representing the memory of this place and of investigating the links of continuity or rupture between one epoch and another, and eventually on how his reading of Mudimbe echoes his own research-creation.

This lively exchange results from a kind of amicable collaboration between Sammy Baloji and myself, over the past ten years or so, from

1. The website of the gallery Framer Framed, in Amsterdam, where the exhibition was held shows several views of the exhibition, and a wealth of documentation, notably the exhibition brochure (Velsen 2018; "Exhibition: A Blueprint for Toads and Snakes" 2018).

Il s'appuie aussi sur une connaissance intime de la ville de Lubumbashi, sa ville natale et la ville où j'ai passé deux ans et demi dans le cadre de ma recherche doctorale.

MLL : Comment as-tu commencé à travailler sur et à partir d'archives visuelles ?

SB : Cela est né de la rencontre entre pratiques, si tu veux, entre une artiste qui fait de la photographie mais qui touche plusieurs sujets, Marie-Françoise Plissard, et un architecte qui est aussi un historien de la période coloniale, Johan Lagae[3]. Johan aborde le bâtiment pour son utilité mais s'intéresse aussi à sa genèse, à la politique et aux enjeux qui vont avec, à la fois au niveau urbain, au niveau de l'administration coloniale, au niveau de la planification… Donc il y a plusieurs couches de lectures. Et à cela venait s'ajouter mon regard, celui d'un autochtone qui, lui, lit cet espace et ces bâtiments en lien avec les histoires des occupants…

MLL : … que tu connais intimement.

SB : … que je connais, ou en tout cas je me fie à ma propre relation à ces lieux et ces espaces-là, et cela me lie instantanément à ma propre histoire, à des trajectoires qui ne sont pas qu'individuelles, qui ne sont pas d'ordre administratif … Et donc c'est comme ça que j'ai découvert les images d'archives.

Avec Hubert [Maheux[4]], l'idée était de mettre en place des journées du patrimoine qui consisteraient en une mise en place d'une exposition mais aussi des conférences, des interventions d'intellectuels dans les différents domaines des sciences sociales, en architecture, etc. Des journées du patrimoine qui favoriseraient le maintien ou la sauvegarde ou la mise en valeur de tout ce patrimoine. Et à ce sujet, Johan [Lagae] a écrit un article qui est intéressant sur la question du partage, la question étant de savoir si cet espace est un patrimoine qui est partagé au niveau des expériences. Est-ce que c'est réellement partagé entre l'administration coloniale et la population qui en hérite ? Peut-on parler de partage d'héritage ?

---

le collectif Libre-Écrire et Picha, nous avons fait une intervention commune à une Journée d'études (« Joseph Kiwele à Élisabethville (1946-1961) : fragments d'un chantier de recherche », Journée d'études « L'"*Archival Turn*" dans l'Art contemporain : Focus sur le Congo », co-organisée par Maureen Murphy et Sandrine Colard, Paris, INHA, 2017). Enfin, j'ai participé au catalogue d'exposition *A Blueprint for Toads and Snakes* (Velsen 2018).

3. Sammy Baloji, Marie-Françoise Plissard, et Johan Lagae, *La Série Likasi*, photomontage panoramique de la Ville de Likasi, 2005-2006.

4. Feu Hubert Maheux fut directeur de la Halle de l'Étoile, ex-CCF, aujourd'hui Institut français de Lubumbashi, entre 2004 et 2008.

Lubumbashi to Paris and Brussels, since we worked on several joint projects.[2] It is also based on an intimate knowledge of the city of Lubumbashi, Sammy's birthplace and the town where I spent two and a half years doing research for my PhD.

MLL: How did you start working on and from visual archives?

SB: That grew out of an encounter between practices, if you like, between an artist who does some photography but who works on several subjects, Marie-Françoise Plissard, and an architect who is also a historian of the colonial period, Johan Lagae.[3] Johan approaches the building from the point of view of its utility but is also interested in its origins, in the policy and issues that go with it, both at the urban level and vis-à-vis the colonial administration, the planning. So there is a reading at several levels. And added to that, there's also my own view—the view of a native, who could read this space and these buildings in relation to the histories of those who live there...

MLL: ...and who you know intimately.

SB: ...who I know, or in any case I rely on my own relationship with these places and these spaces, which instantly brings me back to my own history, to experiences that are not solely individual nor of an administrative nature. And so that's how I got to know the archive images.

With Hubert [Maheux],[4] the idea was to organise Heritage Days which would involve putting on an exhibition and also organising lectures, talks by intellectuals working in various fields of the social sciences, architecture and so on. Heritage Days that would encourage the conservation or the protection or the valorisation of the whole of this heritage. And on this subject, Johan [Lagae] wrote an interesting article on the issue of sharing, the question being to know whether this space is a shared heritage in terms of experiences. Is it really shared between the colonial administration and the population that are heirs to it? Can we talk of shared heritage?

2. After taking part in the 2008 Biennale of Picha contemporary art in Lubumbashi, directed by Sammy Baloji, as part of the collaboration between the collective Libre-Écrire and Picha, we gave a joint lecture during the Journée d'études ("Joseph Kiwele at Élisabethville (1946–61): 'fragments d'un chantier de recherche,' *Journée d'études* 'L' '*Archival Turn*' dans l'art contemporain : Focus sur le Congo,'" co-organised by Maureen Murphy and Sandrine Colard, Paris, INHA, 2017). Finally, I contributed to the catalogue of the exhibition *A Blueprint for Toads and Snakes* (Velsen 2018).

3. Sammy Baloji, Marie-Françoise Plissard, and Johan Lagae, *The Likasi Series* (Panoramic photomontage of the city of Likasi, 2005–6).

4. Late Hubert Maheux was director of the Halle de l'Étoile, ex-CCF, today the Institut français de Lubumbashi, from 2004 to 2008.

MLL : Et d'héritage dans le sens où il serait approprié véritablement…

SB : Oui, mais par les deux parties en même temps, la Belgique postcoloniale et le Congo postcolonial. Cela pose la question de savoir comment on partage cette histoire finalement. Mais quand on partage cette histoire, ça veut aussi dire qu'il faut rendre audibles ces expériences en fait, parce que tout d'abord, tu as l'espace qui est construit mais qui est pensé par d'autres que les autochtones, et, par la suite, tu as les autochtones qui occupent cet espace mais qui ont leurs propres souvenirs et expériences, notamment s'agissant de l'implantation de l'espace de travail, de mémoire moderne tel qu'il est proposé. Pour moi, c'est en travaillant en collaboration avec des disciplines différentes que j'ai pu faire une plongée dans cette histoire coloniale que je ne connaissais pas.

MLL : Que tu ne connaissais pas ? Tu veux dire à l'époque, quand tu commençais la photographie ?

SB : Oui car la question de l'histoire et de la mémoire coloniale n'est pas vraiment étudiée à l'école. Enfin à l'université de Lubumbashi, je n'ai pas souvenir d'avoir eu des cours qui me permettaient de comprendre pourquoi il y a ces villes et pourquoi et comment la Belgique est arrivée…

MLL : Et puis qu'est-ce qu'on fait de ça, de ce qui reste…

SB : Et qu'est-ce qu'on fait de ça après, oui… Je pense que le programme que proposait Hubert [Maheux] devrait faire partie du cursus universitaire. C'est un cours que les gens devraient apprennent à l'école, comme ça ils auraient un lien avec cette période coloniale qui est aussi vraiment de l'ordre d'un héritage…

MLL : Parle-t-on quand même de la colonisation à école ? Et dans quels termes, est-ce qu'il s'agit plus d'un état de faits ? Je veux dire, est-ce que vous dit « Voilà, le Congo a été colonisé par la Belgique », et on ne questionne pas au-delà pour savoir la manière dont ça s'est fait ?

SB : Mais c'est quoi « coloniser », tu vois ? Enfin oui, on a été colonisés, d'accord, mais ça veut dire quoi, « coloniser » ? Qui a joué quel rôle, qu'est-ce qu'il s'est passé et comment on en arrive à avoir son indépendance ? Quels sont les legs coloniaux aujourd'hui ? Si tu me dis : « Les colons sont arrivés, puis ils sont partis et nous avons récupéré le pouvoir », alors c'est très simple de dire : « Les colons sont les mauvais », tu vois, et puis basta ! Mais en même temps, ça ne veut rien dire en fait.

MLL: And of heritage in the sense where it would be really appropriated.

SB: Yes, but by the two parties at the same time; postcolonial Belgium and postcolonial Congo. It raises the question of knowing how we can share this history finally. But when we share this history, it also means making these experiences really audible, because first of all, you have the space which is built but which is planned by people other than the native population, and then you've got the native population who occupy this space but who have their own memories and experiences, in particular as concerns the location of the workplace, of modern memory as it's presented. For me, working in collaboration with different disciplines made me able to delve into this colonial history that I knew nothing about.

MLL: That you knew nothing about? You mean at that time, when you started out in photography?

SB: Yes, because the question of the colonial history and memory is not really studied at school. At Lubumbashi University, I don't remember having any lectures which would have enabled me to understand why there are these towns and why Belgium arrived on the scene.

MLL: And then what do you do with that, with what's left?

SB: And what do we do with that afterwards? Yes... I think the programme Hubert [Maheux] planned should be part of a university course. It's a course people should study at school. That way they'd have a connection with this colonial period which is also really a kind of heritage.

MLL: All the same, do they talk about colonisation at school? And in what terms? Is it more an account of the facts? I mean, did they tell you, "There it is, the Congo was colonised by Belgium," and not to look any further into how it was done?

SB: But what is "colonise," you see? In the end, okay, we were colonised, but what does "colonise" mean? Who played what role, what happened, and how did we manage to get independence? What is the colonial legacy today? If you say "The settlers arrived, then they left and we took back power," then it's easy to say, "The settlers are the baddies," you see, and then that's all! But at the same time, it means nothing, in fact.

MLL: You mean just to say that is not going to help us to really understand what happened?

SB: Yes. But this reading may be explained historically since, for instance, the period of Mobutu was a period marked by a dictatorial regime during which recognition of the traditional power served to recognise or even legitimise the totalitarian aspect of the dictatorial regime.

MLL : Tu veux dire que se contenter de dire cela ne va pas aider à comprendre réellement ce qu'il s'est passé.

SB : Oui. Mais cette lecture peut s'expliquer historiquement puisque par exemple, la période de Mobutu est une période marquée par un pouvoir dictatorial durant laquelle la reconnaissance du pouvoir traditionnel a permis de reconnaître, voire de légitimer le pouvoir dictatorial dans son aspect totalitaire.

MLL : C'est une instrumentalisation.

SB : Oui et c'est en soi une reconduction du dispositif colonial. Le régime dans son établissement, dans son fonctionnement, n'a pas remis en question le legs colonial.

MLL : Est-ce que c'est un des sens de ton film, *Tales of the Copper Grass Garden*, dans lequel tu filmes des images d'aujourd'hui qui se passent à la Gécamines[5] ? Alors qu'avant, dans la série *Mémoire*[6], c'étaient des montages à partir des ruines de cette période ? Est-ce que c'est une façon de montrer ce qui perdure ou ce qui a été transformé, y compris au sens propre puisque tu nous montres justement, dans le film, des étapes de transformation du cuivre… Est-ce que c'est ce rapport au passé que tu as voulu interroger en nous montrant des images de l'exploitation du cuivre dans la GCM (Gécamines) d'aujourd'hui ?

SB : Je pense qu'on peut parler de bibliothèque coloniale… Quand Mudimbe aborde la question de cette bibliothèque coloniale, il suggère que c'est tout un système qui s'est mis en place, ce n'est pas l'affaire d'une personne. Cela implique la société dans ses organes de fonctionnement. Par exemple dans son ouvrage, *Les Corps glorieux des mots et des êtres*, à un certain moment il parle de la manière dont il enseigne aux étudiants, il raconte qu'il favorise la comparaison des documents, par rapport à des sources très très différentes. Et que cette comparaison n'est pas là pour prouver la réalité mais pour permettre plusieurs possibilités de lecture : qu'est-ce qui résulte de cette confrontation ?… Je retrouve dans cette confrontation de documents une part de ma pratique en quelque sorte. Ce ne sont pas des états de faits ou des propositions abouties dans le sens où je proposerais une vérité. C'est plutôt l'idée de confronter des choses,

---

5. Gécamines (Générale des Carrières et des Mines), entreprise minière d'État qui constitua l'épine dorsale de la colonisation belge au Congo, autour de laquelle se construisit la ville de Lubumbashi et l'arc cuprifère urbain où s'était installée la Gécamines (Kolwezi, Likasi, Kambove, Kakanda, Kipushi, Shinkolobwe), anciennement UMHK (Union minière du Haut-Katanga). Elle survit péniblement aujourd'hui.

6. La série *Mémoire* (2004-2006) est une série de montages photographiques qui comptent parmi les pièces les plus connues de Sammy Baloji.

MLL: It's instrumentalisation.

SB: Yes, and in itself it's a continuation of the colonial system. In the way it was set up, the way it functioned, the regime did not question the colonial legacy.

MLL: Is that one of the meanings of your film, *Tales of the Copper Grass Garden*, where you shot images that take place today at Gécamines?[5] While before in the series *Mémoire*,[6] it was a montage using the ruins from that period? Is that a way of showing what is lasting or what has been transformed, including in the literal sense since in the film you show us the stages in the transformation of the copper. Is it that relation with the past that you wanted to look at by showing us images of the exploitation of copper in the GCM (Gécamines) today?

SB: I think we can talk of a colonial library. When Mudimbe deals with the question of the colonial library, he suggests that it is a whole system that was set up, it wasn't one person's doing. It involves the society in all its components. For example, in his work *Les Corps glorieux des mots et des êtres*, at one point, Mudimbe speaks of the way he teaches students, he tells how he encourages the comparison of documents relative to very, very different sources. And that this comparison is not there to prove the reality but to enable several possible readings: what is it that results from this comparison? In a way, in this comparison of documents, I find something of my own practice. These are not statements of facts or definite propositions in the sense that I would be proposing a truth. It is rather the idea of comparing things, different subjects, thoughts, experiences but which are all based on real facts, documented facts, or scientific or theoretical ideas. Comparing them and then seeing what comes out of it. I was trained as a social communicator originally, I have this awareness of semiology, but in the sense of social communication, that is to say, the receptive part is important. In setting up an audible discourse, you have to be aware of who the message is addressed to. At the same time, the specificity of the image is its polysemy. And that's why I feel at home with this comparison of images. It's the very pinnacle of polysemy, in fact.

5. Gécamines (Générale des Carrières et des Mines), the state mining company which constituted the backbone of the Belgian colonisation of the Congo around which the city of Lubumbashi and the urban copper belt (Kolwezi, Likasi, Kambove, Kakanda, Kipushi, Shinkolobwe) were built, and where Gécamines is implanted—formerly the UMHK (Union minière du Haut-Katanga). Today, it has difficulty surviving.

6. The series *Mémoire* (2004–6) is a series of photographic montages which are among the best-known works of Sammy Baloji.

des matières, des pensées, des expériences différentes mais qui sont toutes basées sur des faits réels, documentés, ou bien des pensées scientifiques ou théoriques. Confronter puis voir ce qui se dégage. J'ai été formé en tant que communicateur social donc à la base, j'ai cette sensibilité à la sémiologie, mais dans le sens de communication sociale, c'est-à-dire que la partie réceptive est importante. Dans la mise en place d'un discours audible, il faut prendre conscience des personnes à qui s'adresse le message. En même temps, le propre de l'image c'est sa polysémie. Et c'est pourquoi je me retrouve dans cette confrontation de l'image. C'est l'apogée même de la polysémie en fait.

MLL : C'est ce que j'allais dire, oui : c'est une démultiplication de la polysémie. Parce que si je comprends bien, l'idée de ta pratique, c'est de mettre en lumière certaines images, certaines sources en les confrontant – que ce soit en les juxtaposant, en les collant, en les reliant – à d'autres qui peuvent être d'origine complètement différente (exogène ou éloignée dans le temps)

SB : Oui. En ayant quand même un point de connexion, qu'il soit territorial, qu'il soit généalogique... Proposer différentes lectures par confrontation de choses qui ont une source commune.

MLL : Pour *Tales of the Copper Cross Garden*, on peut rappeler que les images montrent la transformation du cuivre à la Gécamines d'aujourd'hui, images accompagnées d'une bande-son constituée de bruits d'usine. Et on a aussi, en introduction, les chants de la chorale des Chanteurs à la croix de cuivre, dirigée par Joseph Kiwele, qui œuvra à Élisabethville entre 1946 et 1961[7].

SB : Au début, il y a un gros plan sur l'album des Chanteurs à la croix de cuivre[8], la couverture et la page intérieure, la dédicace de Blanche Albane Duhamel[9], la note d'intention puis la gravure représentant deux

7. Il s'agit d'une chorale constituée d'enfants choristes noirs, une chorale dédiée aux chants religieux et folkloriques, dirigée par Joseph Kiwele. Premier chef de chœur noir au Congo, ancien séminariste formé au chant et à la direction de chorale par un chef de chœur religieux (frère Anchaire Lamoral), Joseph Kiwele était reconnu pour ses talents, son sérieux et son dynamisme dans le Katanga colonial. Il restait néanmoins sous étroite surveillance du pouvoir religieux et politique, ainsi qu'en témoignent les traces, dans les archives coloniales attestant de l'attention soutenue dont elle faisait l'objet.

8. Chanteurs à la Croix de Cuivre, *Album n° 2: Chants religieux, classiques et folkloriques* (Belgique: Olympia, 1948). Le début du film (12') est disponible à l'adresse suivante : https://vimeo.com/217717455.

9. Blanche Albane Duhamel était l'épouse de l'écrivain Georges Duhamel, elle était une célèbre comédienne de la Troupe du Vieux Colombier (Paris) dirigée par Jacques Copeau.

MLL: Yes, that's what I was going to say: it's a multifaceted polysemy. Because if I understand it right, the idea of your practice is to highlight certain images, certain sources, by comparing them—whether by setting them side by side, by attaching them, by linking them—to others which may have a completely different origin (from elsewhere or from another time).

SB: Yes. With all the same a point of connection, whether territorial or genealogical. To propose different readings by comparing things which have a common source.

MLL: About *Tales of a Copper Grass Garden*, it's worth recalling that the images show the processing of copper at Gécamines today; images with a soundtrack of foundry noises. And in the introduction, there's also the singing of the choir of the *Chanteurs à la croix de cuivre*, directed by Joseph Kiwele, who was working at Élisabethville from 1946 to 1961.[7]

SB: At the beginning, there's a close-up of the album of the *Chanteurs à la croix de cuivre*,[8] the cover and the inside page, the dedication of Blanche Albane Duhamel,[9] the statement of intent, then the drawing showing two of the choristers and two photographs of the choir. Then, we see the text of the "Congolese mass or Bantu mass," and finally there's the singing: the "Agnus Dei," lamb of God; and it continues over the contemporary images of the Gécamines foundry, the smelting of copper which takes up most of the film. The succession of these images of the choir, the sound of the pages being turned, these are important because it leaves time for the content to emerge. For me, it speaks of the encounter and of the interest for a different world through the creation of this choir...

MLL: ...which is intimately linked with the mining business, the extraction of copper in fact.

SB: I wouldn't necessarily say that the choir is directly linked to the issue of mining. Well, we can look into that further if you like but..

7. This is a choir made up of black child choristers, a choir dedicated to religious songs and folksongs and directed by Joseph Kiwele. The first black choirmaster in the Congo, a former seminarist trained in singing and as a choirmaster by an ordained choirmaster (Frère Anchaire Lamoral), Joseph Kiwele was recognised in colonial Katanga for his talent, his dedication and his dynamism. He nonetheless remained under strict supervision by the religious and political authorities, as attested by reports in the colonial archives showing the sustained interest focused on him.

8. Chanteurs à la croix de cuivre, *Album n° 2: Chants religieux, classiques et folkloriques* (Belgium: Olympia, 1948). The beginning of the film (12') is available at the following website: https://vimeo.com/217717455.

9. Blanche Albane Duhamel was the wife of the writer Georges Duhamel; she was a famous actress in the *Troupe du Vieux Colombier* (Paris) directed by Jacques Copeau.

choristes ainsi que deux photographies de la chorale. Ensuite, on voit le texte de la « Messe Congolaise – Messe Bantoue », enfin un chant s'élève : c'est « Agnus Dei », agneau de Dieu, et il se poursuit sur les images contemporaines de l'usine Gécamines, de la fonte du cuivre qui occupe la majeure partie du film. La succession de ces images de la chorale, le bruit des pages qu'on tourne, c'est important car cela donne le temps au contenu d'émerger. Pour moi ça parle de la rencontre et de l'intérêt pour un monde autre à travers la création de cette chorale…

MLL : … qui est intiment liée à l'exploitation minière, à l'extraction de cuivre en fait.

SB : Je ne dirais pas forcément que la chorale est directement liée à la question de l'exploitation… Enfin on peut aller chercher loin comme ça si tu veux, mais…

MLL : Il me semble qu'il y a quand même eu une représentation pour le Jubilé de l'UMHK (Union minière du Haut-Katanga[10])…

SB : Oui. Mais la présence catholique date déjà de la période léopoldienne…

MLL : Oui, elle est bien antérieure !

SB : Mais elle est bien plus favorisée après le scandale des mains coupées[11]. C'est parce que tous les mouvements religieux protestants vont faire

10. Sur cette chorale propulsée par l'UMHK, Voir Maëline Le Lay, « Joseph Kiwele in Élisabethville (1946-1961) and the Birth of an Urban Culture in the Colonial Era », dans Velsen (2018).

11. En 1908, l'État indépendant du Congo, propriété exclusive du roi Léopold depuis la conférence de Berlin (1885), est transféré à la compétence de la Belgique, suite à un scandale sur sa gestion qui éclabousse l'image du souverain et de sa colonie, pendant plusieurs années. À partir des années 1900 en effet, commencent à circuler en Europe des photographies horrifiques représentant des hommes et des femmes du Congo aux membres mutilés. Ces photographies sont l'œuvre d'Alice Seeley Harris, missionnaire baptiste britannique installée à Boma dans le Bas-Congo (capitale de l'EIC), où les récoltes de caoutchouc étaient menées avec une grande violence. De retour en Europe, elle et son mari les diffusent à la lanterne magique lors de conférences destinées à éclairer ses compatriotes sur l'envers de la mission civilisatrice supposément bienfaitrice. Ces conférences furent amplement suivies en Europe mais aussi aux États-Unis où elles s'exportèrent dans la foulée. Alice S. Harris participa ainsi à donner de l'ampleur à une vaste campagne transatlantique de dénonciation de ce que l'on appelait alors les « atrocités » commises au Congo sous le règne de Léopold II, signalées dès 1904 dans un rapport du Consul britannique à Boma, sir Roger Casement. Ce dernier fut relayé par le journaliste britannique Edmund Dene Morel ainsi que par les œuvres – pamphlétaires pour certaines – d'écrivains bien connus en Angleterre et aux États-Unis : le très célèbre *Heart of Darkness* de Joseph Conrad (1899), *Le Soliloque du Roi Léopold* de Mark Twain (1905) qui paraît accompagné des photos d'Alice Seeley Harris, ou encore *Le Crime du Congo belge* (1909) de Sir Arthur Conan Doyle. À ce sujet, voir Van Reybrouck (2012, Chapitre 2, « Une immense saloperie. Le Congo

MLL: I think there was though a show for the Jubilee of the UMHK (Union minière du Haut-Katanga)[10]...

SB: Yes. But the Catholic presence dates back to the period of Leopold.

MLL: Yes, it was much earlier!

SB: But it was much more favoured after the scandal of the severed hands.[11] That's because all the religious protestant movements applied pressure for the scandal to break out and for Leopold to lose the Congo. From 1908, Belgium took back control of the territory and the faiths other than Catholicism were pushed aside. The Catholic Church had priority. The layout of the city bears the signs of it: Lubumbashi Cathedral was built between the Gouvernorat and the Palais de Justice and it clearly overshadows both. The Methodist Church was placed in the southern part of the town which served as a border area with the native quarter. Even urban planning shows what the priorities were in terms of power by means of a process of strategic occupation.

MLL: In terms of the imprint of power, in fact. This religious power, Catholic power but to which Belgium had delegated a certain number of responsibilities.

10. On this choir promoted by the UMHK, see Maëline Le Lay, "Joseph Kiwele in Élisabethville (1946–1961) and the Birth of an Urban Culture in the Colonial Era," in Velsen (2018).

11. In 1908, the independent State of Congo, the exclusive property of King Léopold since the Berlin Conference (1885), was transferred to the authority of Belgium, following a scandal concerning its management which tarnished the image of the sovereign and his colony for several years. From the 1900s, horrific photographs began to circulate showing men and women in the Congo with severed limbs. These photographs were the work of Alice Seeley Harris, a British Baptist missionary living at Boma in the Bas-Congo (capital of the EIC) where the harvesting of rubber was carried out with great violence. On their return to Europe, she and her husband showed them using magic lanterns during lectures intended to enlighten the British public on the dark side of the allegedly beneficial "mission civilisatrice." These lectures were widely followed in Europe and also in the United States where they were exported soon after. Alice S. Harris thus played a role in driving a vast transatlantic campaign denouncing what was then known as the "atrocities" committed in the Congo under the reign of Léopold II, described in 1904 in a report by the British consul at Boma, Sir Roger Casement. The story was then taken up by a British journalist Edmund Dene Morel and by works—in some case pamphlets—by well-known writers in England and the United States: the very famous *Heart of Darkness* by Joseph Conrad (1899), *King Leopold's Soliloquy* by Mark Twain (1905) which was published with photos by Alice Seeley Harris, or *The Crime of the Congo* by Sir Arthur Conan Doyle (1909). On this subject, see Van Reybrouck (2012, Chapter 2, "Une immense saloperie. Le Congo sous Léopold II (1885–1908)"); Hunt (2013); Wiltz (2015); Hochschild (1998). See too a programme that offers a good survey of this affair, in French: "La petite reine et le terrible roi. Épisode 2/2 : La photo du scandale" (*France Culture*, 12 September 2021). https://www.radiofrance.fr/franceculture/podcasts/une-histoire-particuliere-un-recit-documentaire-en-deux-parties/la-photo-du-scandale-1154201.

pression que le scandale éclate et que Léopold perd le Congo. À partir de 1908, la Belgique reprend le territoire et les confessions autres que le catholicisme vont être mises à l'écart. L'Église catholique va être prioritaire. L'urbanisme en porte la trace : la cathédrale de Lubumbashi est construite entre le gouvernorat et le palais de Justice et fait carrément ombre aux deux. L'église méthodiste, elle, est placée dans le flanc sud de la ville qui sert d'espace de frontière avec la cité indigène. Même le plan urbain marque les priorités en termes de pouvoir par un jeu d'occupations stratégiques.

MLL : En termes d'empreintes du pouvoir en somme. Ce pouvoir religieux, catholique mais auquel la Belgique avait délégué un certain nombre de responsabilités…

SB : Absolument. Et finalement l'éducation passe par l'Église.

MLL : Oui. Et ensuite quelle est la place de l'Église dans le milieu ouvrier de la Gécamines qu'on voit à l'œuvre dans ton film *Tales of the Copper Cross Garden* ?

SB : Je ne sais pas témoigner de cela… Simplement parce que mes parents sont protestants. Ils n'ont pas été dans les mines, ils étaient commerçants. Je n'ai pas d'expérience directe avec les familles ouvrières.

MLL : Quand on lit les archives de *Mwana Shaba*[12], c'est assez clair qu'ils s'adressaient vraiment aux ouvriers (secondairement aux dits « évolués » de l'Union minière) et le background catholique est très prégnant.

SB : La première fois que j'ai présenté *Tales of a Copper Grass Garder* à la Documenta à Athènes, j'y avais inclus une pancarte, une signalétique indiquant cette avenue principale qui était le boulevard Mobutu.

MLL : … la chaussée Kabila ?

SB : Oui, la chaussée Kabila. C'est l'espace qui, pendant le mandat du maire de Lubumbashi, Floribert Kaseba Makonko, a été renommé. L'avenue Tabora a aussi été renommée…

MLL : Je ne me souviens plus où est l'avenue Tabora…

SB (prend son téléphone pour me montrer l'avenue sur un plan de la ville) : Allez, l'Avenue Tabora… Donc, ça c'est [l'avenue] du 30-Juin, tu

sous Léopold II (1885-1908) ») ; Hunt (2013) ; Wiltz (2015) ; Hochschild (1998). Voir aussi cette émission qui propose une bonne synthèse de cette affaire : « La petite reine et le terrible roi. Épisode 2/2 : La photo du scandale » (*France Culture*, 12 septembre 2021). https://www.radiofrance.fr/franceculture/podcasts/une-histoire-particuliere-un-recit-documentaire-en-deux-parties/la-photo-du-scandale-1154201.

12. *Mwana Shaba*, littéralement « l'enfant du cuivre » en swahili, était le journal de l'UMHK/Gécamines destinée aux ouvriers indigènes de l'entreprise minière.

SB: Absolutely. And in the end, education was in the hands of the Church.

MLL: Yes. And then, what is the role of the church among the workers at Gécamines that we see in action in your film *Tales of a Copper Grass Garden*?

SB: I can't say much about that... Simply because my parents are Protestants. They weren't in the mines, they were shopkeepers. I haven't had any direct experience with the workers' families.

MLL: When we read the archives of *Mwana Shaba*,[12] it's fairly clear that they are really talking to the workers (secondarily to the "enlightened" discourse of the Union Minière) and the Catholic background is very striking.

SB: The first time I presented *Tales of a Copper Grass Garden* at the Documenta in Athens, I included a placard, a road sign showing this main avenue, which was Boulevard Mobutu.

MLL: Kabila Road?

SB: Yes, Kabila Road. This is the space which was renamed during the mandate of the mayor of Lubumbashi, Floribert Kaseba Makonko. Avenue Tabora was also renamed.

MLL: I don't remember where Avenue Tabora is.

SB: (taking his telephone to show me the avenue on the map of the city) Avenue Tabora. So, it's [Avenue] du 30 Juin, you see? There, that's what we called Kabila when you lived there, is that it?

MLL: Yes, yes, on Kabila.

SB: There, that's Kabila, which goes as far as the Gécamines. And here is Tabora! And there's the *Gouvernorat...*

MLL: On [avenue] Kasa-Vubu.

SB: So, there we are. So the *Gouvernorat* occupied all this space. And the town really started here, if you like. And what is it that links up the *Gouvernorat* to the rest of the town?

MLL: The Cathédrale Saint-Pierre et Paul, yes.

SB: The cathedral, and when you go along the same street, then you have the *Parquet* (public prosecution authority) of Lubumbashi *(see Figure 1).*

12. *Mwana Shaba*, literally "child of copper" in Swahili, was the UMHK/Gécamines newspaper intended for the native workers in the mining company.

vois ? Alors là, c'est ce qu'on appelait Kabila du temps où toi tu y habitais, c'est ça ?

MLL : Oui, oui, sur Kabila.

SB : Voilà, ça c'est Kabila, qui va jusqu'à la Gécamines hein. Et Tabora c'est ça ! Et là tu as le gouvernorat…

MLL : Sur [l'avenue] Kasa-Vubu.

SB : Voilà. Donc le gouvernorat occupe tout cet espace. Et la ville commence vraiment ici si tu veux. Et qu'est-ce qui fait le pont entre le gouvernorat et le reste de la ville?

MLL : La cathédrale Saint-Pierre et Paul oui,

SB : La cathédrale, et quand tu avances sur la même rue, alors tu as le parquet de Lubumbashi *(voir Figure 1).*

MLL : Et le Cercle Makutano[13] en face.

SB : Tu as le Cercle et quelque part ici, tu as la prison, tu vois ?

MLL : Ah oui… Et la mairie…

SB : Là tu as la mairie ici. Tu vois ? Donc le pouvoir est tel que tu as le pouvoir administratif et le pouvoir religieux qui transfèrent d'un commun accord le pouvoir au parquet, à la mairie, et après quand tu vas sur le fond…

MLL : Tu arrives sur [l'avenue] « du 30-Juin »

SB : Tu arrives sur « du 30-Juin », et tu as la synagogue. Et tout ça, c'est le même angle.

MLL : C'est sur le même axe.

SB : Et c'est l'axe de pouvoir. Le pouvoir administratif ! Et si tu remontes un peu par là, tu as les orthodoxes.

MLL : Oui, c'est ça, vers les arrêts Kasapa[14].

SB : Après, quand tu vas vers le sud.

---

13. Le Cercle Makutano est aujourd'hui un lieu de rassemblement associatif appartenant à la ville où se retrouvent tant des groupes confessionnels que des troupes de théâtre (comme la célèbre troupe Mufwankolo étudiée par Fabian [1990], Le Lay [2014]), il hébergeait autrefois le cercle d'évolués d'Élisabethville.

14. Kasapa est le nom du quartier où se situe l'université de Lubumbashi, désigne par extension l'université. Mobutu avait transféré la faculté de lettres à Lubumbashi afin de tenir les intellectuels (tels que Mudimbe qui y officiait) éloigné du pouvoir. Sur Mudimbe à l'université de Lubumbashi, voir Amuri Mpala-Lutabele et Nestor Diansonsisa Mwana-Bifwelele (2009).

MLL: ...and the Cercle Makutano[13] opposite.

SB: You have the *Cercle* and somewhere here, there's the prison, you see?

MLL: Yes... and the town hall.

SB: There's the town hall, here. You see? So the power is organised so that you have the administrative power and the religious power which by common accord transfer the power to the Parquet, to the town hall, and then when you go to the end...

MLL: ...you get to Avenue du 30 Juin.

SB: You get to 30 Juin, and you've got the synagogue. And all that, it's the same area.

MLL: It's along the same axis.

SB: And it's the axis of power. The administrative power! And if you go a bit further up that way, you've got the Orthodox church.

MLL: Yes, that's it, towards the Kasapa[14] bus stops.

SB: Then when you go south...

MLL: ...towards Kamalondo.[15]

SB: Yes, you've got the Gouvernorat, then the Catholic Church, but in the extreme south which marks the point of separation with Avenue Likasi, there you've got the Methodists.

MLL: And behind Likasi, you've got the *Cité*[16] just behind.

SB: No, you haven't got the *Cité* just behind, you've got what used to be considered as the "neutral zone"[17] *(see Figure 2).*

---

13. The Cercle Makutano is today a place of assembly for associations run by the town hall used by confessional groups or theatre troupes (such as the famous Mufwankolo Troupe studied by Fabian [1990], Le Lay [2014]); it was formerly used by the Cercle d'Evolués d'Élisabethville).

14. Kasapa is the name of the neighbourhood where Lubumbashi University is located, designated by extension as Université. Mobutu had transferred the Faculté de Lettres to Lubumbashi to keep the intellectuals (such as Mudimbe who taught there) at a distance from the seat of power. On Mudimbe at Lubumbashi university, see Amuri Mpala-Lutabele & Diansonsisa Mwana-Bifwelele (2009).

15. Kamalondo is the name of one of the working class neighbourhoods of Lubumbashi (the closest to the town centre). It is the vast ensemble today referred to as "La Cité" and it was previously referred to as "the native quarter," that is, the black township as opposed to the white quarter, which was the city centre formerly known as the "Centre extra-coutumier."

16. La Cité, that is the ex-native quarter, today designates the working class neighbourhoods.

17. The neutral zone or "Cordon sanitaire" was this buffer zone between the white quarter, known as the "Centre extra-coutumier" and the black quarter, La Cité.

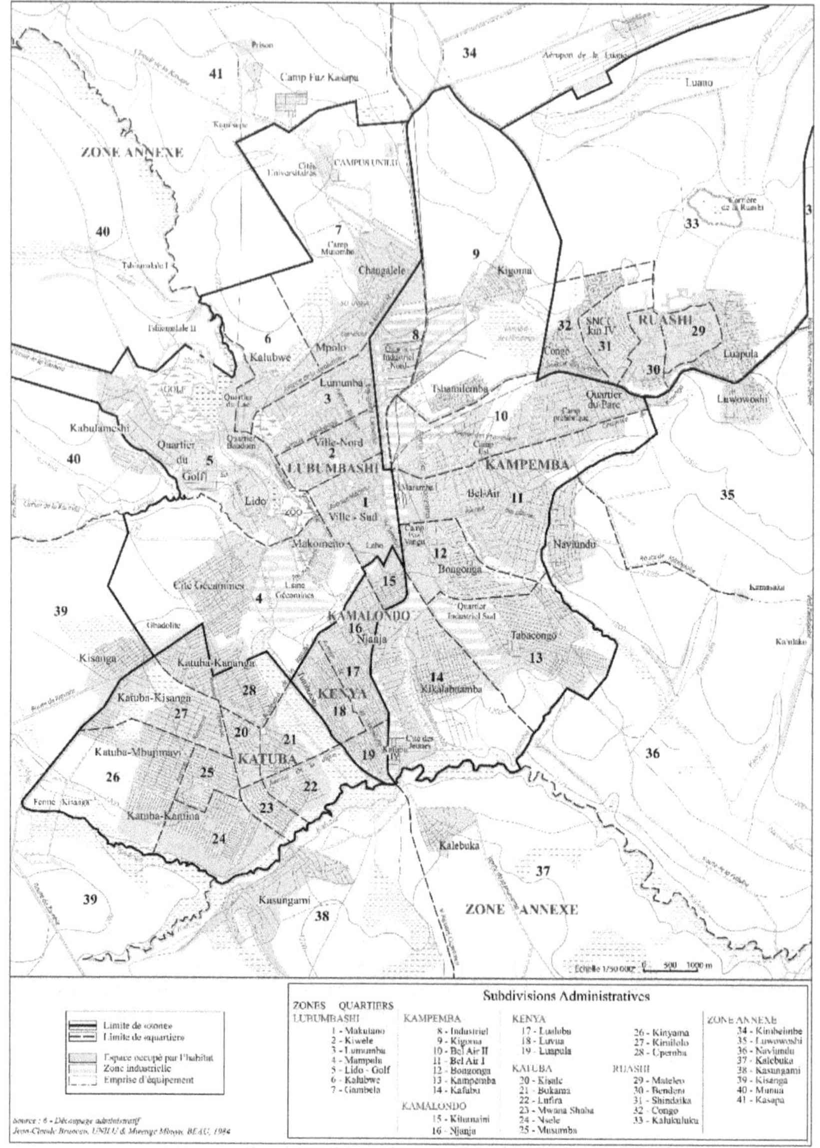

Figure 1. Carte administrative de Lumumbashi – Administrative map of Lumumbashi
Author: Valérie Alfaurt, based on Jean-Claude Bruneau and Mwenge Mbuyu, 1984. Source: Le Lay (2014).

MLL: Oh yes. And that's where the prison is, where Kimbangu[18] was imprisoned?

SB: The prison is on Avenue Likasi. You see, you've got the Methodist Church, it's there. In the course of his research, Johan Lagae came across a whole debate between the Methodist evangelists, the architects and the colonial administration concerning the reason for building this church in this place. Of course, the reason was to convert the natives, by building it just next to the Cité. This wasn't necessarily for the whites because they'd already been converted; it was rather for the natives. So the discussions began to focus on the main entrance of the church. Which way should this church face? If it's aimed at the natives, it should face towards them so they'll come to it. You see? So, there was quite an interesting discussion on, "But no, at the same time the church should face the town!" Because the town, that's the nerve centre!

MLL: These are documents about Élisabethville that he had access to?

SB: Yes and that I haven't yet worked on.

MLL: Is it the text by Bruce Fetter by any chance? He was the author of one of the first theses on Élisabethville in the sixties, known in French under the title: "Plan de la ville d'Élisabethville."[19]

SB: I don't know. But roughly, after some hesitation, the entrance faces the town and not the native quarter because even if the Methodists were there to convert, they were supposed to convert for a mission that belonged to the town. And the town was oriented towards progress, towards the colonial project. That's why the church faces the town and not the Cité although they had come to evangelise it.

MLL: We could say that it's completely against the spirit of the mission. The aim of the mission was precisely to merge into an environment to achieve mass conversions. And that's what Mudimbe describes in *Les Corps glorieux des mots et des êtres.* When he tells the story in that passage that you certainly know better than me, the walk he took on 30th June 1960 between the village of Kapolowe and the mission at

18. Simon Kimbangu was a preacher who proclaimed himself a prophet and miracle-worker. During the 1920s in the province of Léopoldville he won over numerous believers by his charismatic preaching, promising the return of Christ on Earth, in the Congo. Suspected of anticolonialism, he was arrested by the Belgian colonial authorities and imprisoned in Lubumbashi prison in 1921. He was an inspiring figure for Congolese believers such that a religious and political movement emerged from it, Kimbanguism, today still very much alive in the Congo.

19. The exact title of the thesis is "Elisabethville and Lubumbashi: The Segmented Growth of a Colonial City, 1910-1945" (Madison, University of Wisconsin, 1968). It formed the basis of the author's first book (Fetter 1976).

MLL : Vers la Kamalondo[15].

SB : Oui, tu as le gouvernorat, puis l'Église catholique, mais dans la limite sud qui va servir de point de séparation avec avenue Likasi, là tu as les Méthodistes.

MLL : Et derrière Likasi, tu as la cité[16], juste derrière.

SB : Non, tu n'as pas la cité juste derrière, tu as ce qui était considéré comme la « zone neutre »[17] *(voir Figure 2).*

MLL : Ah oui. Et c'est là que se trouve la prison où était emprisonné Kimbangu[18] ?

SB : La prison se trouve sur l'avenue Likasi. Tu vois, tu as l'église méthodiste, bien, elle est là. Johan Lagae était justement tombé dans ses recherches sur tout un débat entre les évangélistes méthodistes, les architectes et l'administration coloniale, portant sur la raison d'implanter cette église à cet endroit. Évidemment, la raison c'était de convertir les autochtones, en s'implantant à la limite de la cité. Ce n'est pas forcément pour les Blancs parce qu'ils sont déjà convertis, c'est plutôt pour les autochtones. Et alors les discussions ont commencé à porter sur l'entrée principale de l'église. Vers où cette église regarde ? Si elle était adressée aux autochtones, elle devait regarder vers eux pour qu'ils viennent vers elle. Tu vois ? Et donc il y a eu une discussion assez intéressante sur : « Mais non en même temps, l'église doit regarder vers la ville ! » Parce que la ville, c'est le point névralgique, quoi!

MLL : Ce sont des documents concernant Élisabethville auxquels il a eu accès ?

SB : Oui, et que moi je n'ai pas encore développés.

15. Kamalondo est le nom d'un des quartiers populaires de Lubumbashi (le plus proche du centre-ville), ce vaste ensemble que l'on nomme aujourd'hui « la cité » et que l'on nommait hier « la cité indigène », autrement dit la ville noire, par opposition à la ville blanche, le centre-ville jadis appelé « centre extra-coutumier ».

16. La cité, c'est-à-dire l'ex-cité indigène, désigne aujourd'hui les quartiers populaires.

17. La zone neutre ou « cordon sanitaire » était cette zone tampon entre la ville blanche, dit « centre extra-coutumier » et la ville noire, la Cité.

18. Simon Kimbangu était un prédicateur se présentant comme prophète et thaumathurge qui, au cours des années 1920 dans la province de Léopoldville, conquit de nombreux fidèles pour son prêche charismatique, promettant le retour du Christ sur terre, au Congo. Soupçonné d'anticolonialisme, il fut arrêté par le pouvoir colonial belge et emprisonné à la prison de Lubumbashi en 1921. Sa figure fut si inspirante pour les croyants congolais qu'elle fit émerger un mouvement religieux et politique, le kimbanguisme, aujourd'hui toujours vivace au Congo.

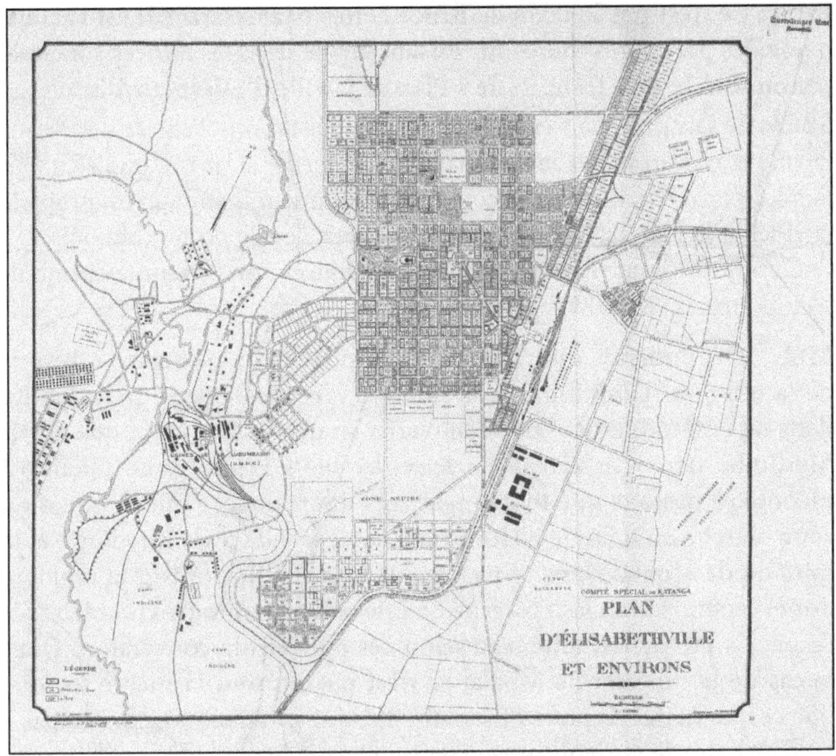

Figure 2. Plan d'Élisabethville et environs
(Map of Elisabethville and surroundings), 1929
Map created in 1927, updated in 1928 and 1929.
Drafted by Ph Vandenbak for the Comité Spécial du Katanga.
Low-res image retrieved from Barry Lawrence Ruderman, Antique Maps Inc. https://www.raremaps.com/gallery/detail/100154/belgian-congo-plan-delisabethville-et-environs-vandenbak.

Mpala. In this passage, he has this reflection on the way the colonisation is enshrined in the built environment, and he measures how the whole space was conceived and constructed according to this goal of conversion. In the case of the mission at Mpala, it wasn't at all the same logic at play as what you have described for Élisabethville: there was no need to face towards the seat of power since they represented the power.

SB: It's what I integrated in the play *A Blueprint for Toads and Snakes*: before the First World War, the workers and the whites lived in this same neutral zone *(see Figure 3)*. Between 1910 (foundation of Élisabethville) and 1918, you have people who occupy these territories and masters and workers do cohabit there.

MLL : Ce n'est pas le texte de Bruce Fetter par hasard ? Il est l'auteur d'une des premières thèses sur Élisabethville dans les années soixante, connu sous le titre français de « Plan de la ville d'Élisabethville »[19].

SB : Je ne sais pas. Mais en gros, après des hésitations, l'entrée donne sur la ville et pas sur la cité indigène parce que même si les méthodistes sont là pour convertir, ils doivent convertir pour une mission qui est propre à la ville. Et la ville est orientée vers le progrès, vers le projet colonial.

C'est pour ça que l'Église donne sur la ville et non pas sur la cité qu'ils sont pourtant venus évangéliser.

MLL : On pourrait dire que c'est complètement contraire à l'esprit de la mission. L'ambition de la mission, c'est justement de se fondre dans un environnement pour convertir en masse. Et c'est ce que décrit Mudimbe dans *Les Corps glorieux des mots et des êtres*. Quand il raconte ce passage que tu connais sans doute encore mieux que moi, cette marche qu'il fait le 30 juin 1960 entre le village de Kapolowe et la mission de Mpala. Dans ce passage, il a cette réflexion sur la manière dont la colonisation s'est inscrite dans le bâti, et il mesure combien tout l'espace a été pensé, aménagé selon cet objectif de conversion. Dans le cas de la mission de Mpala, ce n'est pas du tout la même logique que ce que tu décris pour Élisabethville, qui est à l'œuvre : on n'a pas à regarder vers le pouvoir puisqu'on représente le pouvoir.

SB : C'est ce que j'ai intégré dans la pièce *A Blueprint for Toads and Snakes* : avant la première guerre mondiale, les ouvriers et les Blancs vivent dans cette même zone neutre *(voir Figure 3)*. Entre 1910 (fondation d'Élisabethville) et 1918, tu as des gens qui occupent ces territoires, dans une cohabitation entre maîtres et ouvriers...

MLL : Donc les débuts d'Élisabethville se rapprocheraient plus de l'espace de la mission finalement ?

SB : La même question s'est posée : la création de la zone neutre va venir après la première guerre mondiale. On va déposséder les gens qui habitaient cet espace pour en faire une zone neutre, une zone de séparation physique...

MLL : ... et une zone qui sert de passage, de traversée.

SB : Oui, et il n'y a pas que l'église méthodiste, il y a aussi [l'hôpital] Sendwe par exemple. Au départ, Sendwe était prévu pour pouvoir servir les deux populations, blanche comme noire. Au départ c'était cela qui

19. Le titre exact de la thèse est « Elisabethville and Lubumbashi: The Segmented Growth of a Colonial City, 1910–1945 » (Madison, University of Wisconsin, 1968). Elle a donné lieu au premier ouvrage de l'auteur, dans les années septante (Fetter 1976).

MLL: So, in the end, the beginnings of Élisabethville were closer to the mission space?

SB: It raises the same question: the neutral zone was created after the First World War. The people who lived in this space were dispossessed to create a neutral zone, a zone of physical separation...

MLL: ...And a zone that serves as a passage, a crossing point.

SB: Yes, and there wasn't only the Methodist Church, there was also the Sendwe [hospital] for instance. To begin with, Sendwe was meant to serve the two populations, white as well as black. That's what was planned to begin with. Then afterwards they said, "No, we don't want people to meet, in fact." So in the end, Sendwe was only for the natives. And you see the current administrative building at the university?

MLL: Yes, you mean what's known as "the UNILU building?" Yes, I lived there!

SB: Yes, that was what was planned for the whites. Yes, as a visiting researcher at the university, you could live there, it's true! So the administrative building, when you look at the architectural style of that building, it's a coffin in fact. I realised this through my discussions with Johan.

MLL: Have you read the short story by Ramcy [Kabuya] in *Chroniques du Katanga* about that administrative building?[20]

SB: Yes, a long time ago, I don't remember now.

MLL: It's a good piece of writing. I don't know if he knew that when he wrote it, but it's exactly how he described it: the populations stratified in this building and in particular a family of rats which live in the basement. And in his story, this building is a place marked by death, where the rat family is stoned to death.

SB: But then I think I agree with what you suggest about Mudimbe: that the mission is turned towards the natives. But at the same time, conversion first and foremost serves the administration. Because the administration knows it will acquire these souls. And that leads us to the question of the *Centres extra-coutumiers*, and even of their origins. Because people will no longer respond to the traditional jurisdiction. They are prisoners, retired people, employees, etc., who have to respond to the administration. And that's why Simon Kimbangu got arrested. Or if we go back to the scandal of the severed hands, or even Alice Harris or the Afro-Americans who were brought before the courts in London

20. Ramcy Kabuya, "Et que suis-je maintenant?," in *Chroniques du Katanga* (2007, 101–14).

était prévu. Puis après ils se sont dit : « Non, on ne veut pas que ces gens se rencontrent en fait. » Et donc Sendwe va rester finalement pour les indigènes. Et tu vois l'actuel bâtiment administratif de l'université ?

MLL : Oui, très bien, tu veux parler de ce qu'on appelle « le building de l'UNILU » ? Oui, j'y ai habité !

SB : Oui, oui, c'était ça qui était prévu pour les Blancs. Oui, en tant que chercheuse de passage à l'université, tu as pu y habiter, c'est vrai ! Et donc le bâtiment administratif, quand tu regardes le style architectural de ce bâtiment, c'est un cercueil en fait. C'est en discutant avec Johan que j'ai appris ça.

MLL : Tu as lu la nouvelle de Ramcy [Kabuya] dans *Chroniques du Katanga* sur ce bâtiment administratif[20] ?

SB : Oui mais il y a longtemps, je ne me souviens plus…

MLL : C'est un bon texte. Je ne sais pas s'il avait connaissance de cela quand il a écrit cette nouvelle, mais c'est exactement ce qu'il décrit : les populations stratifiées dans ce building et notamment une famille de rats qui vit au sous-sol. Et dans sa nouvelle, ce building, c'est un endroit marqué par la mort, où la famille rat se fait lapider à mort.

SB : Mais donc je pense que je suis d'accord avec ce que tu évoques par rapport à Mudimbe : que la mission se tourne vers les autochtones… Mais en même temps, cette conversion sert d'abord à l'administration. Parce que l'administration sait qu'elle va récupérer ces âmes. Et cela nous amène à la question des centres extra-coutumiers, et même à leur genèse. Parce que les gens ne vont plus répondre à la juridiction traditionnelle. Ce sont des prisonniers, des retraités, des employés etc., qui doivent répondre à l'administration. Et c'est d'ailleurs pour ça que Simon Kimbangu va être arrêté. Ou si on revient au scandale des mains coupées, ou même Alice Harris ou les Afro-Américains qui vont être portés en justice à Londres pour leurs revendications, c'est qu'on se rend bien compte que si la religion fait valoir une égalité, ce n'est pas pour autant que cette égalité va torpiller la mission administrative.

MLL : Oui, et d'ailleurs, en repensant à ce passage sur Mpala, Mudimbe montre bien que la mission de Mpala est éloignée du village de Kapolowe par cette espèce de zone tampon qu'il décrit bien. Donc il est question de laisser le gros des indigènes dans leur village, et de placer la mission de Mpala à proximité, mais néanmoins

20. Ramcy Kabuya, « Et que suis-je maintenant ? », dans *Chroniques du Katanga* (2007, 101-114).

Figure 3. Sammy Baloji, *A Blueprint for Toads and Snakes*
Installation. Photo at Framer Framed, Amsterdam, 2018.
 See: https://framerframed.nl/en/exposities/solo-exhibition-sammy-baloji/ [image archive].

over their claims, it's [when] we realise that if the religion promotes equality, it doesn't mean that this equality will scupper the mission of the administration.

MLL: Yes and thinking again about this passage on Mpala, Mudimbe shows clearly that the Mpala mission is separated from the village of Kapolowe by this kind of buffer zone which he describes so well. So it is a matter of leaving most of the natives in their village, and putting the Mpala mission nearby but still far enough away. And besides, that's what Mudimbe explains in *Les Corps glorieux*: how he was cut off from his world, his family, through the missions, the seminar that imprinted in him a profound cultural conversion. This brings us back to what you just said, about the way the church which is situated on the outskirts of the village or of the town could also be turned towards the white Centre extra-coutumier even if this church was at the disposal of the village or the native quarter. In other words, the mission mustn't be too close to the natives but a distance needs to be maintained. And a distance that is far less from the seat of power than from those who the power subjugates.

SB: To illustrate the involvement of the Church with the power of the state, let's look at the example of Kimbangu. Simon [Kimbangu] was a passionately religious man who saw himself as a prophet but who also

suffisamment à l'écart. Et d'ailleurs, c'est ce qu'explique Mudimbe dans *Les Corps glorieux* : comment il a été coupé de son milieu, de sa famille, à travers les missions, le séminaire qui ont imprimé en lui une conversion culturelle profonde. Cela revient à ce que tu viens de dire, à savoir la manière dont l'église qui se situait à la lisière du village ou de la ville pouvait tout aussi bien être tournée vers le centre extra-coutumier blanc, même si elle était à disposition du village ou de la cité indigène. Autrement dit, il ne faut que la mission soit à proximité des autochtones, mais une distance est maintenue. Et une distance qui est moins grande avec le pouvoir qu'avec ceux que le pouvoir soumet.

SB : Pour illustrer l'intrication de l'Église dans le pouvoir de l'État, prenons l'exemple de Kimbangu. Simon [Kimbangu] est un illuminé qui va se prendre pour un prophète mais qui va aussi faire valoir la question de l'égalité entre Noirs et Blancs dans sa prédication, ce qui lui vaut d'être envoyé en prison. En même temps, tu as les mouvements socialistes communistes belges de l'époque qui vont adresser des missives à Simon pendant qu'il est en taule mais que l'administration va intercepter. Et ça ne lui parviendra jamais. Tout ça pour dire qu'à partir de 1908, la religion est là mais elle doit faire corps avec le pouvoir administratif.

Un épisode – illustré par Tshibumba[21] – est représentatif de cet entrelacement des pouvoirs : la pendaison qui eut lieu à Lubumbashi *(voir Figure 4)*. Il y a pas mal d'articles là-dessus – Bogumil [Jewsiewicki], etc. – sur cet homme pendu sur la place publique aux environs de l'église catholique[22]. Une pendaison qui fait suite à une histoire de tromperie, genre un agent colonial belge couche avec une femme d'ouvrier et l'ouvrier décide de faire justice lui-même mais en tuant un autre, pas celui qui couche avec sa femme. Mais cette pendaison est cautionnée par l'Église catholique, par l'archevêque Monseigneur de Hemptinne. Cet entrelacement est bien illustré par Tshibumba, regarde… Voilà… On voit l'Église, tu as le drapeau. C'est intéressant…

MLL : C'est quelle année ?

SB : C'est cautionné par Hemptinne de l'Église catholique, ce n'est pas n'importe qui… Et des années plus tard, M. Kaseba, qui est le maire de la ville, décide de changer cette avenue-là, Tabora, par l'avenue Monseigneur de Hemptinne…

21. Peintre populaire de Lubumbashi qui a peint plusieurs épisodes de l'histoire locale et nationale. Voir Jewsiewicki (2003) ; Baloji et Ceuppens (2016) ; Fabian (1996) ; Garnier (2017).

22. Voir Jewsiewicki (1987).

Figure 4. Tshibumba Kana Matula, *La pendaison de François*
The painting reads: "La vraie justice non appliquée – la pendeson de François à Lumumbashi" (True justice not applied—the hanging of François in Lumumbashi). N.d., created in the 1920s.
Personal collection.

proclaimed equality between blacks and whites in his preaching—which got him sent to prison. At the same time, you've got the Belgian communist socialist movements of the time who wrote to Simon while he was in gaol but the administration intercepted the letters. And he never got them. All that just to say that from 1908 onwards, religion was there but it had to be hand in glove with the colonial administration.

One episode—illustrated by Tshibumba[21]—is representative of this intertwining of powers: the hanging that took place at Lubumbashi *(see Figure 4)*. There are quite a lot of articles about it, Bogumil [Jewsiewicki] etc., about this man who was hanged in a public square near the Catholic Church.[22] This hanging was the sequel to a story of cheating; something about a Belgian colonial agent who slept with a worker's wife and the worker decided to take justice into his own hands and killed someone else, not the man who'd slept with his wife. But this hanging was approved by the Catholic Church, by the Archbishop Monseigneur de Hemptinne. This intertwining is well illustrated by Tshibumba, look... There you can see the church, there you have the flag. It's interesting.

21. A popular Lubumbashi painter who painted several episodes of local and national history. See Jewsiewicki (2003); Baloji and Ceuppens (2016); Fabian (1996); Garnier (2017).

22. See Jewsiewicki (1987).

MLL : Ah oui je me souviens de ça, c'est édifiant…

SB : Ce n'est pas anodin. De toute façon, quand tu es sur cette avenue Tabora et que tu regardes vers le gouvernorat, tu ne vois pas le gouvernorat ; la première chose que tu vois, c'est l'Église.

MLL : Juste une autre question pour recentrer sur Mudimbe. Ça me frappe et ça m'intéresse de voir qu'un artiste comme toi travaille à partir de Mudimbe qui reste malheureusement un penseur superficiellement lu. Alors qu'est-ce qui fait que ce penseur qu'est Mudimbe, pourtant si méconnu et pas nécessairement très accessible, t'inspire ? Qu'est-ce qui, dans son œuvre, peut parler à des artistes de ta génération ? En quoi cette pensée sur l'invention de l'Afrique par et depuis le colonialisme est-elle inspirante ?

SB : Je vais répondre de manière détournée, en passant par Pasolini. À l'aube des indépendances, réfléchissant sur ce que l'on appelait alors le « tiers-monde », Pasolini propose d'imaginer dans ces sociétés naissantes un système autre, qui ne soit pas pollué par les systèmes existants, à savoir socialismes/communisme *versus* impérialisme. Il cherche en fait une proposition de sortie de cette dualité communiste ou socialiste *versus* impérialiste. Tu as fait référence à la notion de bibliothèque coloniale, à la question de l'invention de l'Afrique telle que soulevée par Mudimbe ; et moi ce que j'ai donné comme exemple par rapport à la comparaison des documents pour pouvoir trouver des formes : pour moi, tout cela permet de construire des zones de réflexion hors des oppositions idéologiques clivantes.

À un certain moment, toujours dans le livre *Les Corps glorieux*, quand il évoque les arts traditionnels, il dit qu'il faut qu'il y ait une vraie étude qui soit faite par les autochtones. Il demande : « Quand allez-vous proposer une étude faite par vous-même ? » Donc je pense que d'une part il y a la question de l'étude de l'existence ou de l'entité coloniale, mais d'autre part, il y a la perspective coloniale mais il y a aussi la perspective précoloniale. Il va falloir confronter tout ça pour pouvoir trouver des pistes de réflexion. Et nous devons les porter. Que ce soit cette bibliothèque coloniale, que ce soit cet art précolonial, nous les portons à travers ces expériences de trajectoires à la fois individuelles ou collectives. Et ce n'est pas en déconstruisant les formations politiques précoloniales et coloniales que ça n'existe pas encore aujourd'hui, tu vois. C'est pour ça que je suis contre le fait que… je ne pense pas que la restitution des objets va remettre en place des sociétés précoloniales…

MLL : Je pense que c'est une histoire de réparation symbolique.

MLL: What year was that?

SB: It was approved by Hemptinne of the Catholic Church; it wasn't just anyone. And years later, Mr Kaseba who was the mayor of the city decided to change the name of that avenue, Tabora, to Avenue Monseigneur de Hemptinne.

MLL: Ah yes, I remember that, it's instructive.

SB: It's not just a detail. In any case, when you're on this Avenue Tabora and you look towards the Gouvernorat, you don't see the Gouvernorat, the first thing you see is the church.

MLL: Just one more question to refocus on Mudimbe. I'm impressed and it's interesting to see that an artist like you is working on Mudimbe who is a thinker who unfortunately is still only superficially read. So, what is it that explains how the thinker Mudimbe, though little-known and not necessarily very accessible, inspires you? What is it in his work that can speak to artists of your generation? And in what way is this thinking about the invention of Africa by colonialism inspiring?

SB: I'll answer that in a rather indirect way, via Pasolini. At the dawn of independence, thinking about what was then called the Third World, Pasolini suggested imagining in these emerging societies a different system, one that would not be polluted by the existing systems, that is, socialism/communism versus imperialism. He was in fact seeking an alternative to get away from this duality of communist or socialist versus imperialist. You referred to the notion of the colonial library, the question of the invention of Africa as it was evoked by Mudimbe; and what I have given as an example relative to the comparison of the documents to find forms of expression: for me, all that is a way of constructing zones of reflection outside divisive ideological oppositions.

At a certain moment, still in the book *Les Corps glorieux*, when he refers to the traditional arts, he says there's need for a real study undertaken by natives. He asks: "When are you going to produce a study done by yourselves?" So I think that on one hand there is the question of the study of the colonial existence or entity, but on the other hand, there is the precolonial viewpoint. We'll have to confront all that if we're going to be able to find approaches for reflection. And we should take them up. Whether it's the colonial library, or precolonial art, we take them up through these experiences that are at once individual and collective. And this is not because we deconstruct the precolonial and colonial polities that they do not exist today, you see. This is why I'm against the fact that ... I don't think that the restitution of objects will recreate precolonial societies.

SB : C'est une histoire de réparation symbolique. Je ne regarde pas séparément les réalités coloniales, précoloniales, postcoloniales : tout ça est tellement mêlé en réalité. Après, pour des raisons de distanciation, on peut effectivement les présenter comme des périodes avec des moments clés dans l'histoire, etc. Mais dans l'expérience vécue, ces choses-là sont en continu.

MLL : Elles sont intégrées l'une dans l'autre ?

SB : En quelque sorte oui. Et donc, c'est pour cela que des gens comme Mudimbe m'inspirent. Cet ouvrage, *Les Corps glorieux*, rien que sa constitution physique, elle est géniale : tu as un témoignage personnel, des réflexions théoriques et tu as de l'analyse, tout ça inclus dans un même ouvrage. De mon point de vue, de manière brute, j'aurais même tendance à dire que c'est un *kasala*[23] *(rires)* !

MLL *(rires)* : Ah ça y est, tu vois des *kasala* partout maintenant !

SB *(rires)* : Hahaha, oui j'en vois ! Mais graphiquement parlant, c'est très beau. Toutes ces disciplines s'intègrent dans un même ouvrage !

MLL : Et tout s'intègre très bien, cela fait vraiment sens. C'est-à-dire que même au niveau de la forme, *Les Corps glorieux*, dans son approche, dans la manière qu'il a de lier différentes dimensions de l'existence et de l'Histoire, ça se rapprocherait de ta manière de travailler en fait…

SB : C'est pour ça que je parle de *kasala* en fait. Parce que finalement je mêle des histoires autobiographiques, enfin des éléments autobiographiques pourraient être… Mais ça, je l'ai commencé depuis le départ, en fait ! Par exemple la raison pour laquelle j'ai commencé à travailler sur la série *Mémoire*, c'est que je me rendais compte qu'en fait, la création de la ville passait par la constitution d'une société cosmopolite qui n'était pas à l'initiative de l'autochtone mais du pouvoir. Et cela partait d'une lecture personnelle qui trouve ses racines dans les années nonante, pendant lesquelles les Kasaïens vont devenir des sujets à évacuer du territoire [katangais] parce que ce sont des non-autochtones[24]. Et pour moi finalement, en mettant en lumière ces

23. *Kasala* : genre poétique luba, chant héroïque, poème d'(auto)éloge. À l'époque de l'entretien, Sammy Baloji travaillait avec l'écrivain Fiston Mwanza Mujila à un projet plastique et littéraire autour du *kasala*. Les deux compères sont des complices de longue date, ils ont pour points communs de s'être connus, dans leur jeunesse, à Lubumbashi, tandis qu'ils faisaient leurs premières armes (l'un dans l'écriture, l'autre dans l'art plastique et visuel), et de vivre maintenant en Europe (Belgique et Autriche). Ils collaborent sur de nombreux projets. Voir notamment l'exposition de Sammy Baloji, *Kasala: the Slaughterhouse of Dreams or the First Human: Bende's Error* (2020-2021).

24. Sammy Baloji fait ici allusion à un événement historique assez peu connu et trop peu documenté, le « refoulement des Kasaïens » (encore appelés les « non-originaires »)

MLL: I think it's a matter of symbolic reparations.

SB: It's a matter of symbolic reparations. I don't look at the colonial, precolonial, postcolonial realities separately: in reality all that is so intertwined. Then for reasons of distancing, we can indeed present them as periods with key moments in the history, etc. But in the lived experience, these things are a continuum.

MLL: They are integrated with each other?

SB: In a way, yes. So that's why people like Mudimbe inspire me. This work, *Les Corps glorieux*, if only because of its physical construction, is fantastic: you have a personal account, theoretical reflections, you have the analysis, and all that included in a single work. From my point of view, to put it crudely, I'd even be tempted to say it's a *kasala!*[23] *(laughter)*.

MLL *(laughter)*: Ah yes that's it, you see kasala everywhere now!

SB *(laughter)*: Hahaha, yes I see quite a few! But graphically speaking, it's very fine. All these disciplines are integrated within the same work!

MLL: And it all fits together so well, it really makes sense. That is to say even in terms of form, *Les Corps glorieux*, in its approach, in its manner of linking up different dimensions of existence and of history, that seems close to your way of working in fact.

SB: That's why I talk about *kasala* in fact. Because in the end I mingle autobiographical stories, that is, autobiographical elements could be … But I started doing that right from the beginning, in fact! For example, the reason I began to work on the series *Mémoire* is that I realised that in fact, the creation of the town involved the constitution of a cosmopolitan society which wasn't done at the initiative of the natives but of the colonial powers. And that started with a personal reading which had its roots in the nineties, when the Kasaïan people became subjects to be evacuated from the [Katangan] territory because they were not natives of it.[24] And

23. *Kasala*: Luba poetic genre, heroic song, (self-) eulogising poem. At the time of the interview, Sammy Baloji was working with the writer Fiston Mwanza Mujila on a plastic arts and literary project focused on *kasala*. The two partners have long been accomplices, as they got to know each other in their youth in Lubumbashi, when they were starting out (one as a writer, the other in the plastic and visual arts). And both now live in Europe (Belgium and Austria). They have worked together on numerous projects. See in particular Sammy Baloji' exhibition: *Kasala: the Slaughterhouse of Dreams or the First Human, Bende's Error* (2020–21).

24. Sammy Baloji is referring here to a historical event which is little known or documented, the "refoulement des Kasaïens" (deportation of the Kasaïans—still today referred to as the "non-originaires" or non-natives) from Katanga between 1992 and 1994. This "refoulement" consisted of real deportation to Kasaï of populations originally from Kasaï, who had been settled in Katanga for two generations at the initiative of the Belgian settlers (it was a matter of immigration for work). Many of

images-là, je répondais finalement à la question de la fondation de la ville entièrement articulée autour d'un principe cosmopolite quand bien même il y avait de la déportation, ou il y avait des gens qui étaient arrachés à leur société, ou bien que c'étaient pas forcément des Noirs traités au même niveau que les Blancs… Mais je pense que ma première intention a été de démontrer les enjeux qu'il y avait derrière cette présence cosmopolite encore effective aujourd'hui et qui tourne toujours autour de l'économie.

MLL : Donc c'est finalement à partir du refoulement, cette expérience des années nonante que tu as vécue, ces années de retour en force de l'autochtonie prioritaire et exclusive, que tu as lu ou relu l'histoire de la fondation de la ville de Lubumbashi comme étant à rebours de cette autochtonie ?

SB : Oui, oui. Donc quand j'ai découvert l'archive, en quelque sorte, elle justifiait la présence kasaïenne, la présence rwandaise, etc. À la base, il y avait un état de faits politico-économiques qui a fait que ces communautés étaient là. Et c'est pour cela que quand tu regardes la série *Mémoire*, il y a beaucoup plus d'images de groupes que d'individus. Et le choix de faire disparaître l'origine de ces groupes, c'était un choix stratégique de ma part, comme une réplique à cette classification ethnique qui prévaut encore dans le discours politique contemporain.

MLL : Et qui s'est révélée fortement pendant les années nonante.

SB : Oui, voilà. Et ça, c'est par rapport à ma propre expérience. Et donc au départ, ce qui m'a beaucoup plus frappé dans ces archives, ce n'est pas tant la condition de ces gens, par exemple le fait qu'ils soient nus…

MLL : Tu peux re-préciser comment tu as eu accès à ces archives ?

SB : Ces archives se trouvaient dans les services de communication de l'industrie minière, de la Gécamines, à Lubumbashi, dans les bureaux administratifs, que nous sommes allés fouiller ensemble avec Johan [Lagae] et Hubert [Maheux]. C'est Hubert qui avait trouvé le plan pour pouvoir y entrer. Mais moi ce qui m'avait personnellement frappé, c'était que toutes ces caravanes qui débarquaient, et toute cette catégorisation qui se faisait – parce que sur chaque photo, on écrivait l'ethnie de chaque groupe…

MLL : C'étaient quelles années ?

SB : Les années 1910-1920.

---

hors du Katanga entre 1992 et 1994. Ce « refoulement » consista en une véritable déportation au Kasaï de populations originaires du Kasaï, installées au Katanga depuis deux générations sous l'impulsion des colons belges (il s'agissait d'une immigration de travail), déportation qui fut fatale à beaucoup d'entre eux. Voir M'Bokolo (2005) ; Pourtier (1998) ; Mwembu (1999) ; Le Lay (2008).

for me, finally, revealing these images, I'm answering the question of the foundation of the town entirely organised around a cosmopolitan principle when there had nonetheless been deportation, or there had been people torn from their society, or it was not necessarily the blacks treated the same way as the whites. But I think that my initial intention was to show the issues that were behind this cosmopolitan presence that is still there today and which still revolves around the economy.

MLL: So finally it's from this *refoulement* (deportation) of Kasaïans, this experience of the nineties that you lived through, that you read or reread the history of the foundation of the town of Lubumbashi as against this indigenousness.

SB: Yes. So when I discovered the archive, in a way it justified the Kasaïan presence, the Rwandan presence, etc. To begin with, there was a political and economic state of affairs which meant that these communities were there. And that's why when you look at the series *Mémoire*, there are a lot more images of groups than of individuals. And the choice of making the origin of these groups disappear was a strategic choice on my part, as a response to this ethnic classification which still prevails in contemporary political discourse.

MLL: And which was very apparent in the nineties.

SB: Yes, that's it. And that's relative to my own experience. So at the beginning, what struck me the most in these archives is not so much the condition of these people, for instance the fact that they were naked...

MLL: Can you tell me again about how you had access to these archives?

SB: These archives were in the communication service of the mining corporation, of Gécamines, at Lubumbashi, in the administrative offices, where we went to dig around together with Johan [Lagae] and Hubert [Maheux]. It's Hubert who thought up the plan to get in. But what struck me personally, it was all these caravans that arrived, and all that categorisation which was done—because on each photo, they had written the ethnic origins of each group.

MLL: What years [were those]?

SB: The 1910–1920s.

them perished along the journey. See M'Bokolo (2005); Pourtier (1998); Mwembu (1999); Le Lay (2008).

MLL : **Au tout début donc, c'étaient les nouveaux arrivants sur cette terre nouvellement colonisée. Donc on écrivait d'où ils venaient mais pour après les fondre avec les autres ouvriers tout en les laissant monter leurs associations culturelles qui étaient aussi des associations ethniques.**

SB : Oui et non… Par exemple, dans *A Blueprint for Toads and Snakes*, ce que j'essayais de montrer, c'est que dans l'établissement de la cité indigène dans sa constitution physique, les communautés sont mélangées. Sauf que les noms des avenues portent les noms des ethnies qui ne sont pas forcément représentatives des personnes qui habitent là… Tu as encore ça aujourd'hui… À la Kamalondo jusqu'à aujourd'hui, tu as la rue des Baluba, tu as l'avenue de ceci… Mais finalement, d'après Johan, cette grille des noms des avenues se fait d'après une idéologie consistant à faire valoir l'identité ethnique dans les territoires. Ce qui avait pour objectif d'empêcher que les gens puissent être unis dans cette « nouvelle mémoire », comme l'appelle justement Mudimbe, c'est-à-dire empêcher que les gens se réunissent autour de revendications purement syndicalistes (conditions de travail, salaires). Au lieu de cela, ils peuvent se rassembler derrière des identités ethniques qui vont en gros les défavoriser… Et donc voilà…

Je commence à avoir faim… On va commencer à préparer là *(rires)*. Mais c'était quoi la question, au fait ?

MLL *(rires)* : **La question, c'était en quoi Mudimbe nous aide à penser notre compréhension de l'Afrique ? Mais je pense que tu y as répondu, notamment sur le fait qu'il est, lui, dans un refus très fort de l'ethnisme, du tribalisme, comme on dit au Congo. C'est une chose contre laquelle il est en résistance dans toute son œuvre.**

SB : Ben, oui ! Mudimbe est vachement intéressant parce que, encore une fois, il démembre très bien ces deux espaces – la mémoire ancienne/l'espace traditionnel et la mémoire nouvelle – et il t'explique comment ces deux mémoires se composent. Et aussi comment ces mémoires peuvent s'imbriquer. Que ce soit le centre extra-coutumier, le centre-ville ou l'espace de la cité indigène, tous ces espaces sont purement modernes en fait. Et je pense que faire valoir une identité ethnique ne répond pas au projet de la modernité duquel nous sommes héritiers. En même temps, il dit aussi – et c'est très bien vu – qu'on peut faire partie de ces deux espaces : l'un ne contredit pas forcément l'autre.

MLL: So right at the beginning, it was the new arrivals in this newly-colonised land. So, where they had come from was written down, but afterwards they were merged with other workers, leaving them to start their cultural associations which were also ethnic associations.

SB: Yes and no. For example, in *A Blueprint for Toads and Snakes*, what I was trying to show is that in establishing the native quarter in its physical constitution, the communities were mixed together. Except that the names of the avenues bore the names of the ethnic groups which were not necessarily representative of the people who lived there. You've still got that today. At Kamalondo still today, you've got the *Rue des Baluba*, you've got the avenue of this or that. But finally, according to Johan, this grid of the names of avenues follows a consistent ideology to valorise ethnic identity in the territories. The purpose of that was to prevent people from being united in this "new memory," as Mudimbe rightly calls it, that is to prevent people from uniting on the basis of purely trade union claims (working conditions, wages). Instead of that, they could get together through their ethnic identities which would, broadly speaking, be against their interests. That's it.

I'm beginning to get hungry. We'll start cooking *(laughter)*. But what was the question, in fact?

MLL *(laughter)*: **The question was how does Mudimbe help us to conceive our understanding of Africa? But I think that you've answered that, in particular in the fact that he's in a position of categorical refusal of ethnicism, of tribalism as they say in Congo. That's something he's in opposition to throughout his work.**

SB: Yes! Mudimbe is really fantastically interesting because once again, he's very good at dismembering these two spaces—the ancient memory/traditional space and the new memory—and he explains how these two memories are composed. And also how these memories may overlap. Whether it's the *Centre extra-coutumier*, the town centre or the native quarter, all these spaces are purely modern in fact. And I think that valorising an ethnic identity is not compatible with the project of modernity which we are heir to. At the same time, he also said—and it's a good point—we can be part of both of these two spaces: one is not necessarily in contradiction with the other.

References

Amuri Mpala-Lutabele, Maurice, and Nestor Diansonsisa Mwana-Bifwelele. 2009. "La querelle littéraire de Lubumbashi : Mudimbe contre Ngal." *Études littéraires africaines,* no. 27 (Special Issue: "Lubumbashi, épicentre littéraire"): 28–35. https://doi.org/10.7202/1034303ar.

Baloji, Sammy, and Bambi Ceuppens. 2016. *Congo Art Works. Peinture populaire.* Bruxelles: Racine-Musée royal de l'Afrique centrale.

Bernard, Christine, prod. 2021. "La petite reine et le terrible roi. Épisode 2/2 : La photo du scandale." *France Culture* ("Une histoire particulière, un récit documentaire en deux parties"), 12 September 2021. https://www.radiofrance.fr/franceculture/podcasts/une-histoire-particuliere-un-recit-documentaire-en-deux-parties/la-photo-du-scandale-1154201

Chanteurs à la croix de cuivre. 1948. *Album n° 2: Chants religieux, classiques et folkloriques.* African Serie. N.l. (Belgium): Olympia.

"Exhibition: A Blueprint for Toads and Snakes." 2018. *Framer Framed.* https://framerframed.nl/en/exposities/solo-exhibition-sammy-baloji/ [archive]

Fabian, Johannes. 1990. *Power and Performance: Ethnographic Explorations Through Proverbial Wisdom and Theater in Shaba, Zaire.* Madison, WI: University of Wisconsin Press.

Fabian, Johannes. 1996. *Remembering the Present: Painting and Popular History in Zaïre.* Berkeley, CA: University of California Press.

Fetter, Bruce. 1976. *The Creation of Élisabethville 1910–1940.* Hoover Colonial Studies. Stanford, CA: Hoover Institution Press, Stanford University Press.

Fiston Mwanza Mujila. 2021. *Kasala pour mon Kaku et autres poèmes.* Amay (Belgium): Éditions de l'Arbre à paroles.

Garnier, Xavier. 2017. "L'Histoire du Zaïre entre peinture et écriture. Le cas de Tshibumba Kanda Matulu." *Écrire l'histoire,* no. 17: 198–201. https://doi.org/10.4000/elh.1258.

Hochschild, Adam. 1998. *Les fantômes du Roi Léopold. La terreur coloniale dans l'État du Congo.* Paris: Belfond.

Hunt, Nancy Rose. 2013. "An Acoustic Register: Rape and Repetition in Congo." In *Imperial Debris: On Ruins and Ruination,* edited by Ann Laura Stoler, 39–66. Durham, NC: Duke University Press. https://doi.org/10.1215/9780822395850-002.

Jewsiewicki, Bogumil. 1987. "La mort de Bwana François à Elisabethville: la mémoire, l'imaginaire et la connaissance du passé." *Annales Aequatoria* 8, 405–13. https://www.jstor.org/stable/25836453.

Jewsiewicki, Bogumil. 2003. *Mami Wata. La peinture urbaine au Congo.* Le Temps des images. Paris: Gallimard.

Kabuya, Ramcy. 2007. "Et que suis-je maintenant?" In *Chroniques du Katanga,* short stories collected by Dominique Ranaivoson, 101–14. Saint-Maur-des-Fossés: Sépia.

Le Lay, Maëline. 2008. "Où est le territoire?" Les écrits pour mémoire au Katanga (RDC)." In *Littératures africaines et territoires*, edited by Christiane Albert, Marie-Rose Abomo-Morin, Xavier Garnier, and Gisèle Prignitz, 165–76. Lettres du Sud. Paris: Karthala. https://doi.org/10.3917/kart.alber.2011.01.0165.

Le Lay, Maëline. 2014. *"La parole construit le pays." Théâtre, langues et didactisme au Katanga (République démocratique du Congo).* Francophonies. Paris: Honoré Champion.

Lucchetti, Matteo, ed. 2020. *Sammy Baloji: Other Tales*. Lund, Sweden: Lundskonsthall; Aarhus, Denmark: Kunsthal Aarhus. https://framerframed.nl/wp-content/uploads/2020/05/Sammy-Baloji-Other-Tales-2020.pdf [archive].

M'Bokolo, Elikia. 2005. "Le 'séparatisme katangais'". In *Au cœur de l'ethnie: Ethnie, tribalisme et État en Afrique*, edited by Elikia M'Bokolo and Jean-Loup Amselle, 185–226. Paris: La Découverte. https://doi.org/10.3917/dec.amse.2005.01.0185.

Mwembu, Donatien dia. 1999. "L'épuration ethnique au Katanga et l'éthique du redressement des torts du passé." *Canadian Journal of African Studies / Revue canadienne des études africaines* 33, no. 2–3: 483–99. https://doi.org/10.1080/00083968.1999.10751170.

Pourtier, Roland. 1998. "Les refoulés du Zaïre : identité, autochtonie et enjeux politiques." Autrepart, no. 51: 137–54. https://www.documentation.ird.fr/hor/fdi:010013211.

Van Reybrouck, David. 2012. *Congo. Une Histoire*. Arles: Actes Sud.

Velsen, Vincent van, ed. 2018. *A Blueprint for Toads and Snakes: A Solo Exhibition by Sammy Baloji*. Amsterdam: Framer Framed. https://framerframed.nl/wp-content/uploads/2018/06/ABFTAS-HANDOUT-DIGITAAL_C.pdf [archive].

Wiltz, Marc. 2015. *Il pleut des mains sur le Congo*. Paris: Magellan & Cie.

Artworks cited

Baloji, Sammy. 2004–6. *Mémoire*. Series of photomontages.

Baloji, Sammy. 2017. *Tales of a Copper Grass Garden*. Installation. Video, photographs, copper plate, copper crosses, and coins.

Baloji, Sammy. 2018. *A Blueprint for Toads and Snakes*. Installation. Wood and canvas, digital photographic prints on paper and photographs. https://kanal.brussels/en/inventaire/sammy-baloji/a-blueprint-toads-and-snakes-1 [archive].

Baloji, Sammy. 2020. *Kasala: the Slaughterhouse of Dreams or the First Human, Bende's Error.* Exhibition. Series of works, multiple mediums. Paris: Galerie Imane Farès. https://imanefares.com/en/expositions/1328/; https://imanefares.com/wp-content/uploads/2020/05/imane_fares_journal_baloji_munken_print_2.pdf [archive].

Baloji, Sammy, Marie-Françoise Plissard, and Johan Lagae. 2005–6. *The Likasi Series*. Collective work. Panoramic photomontage of the city of Likasi.

Tshibumba Kana Matula. N.d. (Created in the 1920s). *La pendaison de François* ["La vraie justice non appliquée – la pendeson de François à Lumumbashi"]. Painting. Personal collection.

Africa and Dialectics

Reading V.Y. Mudimbe Towards a Concept of Africa

Salim Abdelmadjid[1]

For Shehrazade, my mother

What is Africa? The question does not necessarily presuppose the thingness or the fixity or an essence of Africa, nor does it necessarily call for a descriptive-only answer. It can be posed as a philosophical question, for which "What is" corresponds to the eminent form of the philosophical question, as we have known it since Plato: "What is justice?" "What is courage?" "What is beauty?" Its singularity lies in that it is asked not about

1. This chapter was prepared by several papers: at the colloquium "*Autour de V.Y. Mudimbe: introduction à l'œuvre de Valentin Yves Mudimbe*" organised by Dominique Combe, Nadia Yala Kisukidi, Frédéric Worms and myself, on 6 June 2013 at the École Normale Supérieure in Paris (ENS Paris); at the colloquium "Mudimbe" organised by Marie-Aude Fouéré, Maëline Le Lay and Karori Mbugua, on 17 December 2019 at the University of Nairobi; for the lecture "Africa and Dialectics: Reading V.Y. Mudimbe Towards a Concept of Africa" given on 18 February 2020 at the invitation of Andrew Aisenberg at the Claremont Colleges; in the session on 5 March 2021 of the seminar "*Race et culture: questionnements philosophiques*" organised by Magali Bessone, Sophie Guérard de Latour and Jamila Mascat at Université Paris 1 Panthéon-Sorbonne, ENS Lyon and Utrecht University, with Delphine Abadie as respondent; in the session on 26 June 2021 of the doctoral seminar organised by Bado Ndoye at Université Cheikh Anta Diop. I thank all the organisers and participants for their invitations, attention and criticisms. I thank V.Y. Mudimbe for his kindness at the congress "*Epistémè africaine. Africa N'Ko, dire l'Afrique dans le monde. La bibliothèque coloniale en débat*," organised by Rémy Bazenguissa-Ganga, Mamadou Diawara, Mamadou Diouf, Frieda Ekotto, Kelly Gillespie, Achille Mbembe, Ebrima Sall and Rawya Tawfik Amer for the Programme Point Sud, the Council for the Development of Social Science in Research in Africa, the Deutsche Forschungsgemeinschaft and Goethe-Universität Frankfurt am Main, from 27 to 31 January 2013 in Dakar, where we met, and for accepting my invitation to ENS Paris, where we took part in three colloquia together: "*Autour de V.Y. Mudimbe*," "*Négritude et philosophie en France au xx*[e] *siècle: problèmes, histoires et controverses*" organised by Nadia Yala Kisukidi on 25 May 2013, "*Sartre et l'Afrique*" which I organised on 7 June 2013. I thank Jean-Philippe Dedieu, whom I met at the social sciences seminar devoted to Africa organised by Aïssatou Mbodj at ENS Paris in 2003, for the generosity with which, to encourage my interest in African philosophy, he offered me four books of his own, then virtually unknown and hard to find in France, including three by V.Y. Mudimbe whose work he introduced me to: *L'odeur du père*, *The Invention of Africa* and *Parables and Fables*, in their original editions. I thank Marie-Aude Fouéré and Maëline Le Lay for their critical and kind reviews. I take sole responsibility for this text.

a general idea but about a singular empirical reality, and the one that has been most denied philosophical interest, philosophical legitimacy, philosophical meaning, and even the ability to philosophise.[2] The question "What is Africa?" presupposes that Africa has a philosophical meaning which it is possible and necessary to meditate, grasp and express to the point of creating a philosophical concept of Africa.[3] Fundamentally, this is what thinking Africa consists of; and thinking Africa with V.Y. Mudimbe, as the title of this collective work suggests, consists of relying on him to make this effort.

He undertook it explicitly, notably in *The Idea of Africa* in 1994, in the preface to which he announced his intention "to approach the questions 'What is Africa?' or 'How do we define African cultures?'" (Mudimbe 1994, xiv) and to "explore the concept of Africa" (Mudimbe 1994, xv). To

2. One is obviously thinking of Hegel, to whom I will refer later, but one might also think of such cardinal authors in the repertoire of modern European philosophy as Hume or Kant. In his essay "Of National Characters," Hume wrote: "I am apt to suspect the Negroes to be naturally inferior to the Whites. There scarcely ever was a civilized nation of that complexion, nor even any individual, eminent either in action or speculation. No ingenious manufactures amongst them, no arts, no sciences. On the other hand, the most rude and barbarous of the Whites, such as the ancient Germans, the present Tartars, have still something eminent about them, in their valour, form of government, or some other particular. Such a uniform and constant difference could not happen, in so many countries and ages, if nature had not made an original distinction between these breeds of men. Not to mention our colonies, there are Negro slaves dispersed all over Europe, of whom none ever discovered any symptoms of ingenuity; though low people, without education, will start up amongst us, and distinguish themselves in every profession. In Jamaica, indeed, they talk of one Negro as a man of parts and learning; but it is likely he is admired for slender accomplishments, like a parrot who speaks a few words plainly." (Hume 1825, 521–22; the essay was first published in 1748, this note was added in 1753, the first two sentences were revised in 1777). In *Observations on the Feeling of the Beautiful and Sublime* in 1764, Kant wrote: "The Negroes of Africa have by nature no feeling that rises above the ridiculous. Mr. Hume challenges anyone to adduce a single example where a Negro has demonstrated talents, and asserts that among the hundreds of thousands of blacks who have been transported elsewhere from their countries, although very many of them have been set free, nevertheless not a single one has ever been found who has accomplished something great in art or science or shown any other praiseworthy quality, while among the whites there are always those who rise up from the lowest rabble and through extraordinary gifts earn respect in the world. So essential is the difference between these two human kinds, and it seems to be just as great with regard to the capacities of mind as it is with respect to color. The religion of fetishes which is widespread among them is perhaps a sort of idolatry, which sinks so deeply into the ridiculous as ever seems to be possible for human nature. A bird's feather, a cow's horn, a shell, or any other common thing, as soon as it is consecrated with some words, is an object of veneration and of invocation in swearing oaths. The blacks are very vain, but in the Negro's way, and so talkative that they must be driven apart from each other by blows." (Kant 2011, 58-59).

3. This is what I set out to do in my PhD thesis, "Un concept d'Afrique" (Abdelmadjid 2015). The ideas presented in this chapter are largely based on it.

my knowledge, he was the first African philosopher—by which I mean, here, both a philosopher who is African and a participant in the field of African philosophy—to do so in such an explicit manner. The field of African philosophy had been largely structured by the contradiction between ethnophilosophy[4] and "rational, or theoretical, or critical, or professional philosophy"[5] (Fløistad 1987, 1), which certainly involved the problem of defining African philosophy, but more by involving the problem of defining philosophy than that of defining Africa. Of course, the question "What is Africa?" had been constantly present, at least implicitly, in the history of pan-Africanism, eminently during independences, for example in Fanon or Nkrumah among so many; but the explicit and properly philosophical nature of the position of the question set Mudimbe apart. If one replaced "African philosopher" with "philosopher of Africa," to refer to someone who philosophises about Africa, it may seem that one could not say that he was the first to so explicitly "explore the concept of Africa," since Hegel went so far as to formulate one, in his lectures on the philosophy of history, in 1830: "What we properly understand by Africa, is the Unhistorical, Underdeveloped Spirit, still involved in the conditions of mere nature, and which had to be presented here only as on the threshold of the World's History" (Hegel 2004, 99). But then one would have to say that Mudimbe was the first to do so with methodological rigour and with respect for Africans, that is to say to produce an effort that, unlike Hegel's, was truly philosophical. Mudimbe's method, which I could firstly define with Dismas A. Masolo (1991) as "an archaeology of African knowledge," has made possible a decisive result for the conceptualisation of Africa, which will be central in this chapter: the analysis of the meaning inherent in the historical construction of Africa. The combination of this methodological contribution and his primacy in the philosophical position of the question "What is Africa?" explains the need to refer to Mudimbe in order to elaborate a concept of Africa.

Conversely, reading Mudimbe in the light of the question "What is Africa?" and with a view to elaborating a concept of Africa helps to understand him. It is true that his work, both philosophical and literary, deals with a variety of fields—epistemology, history, politics, religion and others—and that there are several possible perspectives to approach it:

4. The practice initiated by the Belgian missionary in Congo Placide Tempels in *La philosophie bantoue* in 1945—translated as *Bantu Philosophy* in 1959—consisting in extracting a "worldview" from the observation of a society.

5. Represented notably by the Beninese philosopher Paulin Jidenu Hountondji in *Sur la "philosophie africaine"* in 1977—translated in 1983 as *African Philosophy: Myth and Reality*. Hountondji is the creator of the concept of ethnophilosophy, which he criticises.

the relation between philosophy and literature, between epistemology and politics, English and French, or even the Congo and the United States. But, as the titles of so many of his texts suffice to show (for example, *L'odeur du père. Essai sur des limites de la science et de la vie en Afrique Noire* in 1982—which can be translated as *The Smell of the Father. Essay on Limits of Science and Life in Black Africa*[6]—; *The Invention of Africa: Gnosis, Philosophy, and the Order of Knowledge* in 1988; *Parables and Fables: Exegesis, Textuality and Politics in Central Africa* in 1991; *The Idea of Africa* in 1994; *Tales of Faith: Religion as Political Performance in Central Africa* in 1997; or even *On African Fault Lines: Meditations on Alterity Politics* in 2013), the search for the meaning of Africa is at the heart of his work and shines through in all these perspectives.

Under the title "Africa and Dialectics: Reading V.Y. Mudimbe Towards a Concept of Africa," I intend to show how one can draw on the work of Mudimbe to elaborate a concept of Africa, with the hope that this also contributes to understanding his work. I will explain in particular how he helps to problematise both the unity of Africa—the justification of which is a priority condition for a concept of Africa—and—this is the meaning of the expression "Africa and dialectics"—the logic and method necessary to think this unity. To do so, I will concentrate on Mudimbe's philosophical works; but on the assumption that fully understanding them requires an understanding of their relationship with his literary works, because the specific logic he deploys to think Africa lies at the crossroads of philosophy and literature; on the assumption therefore that this chapter requires, for its completion, a critical rereading based on the knowledge of Mudimbe's literary works. I will especially refer to *The Invention of Africa* and *The Idea of Africa*. As Mudimbe indicates in the preface to *The Idea of Africa*, writing that, "*The Idea of Africa* is both the product and the continuation of *The Invention of Africa*" (Mudimbe 1994, xv), these two books should be read together, *The Idea of Africa* extending *The Invention of Africa* to set out what one could call "the idea of the invention of Africa," that is to say: the idea that corresponded to the violent colonial and neocolonial construction of Africa, and that has had to be criticised and replaced throughout the still unfinished African reappropriation of Africa. I will also refer to *L'odeur du père*, in which Mudimbe develops an epistemological reflection on the conditions for real philosophical and scientific independence for Africa;

6. *L'odeur du père* has recently been translated into English as *The Scent of the Father: Essay on the Limits of Life and Science in Sub-Saharan Africa* by Jonathan Adjemian (Mudimbe 2023). I suggest *The Smell* rather than *The Scent* or *The Odour* to express the possibility, depending on who the father is, that the "odeur" stinks and sticks.

that, moreover, helps to understand his method in *The Invention of Africa* and *The Idea of Africa*.

So, how does Mudimbe, notably in *The Invention of Africa*, *The Idea of Africa* and *L'odeur du père*, help to elaborate a philosophical concept of Africa?

I will emphasise two main contributions: how Mudimbe's constructivist historicisation of Africa helps to justify the unity of Africa (1); and how the logic and method he uses, by differentiation from dialectics, to carry out this historicisation, enables him to grasp what I will call "the discursive concept of Africa" (2).

1. Negativity or otherness: The unity of Africa

Elaborating a philosophical concept of Africa signifies raising the question "What is Africa?" as a philosophical question and, to answer it, constructing an idea that corresponds to the reality of Africa, expresses its meaning, and constitutes both a norm of knowledge of Africa and a norm of action in its situation.

There are various conditions of possibility of a concept of Africa: as for the object of any concept, the unity of Africa; by definition of concept—a mental analytical unit—, its universality—at least in the sense of its communicability to any understanding—; or even the anchoring of the concept in the empirical singularity of Africa—which raises notably the question of the epistemological arrangement of philosophy and the sciences that can relate to Africa.

Mudimbe's work is primarily decisive to justify the unity of Africa. To bring out the singularity of his contribution, I will explain why, while a concept of negativity seems to justify the unity of Africa in line with the constructivist historicisation of Africa that he undertakes in *The Invention of Africa* and *The Idea of Africa* (1.1), he uses a non-dialectical terminology of otherness (1.2).

1.1. African negativity

At first glance, it seems obvious that the unity of Africa cannot be justified empirically. Whatever the ordinary definition one opts for—whether geographical (Africa as the African continent), racial (as "Black Africa"), political (as the African Union or a supposedly sufficient number of states located on the African continent), or demographical (as all Africans)—, what one calls "Africa" corresponds to an incalculable number of differences and even contradictions. Conceptualising Africa, therefore, seems impossible and any attempt to do so doomed to produce: scientifically, an abstraction;

and, politically, a totalitarian notion, which would consist of a massifying assignation of a supposed identity.

And yet, there have been African affirmations of the unity of Africa, the most remarkable of them being, during the struggles for independence, the call for African unity, endorsed by almost all independentist organisations and institutionalised as early as 1963 in the Organisation of African Unity. How can one understand this apparent contradiction between such a proclamation of African unity, and all the differences and contradictions that one can observe throughout the areas which and among the populations who call themselves or are called "African"?

To begin to clarify this apparent contradiction, and in a way that allows one to understand the interest of referring to Mudimbe to problematise the unity of Africa, I will briefly recall the history of the name "Africa." It comes from the Latin *"Africa"* with which Rome designated the area that approximately corresponds to today's Tunisia (Map 1), before extending it to its provinces in what is today called "North Africa" (Map 2). *"Africa"* was later appropriated by the Arabs as إفريقية (*Ifriqiya*) (Sayadi 2012). It was not until the end of the 15th century, with events such as the beginning of the slave trade, the European circumnavigation of Africa, the beginning of the European invasion of Africa, that the name *"Africa"* was progressively extended, by the Europeans, to the whole of what was becoming the continent and its inhabitants (Maps 3–7). The African continent is not a natural entity, but the result of a historical construction; and Africa is not an essence: it was, as Mudimbe says, invented. The constructivist historicisation of Africa, the demonstration that it was invented and the explanation of how it was invented constitute a decisive contribution of *The Invention of Africa* to the problematisation of African unity. Right from the first chapter of the book, "Discourse of Power and Knowledge of Otherness," this inaugural moment, the end of the 15th century and the beginning of the 16th, is thoroughly reflected—notably by analysing "Hans Burgkmair's painting *Exotic Tribe* [which dates from 1508, to which I will return to later in the chapter] and some contemporary works directly or indirectly dealing with black figures, such as Erasmus Grasser's *Moor Dancers* (1480), Hieronymus Bosch's *Garden of Delights* (1500), *Katleen the Moor Woman* (1521) by Albrecht Dürer, and at the very end of the century, Cornelisz van Haarlem's *Batseba* (1594)" (Mudimbe 1988, 6–7).

The observation of this violent unifying invention subordinates my previous question—how can one understand this apparent contradiction between such a proclamation of African unity, and all the differences and contradictions that one can observe throughout the areas which and

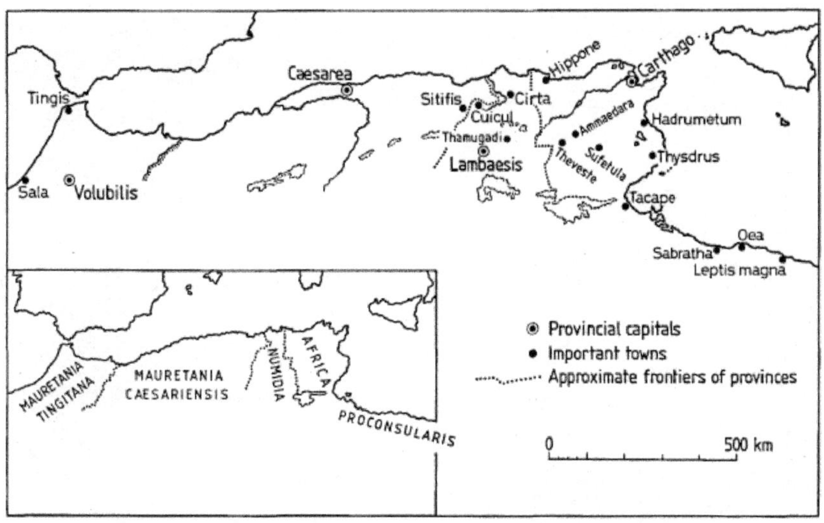

Map 1. "Roman provinces in North Africa at the end of the second century of our era"
Source: Mahjoubi (2000, 467).

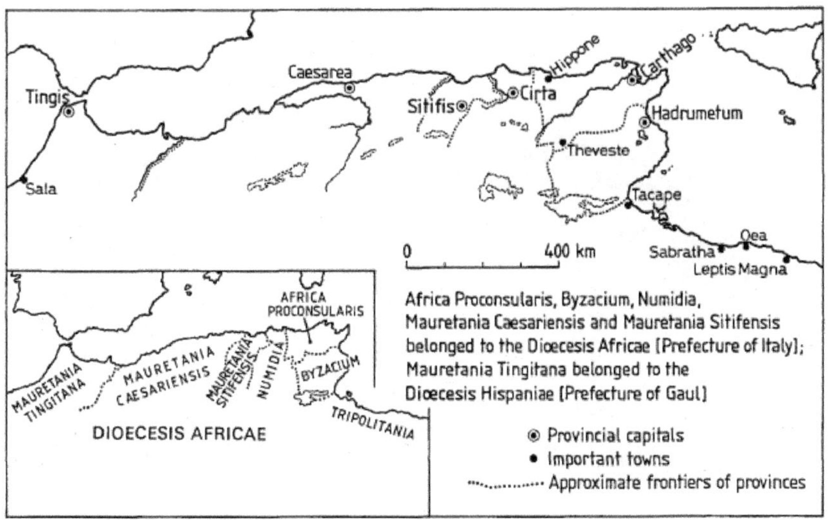

Map 2. "Roman provinces in North Africa in the fourth century of our era"
Source: Mahjoubi (2000, 473).

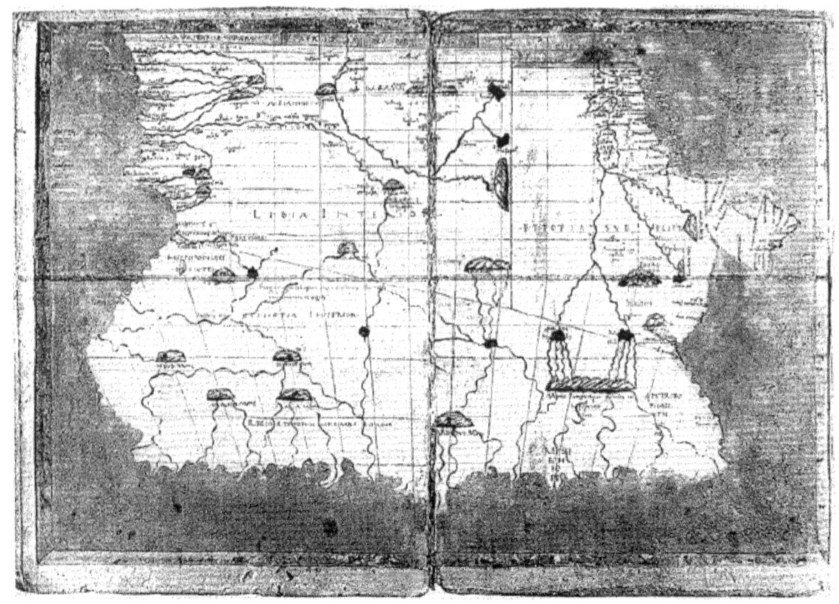

Map 3. "Ptolemy–Wilczek Brown (c. 1450). Original in John Carter Brown Library, Brown University, Providence, USA"
Source: Norwich (1997, xiii).

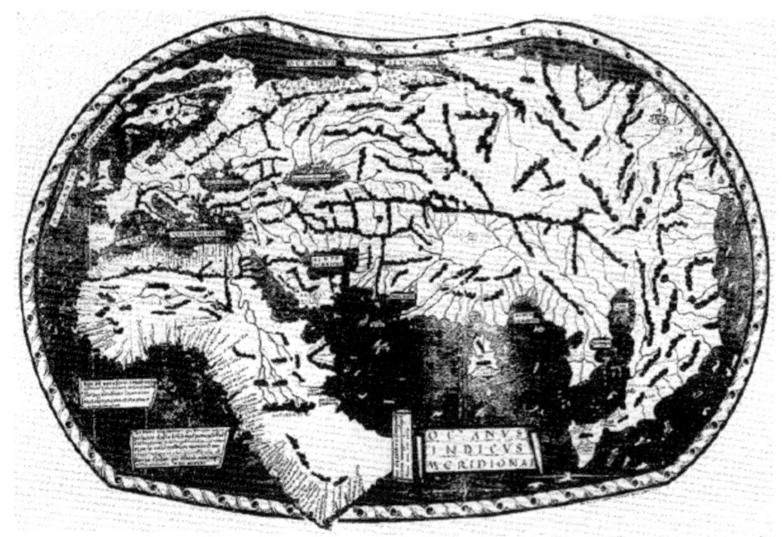

Map 4. "Martellus (1489). Original in British Library"
Source: Norwich (1997, xiv).

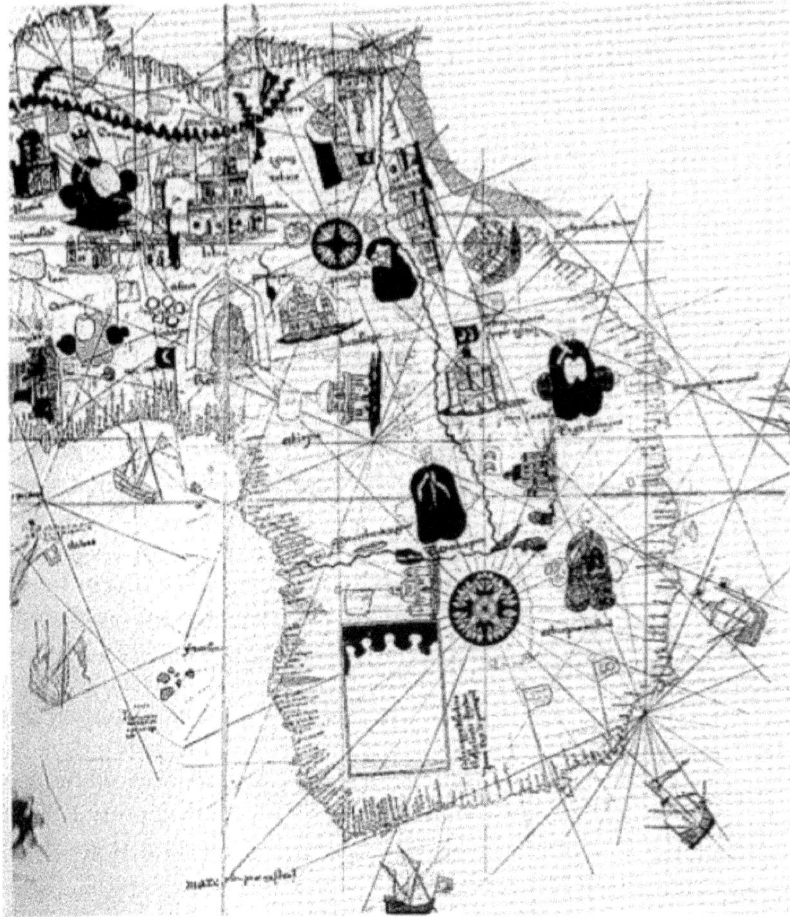

Map 5. "Juan de la Cosa (1500). Original in Naval Museum, Madrid"
Source: Norwich (1997, xv).

among the populations who call themselves or are called "African?"—to this one: why, the unity of Africa having first been imposed by force by the colonialists, did the African independentists assert the unity of Africa for and in the liberation? Or, to put it in terms of the history of the name "Africa": how could the name of oppression also be the name of liberation?

It *became* the name of liberation, following a process which led: from the colonial European negation of what was not yet Africa—which was also the negation of the diversity of those who did not yet call themselves "Africans"—; to the African negation of this initial negation, which would imply the assumption by Africans of their alienation as Africans, and the recognition of the framework of oppression, in particular the geographical

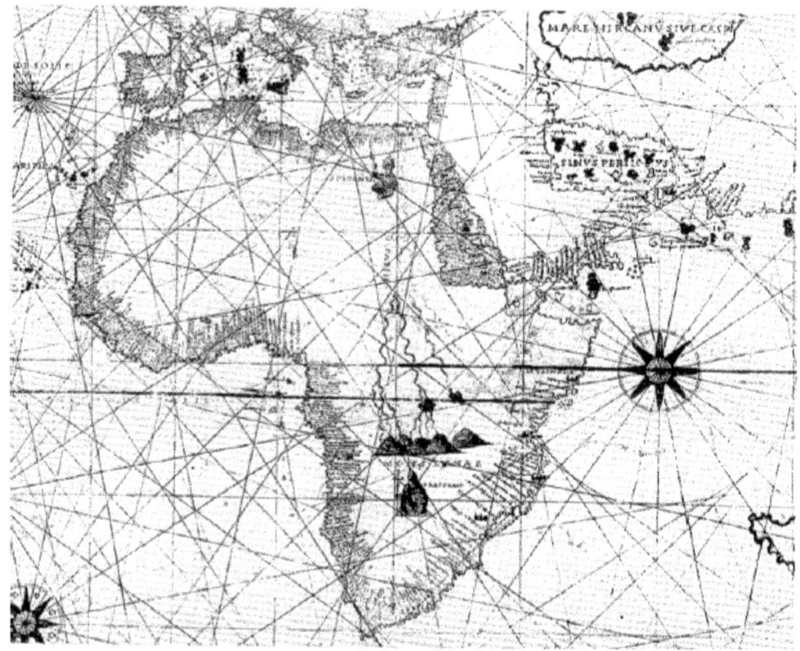

Map 6. "King-Hamy map (ca. 1504). Original in Henry E. Huntington Library, San Martino, California, USA"
Source: Norwich (1997, xvi).

and demographic delimitations of Africa, as that necessary for liberation; and from this negation of negation to the pan-African solidarities, the call for political unity and the beginning of its realisation, in which will have resulted the African negation of the colonial European negation of what and who, in the meantime, had become Africa and Africans. I propose to call "African negativity" this unifying and liberating productivity of the African negation of the colonial European negation of what, thereby, was becoming Africa. The unity of Africa is justifiable by means of this concept.[7]

1.2. African otherness

Mudimbe does not use this terminology. It is true that, in the preface to *The Idea of Africa*, he writes, following on from *The Invention of Africa*, that Africa was invented by colonial Europe as its "negated double" (Mudimbe 1994, xii). One can observe it, for example, in the history

7. This concept confirms that the question "what is Africa?" does not necessarily presuppose the thingness or the fixity or an essence of Africa; nor, may I add, the identity of being and essence, nor an essentialist understanding of being. The concept of African negativity entails an event-driven understanding of being, and points towards an answer to the question "what is Africa?" of the type: there is Africa where-when there is African negativity.

Map 7. "Bünting, Heinrich (1545–1606). *Die eigentliche und warhafftige gestalt der Erden und des Meers. Cosmographica Universalis* (The true shape of the world and the oceans) (Hanover, H. Bünting, 1592). Map, 27x36 cm, woodcut. Top left: 8. Top right: 9"
Source: Norwich (1997, 26).

of modern European philosophy: a concept of Europe emerged from it, for instance in the works of Kant, Hegel or Husserl, who, in order to ensure the uniqueness of the idea of Europe, believed it necessary to produce a specific differentiation, always involving Africa as all or part of an anti-Europe, as a negative mirror enabling Europe to think itself as anti-Africa.[8] Mudimbe shows, in anthropology in particular, and in the human and social sciences in general, how this "negated double" was epistemologically constructed. In the introduction of *The Invention of Africa*, he writes: "These disciplines do not provide a real comprehension of the *Weltanschauungen* studied. Yet one can also say that it is in these very discourses that African worlds have been established as realities for knowledge." (Mudimbe 1988, xi). This is another major contribution of *The Invention of Africa*, analogous for Africa to that of Said for the Orient in

8. For instance, in *The Vienna Lecture* in 1935, Husserl wrote: "we had to work out the *concept of Europe as the historical teleology of the infinite goals of reason*" (Husserl 1970, 299). In this text, he differentiated Europe from "Eskimos," "Indians," "Gypsies," or even "the Papuan"; in *Phänomenologische Psychologie: Vorlesungen Sommersemester 1925*, he referred to the "Bantu" (Husserl 1962, 497–98).

Orientalism[9]: the invention of Africa has not only been political, economic, military, but also scientific; its liberation must therefore also be scientific, epistemological, methodological.[10]

Even if Mudimbe recognises the construction of Africa as the negated double of Europe and more broadly of the West, he does not use a concept of negativity to think this liberation. This, however, immediately appears consistent with his epistemological critique, since the terminology of negativity was first brought forward in Europe by Hegel who conceptualised Africa precisely by the absence of negativity. Negativity, for Hegel, characterises the speculative productivity of contradiction, which can also be phrased as the affirmative productivity of the negation of the negation.[11] As such, negativity specifies dialectics and dialectical logic, as opposed to analytics and analytical logic which are based on the principle of non-contradiction. Negativity, moreover, is for Hegel an activity of the spirit, that is to say, according to his concept of spirit, both rational and effective in history[12] which he conceives as the exteriorisation of reason in time.[13] It can therefore be understood why saying that "Hegel conceptualised Africa by the absence of negativity" is equivalent to saying, in his conceptuality, that he conceptualised it by the absence of the spirit, and therefore of history, which appears more explicitly than the absence of negativity in the formula by which he states his concept of Africa in his lectures on the philosophy of history.

Rather than elaborating another concept of negativity and affirming, by negating the Hegelian negativity not applied to Africa, the existence of a non-Hegelian African negativity, Mudimbe writes, in the preface to *The Idea of Africa*—shortly before he uses the expression "negated double"—that Africa is conceived, in the European construction of it, "as a paradigm of difference" and —shortly after "negated double"—as "deviation" (Mudimbe 1994, xii). "Difference," "deviation" or, elsewhere, "otherness" are words and concepts that Mudimbe prefers to negativity. It does not mean that he does not recognise the relation between Africa and Europe, and more broadly the West, as a dialectical relation of oppression and liberation. Moreover, not only does he know Hegel's work perfectly,[14] but also Sartre's, whom he

9. On the analogy between Mudimbe and Said, see Alix (2008).

10. On this understanding of liberation by Mudimbe, see Bisanswa (2000, 706–8).

11. See paragraphs 79 to 82 of *Encyclopaedia of the Philosophical Sciences*.

12. See the preface and paragraphs 341 to 360 (devoted to world history) of *Elements of the Philosophy of Right*.

13. See *Lectures on the Philosophy of History*.

14. In that regard, let us note, in *The Idea of Africa*, his quotation of Cailler quoting Glissant quoting Hegel's conceptualisation of Africa: "Truly, every history (and

calls "an African philosopher" in *The Invention of Africa* (Mudimbe 1988, 83), and who famously used, in "Black Orpheus," in 1948, a concept of negativity which was supposed[15] to be contrary to Hegel's—for example in this occurrence: "Black faces—these night memories which haunt our days—embody the dark work of Negativity which patiently gnaws at concepts." (Sartre 1964–65, 28). In *The Invention of Africa*, Mudimbe writes: "What Sartre did was to impose philosophically the political dimension of a negativity in the colonial history." (Mudimbe 1988, 85); and, in the chapter dedicated to Blyden (the Caribbean and then Liberian intellectual and politician of the 19th and very beginning of the 20th century, who is one of the historical figures of pan-Africanism): "[for Blyden] the prospect of Africa's transformation would appear to institutionalize a negativity. Sartre put forward a similar theoretical perspective in *Black Orpheus*." (Mudimbe 1988, 132). So, the fact that Mudimbe himself does not use the concept of negativity does not mean that he does not recognise the dialectical nature of the relation of oppression and liberation between Africa and Europe, and more broadly the West, nor that he does not consider its critics who use a concept of negativity. Rather, it is the reverse side of the assertion that if, as is the case, this dialectical relation has been imposed upon Africa, along with the dialectical logic presented as necessary for thinking it, then liberation will be politically, philosophically, logically, metaphysically, strategically, both a liberation from this dialectical relation

consequently, every Reason of History conceived projected therein) has decidedly been to the exclusion of the others: which is what consoles me for having been excluded by Hegel from the historical movement. / 'What we understand under the name Africa, is an ahistoric, underdeveloped world, entirely prisoner to natural spirit, whose place is still at the threshold of universal history.' Wherein totalizing Reason was less poetic, shrewd, than the tolerant relativism of Montaigne. The Hegelian investigation of the world, so beautifully systematic and so advantageous to the Western methodologies, often stumbles against the details in which Montaigne's very vigorous interest is practiced." (Mudimbe 1994, 194).

15. I say "supposed" to emphasise that the concept of African negativity that I propose, and the concept of negativity that it implies, not only oppose Hegelian dialectics, but also differ from the concept of negativity of Négritude that Sartre elaborated in 1948, and from the concept of negativity that it implied. For example, according to the concept of African negativity, Négritude does not appear "like the up-beat [un-accented beat] of a dialectical progression" (Sartre 1964-65, 49), but in its absoluteness; and I understand Fanon's critique of Sartre's dialectisation of Négritude in the fifth chapter, "The Lived Experience of the Black Man," of *Black Skin, White Masks* (Fanon 2008, 89). This is not the place to explain these differences; but it is important to note them and to record, for programmatic purposes, the importance of explaining them. The main point here is—in order to specify Mudimbe's logic, and for that to differentiate between Mudimbe's conceptuality and Hegel's negativity—to acknowledge that Mudimbe recognises the dialecticity of African history and that he masters perfectly the thoughts of dialectics and negativity.

and, in order to think it—that is also to say to think its end, its exit, the way out of it—a liberation from dialectical logic and conceptuality.

But how to get out of dialectics—and without returning to an analytical logic that would not allow one to think a process of oppression and liberation? Hegel, who needed getting out to be impossible, anticipated this question. For him, the overcoming of contradictions is subordinated to the objective, expressed by the very title of the *Encyclopaedia of the Philosophical Sciences*, of grasping and expressing the wholeness of the whole, which indeed requires explaining the coherence of all the contradictions one can observe in reality. This is why one can say that Hegel dialectically built his system, in which Africa was doomed to slavery, colonisation and Europeanisation, in such a way that it was as impossible to get out of it as it was to get out of the whole of reality;[16] in other words, in such a way as to make any criticism of the system an element of the system, as a contradiction among the contradictions that dialectics explains in their coherence.[17] And yet, Mudimbe leads to think, if Africans want to be authentically free, we have to theoretically and practically get out of dialectics.

How do we get out of dialectics?[18]

2. Hegel or Foucault: The discursive concept of Africa

Mudimbe hypothesises that a dialogue with Foucault, centred on the African history and situation, is a possible way out of dialectics. To introduce this hypothesis, I can refer to this singular quotation from *The Discourse on Language*[19] by Mudimbe in *L'odeur du père*, both in the foreword and in the second text of the book, "Quel ordre du discours africain?" ("Which Order of the African Discourse?"), in which he situates himself within Foucault's writing, where Foucault invokes Hegel, and substitutes "the West" for "Hegel": "for Africa," Mudimbe begins in the foreword, "truly to escape the West [instead of Hegel] involves an exact appreciation of the price we have to pay to detach ourselves from it [him]. It assumes that we are aware of the extent to which the West [Hegel], insidiously perhaps, is close to us; it implies a knowledge, in that which permits us to think against

16. Among many possible texts, see the first sentence of the sixth chapter—"Spirit"—of *Phenomenology of Spirit*: "Reason is Spirit when its certainty of being all reality has been raised to truth, and it is conscious of itself as its own world, and of the world as itself." (Hegel 1998, 263).

17. Among many possible texts, see the preface to *Phenomenology of Spirit*.

18. *Get out* by Jordan Peele conveys a sense of this idea.

19. In the Anglophone edition I refer to, the book title *The Discourse on Language* translates the French original *L'ordre du discours*, which literally translates as *The Order of the Discourse*.

the West [Hegel], of that which remains Western [Hegelian]. We have to determine the extent to which our anti-Westernism [anti-Hegelianism] is possibly one of its [his] tricks directed against us, at the end of which it [he] stands, motionless, waiting for us." (Mudimbe 1982, 12, 44; Foucault 1972, 235). On these lines, I will limit myself to three comments: on the explanation they provide of what "getting out of dialectics" means for Mudimbe (2.1); on the method they call for, which I could call an "African supra-dialectical archaeology-genealogy of the Africa-West dialectics" to formulate synthetically the idea of an archaeology and a genealogy of the dialectical relation of oppression and liberation between Africa and the West, which would be situated in Africa and would make it possible to go beyond dialectics (2.2); and on the epistemological injunction they contain to Africanise the concept (2.3).

2.1. Getting out of dialectics

Firstly, meaning that "Hegel" and "the West" are substitutable, that is to say synonyms, Mudimbe claims that Hegel expressed the thought of the West by itself, which made of Africa the being in-itself of Europe and of Europe the being for-itself of Africa—one might say, echoing the terms of the first page of the preface to *The Idea of Africa*, which are borrowed from Hegel's, and Sartre's terminology and implicitly refer to Hegel's conceptualisation of Africa, and Sartre's criticism—: "[In the West's self-representations from Herodotus onward, peoples situated outside of its cultural and imaginary frontiers] were [...] imagined and rejected as the intimate and other side of the European-thinking subject, on the analogical model of the tension between the being In-Itself and the being For-Itself." (Mudimbe 1994, xi)—the for-itself specifically designating in this distinction "the knowledge that the conscious being has of itself, as opposed to existence in itself" (Lalande 1997, 799–800, my translation). Thus, Mudimbe asserts that, again, Africa is conceptually involved in a dialectical relation with dialectics, whose end, exit and way out—if they are to be political and spiritual liberation—seem to have not to be dialectical; and one understands, Mudimbe quoting Foucault on Hegel, that Foucault's conceptuality constitutes for Mudimbe a possible way out.

2.2. African supra-dialectical archaeology-genealogy of the Africa-West dialectics

Secondly, substituting "the West" for "Hegel," Mudimbe points out that the dialectal relation between Africa and the West is not a relation of essences, but a historic relation, of which it is possible and necessary—against Hegel who brings the essences into history notably by identifying and generalising national expressions of the spirit[20]—to make the archaeology and the genealogy in the sense of Foucault. In *Le vocabulaire de Foucault* (Foucault's vocabulary), Judith Revel gives these clear, synthetic definitions: "The term 'archaeology' appears three times in the titles of Foucault's works—*Naissance de la clinique. Une archéologie du regard médical* (1963), *Les Mots et les choses. Une archéologie des sciences humaines* (1966), and *L'Archéologie du savoir*[21] (1969)—and characterised the philosopher's research method until the early 1970s. An archaeology is not a 'history' in the sense that, while it is indeed a question of reconstituting a historical field, Foucault in fact brings different dimensions into play (philosophical, economic, scientific, political, etc.) in order to obtain the conditions of emergence of discourses of knowledge in general, at a given period. [...] The abandonment of the term 'archaeology' in favour of the concept of 'genealogy', at the very beginning of the 1970s, emphasised the need to double the 'horizontal' reading of discursivities with a vertical analysis—oriented towards the present—of the historical determinations of our own regime of discourse." (Revel 2009, 10–12, my translation); "genealogy is a historical enquiry that opposes the 'metahistorical deployment of ideal significations and indefinite teleologies,'[22] that opposes the uniqueness of the historical narrative and the search for origin, and that seeks on the contrary the 'singularity of events outside any monotonous finality.'[23] Genealogy therefore works from diversity and dispersion, from the chance of beginnings and accidents: in no case does it claim to go back in time to reestablish the continuity of history, but on the contrary it seeks to restore events in their singularity." (Revel 2009, 60–61, my translation). *The Invention of Africa* and *The Idea of Africa* can be read as an African supra-dialectical archaeology and genealogy of the dialectal relation between Africa and the West.

Archaeology in the sense of Foucault implies making "a horizontal cut" (Revel 2009, 12, my translation) in history and exhibiting a certain period that corresponds to an *episteme*—that is, Foucault writes in *The Order of Things*, as quoted by Mudimbe in *The Invention of Africa* (Mudimbe 1988, 24), what "defines the conditions of possibility of all knowledge,

20. See *Lectures on the Philosophy of History* and paragraphs 341 to 360 of *Elements of the Philosophy of Right*.

21. Which translates literally as *The Birth of the Clinic: An Archaeology of the Medical Gaze, Words and Things: An Archaeology of the Human Sciences* and *The Archaeology of Knowledge*.

22. Revel quotes Foucault in "Nietzsche, la généalogie, l'histoire" ("Nietzsche, Genealogy, History"), published in 1971.

23. Foucault 1971.

whether expressed in a theory or silently invested in practice" (Foucault 1973, 168). The very word "invention" similarly indicates an inaugural event, whose meaning must be grasped by relating it genealogically to the present. Such a method, archaeological-genealogical, relies on a different logic from the Hegelian dialectics—which is monological, proceeding systematically by identification of identity and difference[24]—, and corresponds to different politics.

To explain this correspondence between logic and politics, one can start with the title of the text that concludes *L'odeur du père*: "Quel meurtre du père?" (Which Murder of the Father?). This question is inseparable from this one: Which mourning for the father? *The Invention of Africa* indeed reminds us of the fact that it was not Africa what was made Africa,[25] and that what was not yet Africa does not and will never exist anymore; except as a ghost, as an incalculable number of ghosts—all those who suffered violence because they were Africans—who demand, for their dialogue, a logic other than dialectics. Here in particular, one should read philosophically Mudimbe's literary works, and consider *Air*, *Déchirures*, *Entretailles*, *Entre les eaux*, *L'écart*, or *Les Corps glorieux des mots et des êtres*, as also terms of such other logic.[26]

This mourning is a tragic motive and motif of emancipation. I assume that the recurrence of Greece in Mudimbe's work—for instance, the third chapter of *The Idea of Africa* is titled "The Power of the Greek Paradigm"—is intended not only to reestablish the difference between *ratio* and *logos*, nor merely to conclude the genealogy of the paradigm of difference—Ancient Greece being, for Mudimbe, its final and inaugural

24. Among many possible texts, see paragraphs 79 to 82 of *Encyclopaedia of the Philosophical Sciences*.

25. It is thus immediately clear that African history cannot correspond to the Hegelian process of identification of identity and difference: at the beginning rather than at the origin, there is difference rather than identity, and perhaps even something other than difference.

26. Mudimbe devoted his PhD thesis, submitted at the University of Louvain in 1970, to the semantic study of the word "air" (Mudimbe 1979; Mudimbe 1991, x; Fraiture 2013, 41). *Déchirures* is a collection of poems published in 1971 of which there is, as far as I know, no English translation, whose title could be translated as *Tears*—not those which run down cheeks, but those which tear pages or muscles. *Entretailles* is also a collection of poems, published in 1973, of which there is, as far as I know, no English translation either, whose title is harder to translate, the word being used in French both for intaglio and for cuts, especially for horses, between legs kicking themselves. *Entre les eaux* is a novel published in 1973, translated into English in 1991 as *Between Tides*. *L'écart* is also a novel, published in 1979, translated into English in 1993 as *The Rift*. *Les Corps glorieux des mots et des êtres* is an autobiography published in 1994, of which there is, as far as I know, no English translation, whose title could be translated as *The Glorious Bodies of Words and Beings*.

point—, but intimately pertains to the acute awareness of tragedy in the history of Africans. The mourning for that which was not yet Africa, of which however we Africans cannot say that it was not already us, is a motive and motif of emancipation in this specific and practical sense that it is a remedy for these quests of origin which always end up with the subordination of the possibility to invent oneself to the norm of identity. Reading Mudimbe, one can understand why, practically, all traditionalisms and fundamentalisms, even under the cloak of fighting against what remains of colonial oppression, are in fact expressions of colonial alienation; and that any real liberation requires both fighting and inventing oneself. *The Invention of Africa* expresses this immanent African historical movement, from Africa and Africans violently and falsely invented by their oppressors, to Africa and Africans inventing themselves.

2.3. The Africanisation of the concept

Thirdly, these lines from *L'odeur du père* help to explain the epistemological necessity of the Africanisation of the concept. Mudimbe recalls this in the introduction to *The Invention of Africa,* using the more general expression "'Africanizing' knowledge": "The book attempts [...] a sort of archaeology of African *gnosis* as a system of knowledge in which major philosophical questions recently have arisen: first, concerning the form, the content, and the style of 'Africanizing' knowledge; second, concerning the status of traditional systems of thought and their possible relation to the normative genre of knowledge" (Mudimbe 1988, x). The need to Africanise the concept is implied in any project to elaborate a concept of Africa, which can be explained from the expression itself. In "concept of Africa," the preposition "of" must be understood as the sign of both the objective genitive, meaning that Africa is the object of the concept, and the subjective genitive, meaning that a concept of Africa is a concept coming from and by Africa; the meaning of the objective genitive and that of the subjective genitive being linked at least in that Africa determines, as any properly conceptualised object, the mode of its concept—in other words in that any conceptualisation of Africa implies an Africanisation of the concept. To avoid a misunderstanding—the inverted commas placed by Mudimbe around "Africanizing" are also to point out this risk—, I underline that, in writing "Africanisation of the concept," I do not mean that there are different rationalities, a typically African rationality for instance. I mean that it is not certain that the objects that have been most conceptualised in the Western philosophical tradition, and that the most frequent ways in which the concept has been used in the Western philosophical tradition, do not constitute a bias—which we could study by means of distinctions between, for example, general concept and singular concept, ideal concept and empirical concept, concept and intuition, or identity of the concept and identity of its object[27]—; and that it is possible that, applied to Africa without methodological precaution, these ways of using the concept make it, as Mudimbe says of ethnology, "a distorting prism" (Mudimbe 1982, 25, my translation), which would only show an Africa such as the West wants it to be African. In the first text of *L'odeur du père*, "Un signe, une odeur" (A Sign, a Smell), Mudimbe writes, following on from Foucault and Adotevi, that: "ethnology, a European science, has always been, even at its best,[28] the expression of epistemological and cultural configurations foreign to Africa. In sum, in a simple and brutal way, we can say that it has—until now—been a "lie" in the precise sense that under the guise of discovering and telling Africa, it presented Africa through a distorting prism." (Mudimbe 1982, 24–25, my translation). Africanising the concept signifies, on the contrary, empirically anchoring the conceptualisation of Africa in the African history and situation.

Precisely, Mudimbe helps to problematise, in addition to the unity of Africa and the logic for thinking it, this other condition of any proper conceptualisation of Africa, which is the empiricality of the concept—its anchoring in the empirical reality of the African history and situation—and to establish a method for satisfying it. In *The Invention of Africa* and *The Idea of Africa*, such an anchoring makes it possible to reveal the content and structure of the discourse on Africa, and to express the meaning of Africa as an object of discourse—the discourse being understood in the sense of Foucault as "the whole of constrained and constraining significations which pass through social relationships" (Foucault 2001, 123, my translation). For instance, in the first chapter of *The Invention of Africa*, "Discourse of Power and Knowledge of Otherness," under the second subtitle, "Discursive Formations and Otherness," Mudimbe transposes the method used by Foucault for the pictorial commentary of *Las Meninas* by Velázquez in the first chapter of *The Order of Things*. To study the link between the European discourse on Africa, the *episteme* that was contemporary of its emergence and the events taking place in Africa at the same time, Mudimbe chooses to "consider Hans Burgkmair's painting *Exotic Tribe[s]*" (Mudimbe 1988, 6)—and more precisely "the first picture of the series [in which the painting consists]," *In Gennea* (Fig.

27. For such a reflection, see *Concepts* by Jocelyn Benoist (Benoist 2010).

28. The expression "even at its best" translates "même dans ses meilleurs envols," which signifies literally "even in its best fly-offs."

1)—, which, dating back to 1508, was contemporary of the inaugural events of the colonial European invention of Africa. Mudimbe quotes the description given by art historian Hans Joachim Kunst in *L'Africain dans l'art européen* (The African in European Art): "The nude African depicted from behind conforms to the classical rule of contraposto expressed in the compensatory balance of symmetrical parts of the body in movement: one shoulder leaning on one leg and the other, raised above the free leg. One guesses that this nude man was copied from a classic model to which the artist gave characteristics, jewelry and swords, of an exotic people still strongly attached to nature." (Kunst 1967, 19–20; Mudimbe 1988, 7). Only, this time, the body, "perhaps" based on a "presumably white" model (Mudimbe 1988, 7), or at least, given the situation, imagined as a "pale body" (Mudimbe 1988, 7), is painted black. That is how, Mudimbe writes, "[t]he contrasts between black and white tell a story which probably duplicates a silent but powerful epistemological configuration" (Mudimbe 1988, 8) and reveals the order of the colonial European discourse on Africa. To represent black characters, Burgkmair represented blackened white characters. A double meaning then emerges: firstly, the subordination of the differences to the identity of the white norm; secondly, through the colours, through the lines, the subordination of the black-white identity to the asymmetrical white-black difference. The painting thus reveals two characteristics of the *episteme* contemporary of the inaugural events of the invention of Africa: firstly, at the most general level, the substitution of identity and difference for resemblance and dissimilarity, and the subordination of difference to identity; and secondly, brought back to its African ramification, the exacerbated, op-positioned, thwarted, hierarchised difference—in the sense that there is no bigger apparent difference than that which arises from the biggest resemblance. Again: Africa is anti-Europe, Europe is anti-Africa. In this example, the blackening of the white model indicates furthermore the reason of such a discourse, and the meaning and direction of its materialisation: the unbearable violence of the undertaking of the whitening of black people. Africa was to be Europeanised, that is to say to be suppressed as such. The distance between resemblance and difference is emphasised in order to be filled: in bringing, through its suppression, the black into the white.

Figure 1. Hans Burgkmair, *Exotic Tribes—In Gennea*, 1508–1570
Woodcut. Height: 175 millimetres, Width: 244 millimetres.
The British Museum, 2023.

With this example, Mudimbe, furthermore, makes conceivable the possibility of articulating the Foucauldian concepts of discourse and dispositif,[29] even though in the 1970s Foucault rather substituted, for the concept of discourse, the concept of dispositif—of which the analysis of the panopticon in *Surveiller et punir* in 1975 (later translated as *Discipline and Punish*) is probably the best-known example of application (Foucault 1995, 195–228). Their articulation enables to anchor empirically the philosophical analysis of the discursive concept of Africa—that is to say, the concept of Africa conveyed by the discourse on Africa. To explain it, this formula from Jocelyn Benoist in "*Rompre avec l'idéalisme historique: re-spatialiser nos concepts*" (Breaking With Historical Idealism: Re-spatialising Our Concepts) is very clear: "[The meaning] is 'outside'" (Benoist 2001, 111, my translation). Defining the dispositif as the material operator of the discourse, and identifying dispositifs in the empirical reality of Africa, enable to grasp the meaning of the discourse on Africa in its outside, in the empirical reality in which it expresses itself. For example, one can say that the panopticon is a material operator of the discourse of surveillance and punishment at the end of the 18th century. In the same way, one can

29. I maintain the French word *dispositif* in English because the words by which it could be translated, such as "apparatus," cannot convey the singularity of its meaning in Foucault.

identify colonial dispositifs specifically designed and produced for Africa, and the analysis of which can provide a more precise grasp of the discursive meaning of Africa. In fact, the colonial discourse on Africa was expressed by and passed through its dispositifs: the chains, the trading posts, the holds of the ships, the plantations.

Mudimbe's articulation of these methodological concepts—in particular discourse and dispositif, but also archaeology, genealogy, *episteme*, event, or even archive which should be emphasised with reference to Mudimbe's quite widespread concept of the colonial library[30]—, by enabling him to reveal the discursive concept of Africa as the negated double of Europe and by exposing and thus making this negation more negatable, contributes decisively to making possible the empirical anchoring of a potential philosophical conceptualisation of Africa—which would imply a negation of this negation of Africa.

Conclusion: African philosophy and concept of Africa

The exposition of this double alternative—negativity or otherness; Hegel or Foucault—makes it possible to propose a situation of Mudimbe in the contemporary history of African philosophy, and an interpretation of this history—which he himself helps to do in, notably, the final chapter of *The Invention of Africa*, "The Patience of Philosophy."

To explain the novelty of Mudimbe in African philosophy, I will first recall two of the main moments of its contemporary history. The appearance of the field of African philosophy is often dated to 1945 with the publication of *La philosophie bantoue* by Tempels, in which, observing Congolese society, he claims to set out its system of thought. This colonial beginning was the object of a critical reflection—for example by Césaire in his *Discours sur le*

30. Mudimbe gives this definition in *The Idea of Africa*: "It was, I think, fifteenth- and sixteenth-century Europe that invented the savage as a representation of its own negated double. Exploiting travelers' and explorers' writings, at the end of the nineteenth century a 'colonial library' begins to take shape. It represents a body of knowledge constructed with the explicit purpose of faithfully translating and deciphering the African object. Indeed, it fulfilled a political project in which, supposedly, the object unveils its being, its secrets, and its potential to a master who could, finally, domesticate it. Certainly, the depth as well as the ambition of the colonial library disseminates the concept of deviation as the best symbol of the idea of Africa. I do refer to this colonial library, which beyond its adjustments and arrangements offers traces or reflections of a longer tradition. In fact, I have tried to circumvent its epistemological violence by including its nightmares as well as the fragile presuppositions of its ponderous knowledge" (Mudimbe 1994, xii). It is around this concept that the congress "Épistémè africaine. Africa N'Ko, dire l'Afrique dans le monde. La bibliothèque coloniale en débat" was organised; and that the collective work to which it gave rise was published in 2022: *Africa N'Ko. La bibliothèque coloniale en débat*, edited by Mamadou Diawara, Mamadou Diouf and Jean-Bernard Ouédraogo (2022).

colonialisme (*Discourse on Colonialism*) in 1950—which involved the very definition of African philosophy. One can understand, from this point of view, why *Sur la "philosophie africaine"* by Hountondji in 1977 has been a cardinal book in the field. Against what he called "ethnophilosophy," Hountondji proposed to stick to a simple and thorough definition of African philosophy as, following the concept of philosophy applied to the European corpus: "a set of texts, specifically the set of texts written by Africans and described as philosophical by their authors themselves." (Hountondji 1996, 33).

As indicated in the introduction, the field of African philosophy has been largely structured by these two currents: ethnophilosophy and "rational, or theoretical, or critical, or professional philosophy" (Fløistad 1987, 1). It is astonishing to observe that their contradiction was on the definition of philosophy, rather than the definition of Africa, as if, even for African philosophers, Africa could not be a subject for philosophy. This can be understood in the African context of the aftermath of the Second World War and of the African independences: the priority was to demonstrate the existence of an African philosophy and of African philosophers, and, thereby, to provide, against the colonial denial of the very possibility of an African philosophy and for Africans to philosophise, supplemental evidence of the common humanity of Africans and colonisers.

It seems that it was only in the following period that the impossibility was more widely recognised of defining African philosophy without elucidating the meaning of the concept of Africa. Mudimbe's work is decisive in this respect. In *The Invention of Africa* and *The Idea of Africa*, he raised the question "What is Africa?" (Mudimbe 1994, xiv) and "[explored] the concept of Africa" (Mudimbe 1994, xv). Explaining, in *The Invention of Africa*, how Africa resulted from a historical construction and was made the object of a discourse, he could, in *The Idea of Africa*, articulate the characteristics of the colonial European and Western representation of Africa and analyse the discursive concept of Africa as the "negated double" of Europe and the West—making thus this discursive concept more negatable. This is a third moment in the definition of African philosophy: not anymore as the African collective system of thought of ethnophilosophy; nor only as "the set of texts written by Africans and described as philosophical by their authors"; but also as the philosophical analysis of the discursive concept of Africa. By thus enabling us to understand that the definition of African philosophy, and the delimitations of its corpus, of its field, of its geography, of its history, always depend on a certain concept of Africa, Mudimbe made it clear that any new concept of Africa would modify the definition and delimitations of African philosophy; all the more so if it resulted from a philosophical elaboration, and would engage, in their connection, the definition of philosophy and the definition of Africa.[31]

Elucidating the meaning of the discursive concept of Africa was a necessary condition for the independentist philosophical reappropriation of the meaning of the colonial construction of Africa, and for the creation of a meaning of a new construction, which would be authentically a construction. More specifically, the philosophical exhibition of the discursive concept of Africa was a necessary condition for the elaboration of a philosophical concept of Africa. By answering the questions "What is it that Africa has been said to be?" and "What is it that Africa has been forced to be?," Mudimbe contributed decisively to making it possible for our generations to take a step further in the deployment of the question "What is Africa?," to elaborate a philosophical concept of Africa and to make it an orientation to complete the liberation that has been handed down to us.

References

Abdelmadjid, Salim. 2015. "Un concept d'Afrique." PhD Thesis, Université Paris-Sorbonne. https://theses.fr/2015PA040115.

Alix, Florian. 2008. "Foucault déplacé: réécriture chez E.W. Said et V.Y. Mudimbe." *Malfini: Publication exploratoire des espaces francophones.* http://malfini.ens-lyon.fr/document.php?id=124 [archive].

Bates, Robert H., V.Y. Mudimbe, and Jean O'Barr, eds. 1993. *Africa and the Disciplines. The Contributions of Research in Africa to the Social Sciences and Humanities.* Chicago, IL, and London: The University of Chicago Press.

Benoist, Jocelyn. 2001. "Rompre avec l'idéalisme historique: re-spatialiser nos concepts." In *Historicité et spatialité. Le problème de l'espace dans la pensée contemporaine*, edited by Jocelyn Benoist and Fabio Merlini, 97–113. Paris: Vrin.

Benoist, Jocelyn. 2010. *Concepts. Introduction à l'analyse.* Paris: Cerf.

Bisanswa, Justin Kalulu. 2000. "V.Y. Mudimbe. Réflexion sur les sciences humaines et sociales en Afrique." *Cahiers d'Études africaines*, no. 160: 705–22. https://doi.org/10.4000/etudesafricaines.45.

The British Museum. "The British Museum. Object: In Gennea (In Guinea)." https://www.britishmuseum.org/collection/object/P_1913-0317-1.

Césaire, Aimé. 1950. *Discours sur le colonialisme.* Paris: Réclame.

31. For a reflection of Mudimbe on this connection, see *Africa and the Disciplines. The Contributions of Research in Africa to the Social Sciences and Humanities* he edited with Robert H. Bates and Jean O'Barr in 1993 (Bates, Mudimbe, and O'Barr 1993), and the chapter he wrote with Kwame Anthony Appiah: "The Impact of African Studies on Philosophy" (Mudimbe and Appiah 1993, 113–38).

Diawara, Mamadou, Mamadou Diouf, and Jean-Bernard Ouédraogo, eds. 2022. *Africa N'Ko. La bibliothèque coloniale en débat*. Paris: Présence africaine.

Fanon, Frantz. 2008. *Black Skin, White Masks*. Translated by Richard Philcox. New York: Grove Press.

Fløistad, Guttorm. 1987. "Introduction." In *Contemporary Philosophy. A New Survey. Vol. 5: African Philosophy*, edited by Guttorm Fløistad, 1–7. Dordrecht, Boston and Lancaster: Martinus Nijhoff.

Foucault, Michel. 1971. "Nietzsche, la généalogie, l'histoire." In *Hommage à Jean Hyppolite*. Épiméthée. Paris: Presses universitaires de France.

Foucault, Michel. 1972. *The Archaeology of Knowledge & The Discourse on Language*. Translated by Alan Mark Sheridan Smith. New York: Pantheon Books.

Foucault, Michel. 1973. *The Order of Things: An Archaeology of the Human Sciences*. New York: Pantheon Books.

Foucault, Michel. 1975. *Surveiller et punir*. Paris: Gallimard.

Foucault, Michel. 1995. *Discipline and Punish: The Birth of the Prison*. Translated by Alan Sheridan. New York: Random House, Vintage Books.

Foucault, Michel. 2001. "Le discours ne doit pas être pris comme…." In Michel Foucault, *Dits et écrits II*, edited by Daniel Defert and François Ewald, 123–24. Paris: Gallimard.

Fraiture, Pierre-Philippe. 2013. *V.Y. Mudimbe: Undisciplined Africanism*. Liverpool: Liverpool University Press.

Hegel, Georg Wilhelm Friedrich. 1998. *Phenomenology of Spirit*. Translated by A.V. Miller. Delhi: Motilal Banarsidass Publishers.

Hegel, Georg Wilhelm Friedrich. 2004. *The Philosophy of History*. Translated by John Sibree. Mineola, New York: Dover Publications, Inc.

Hountondji, Paulin Jidenu. 1977. *Sur la "philosophie africaine": Critique de l'ethnophilosophie*. Paris: Maspero.

Hountondji, Paulin Jidenu. 1983. *African Philosophy: Myth and Reality*. Translated by Henri Evans with the collaboration of Jonathan Rée. Bloomington and Indianapolis, IN: Indiana University Press.

Hountondji, Paulin Jidenu. 1996. *African Philosophy: Myth and Reality*. Second Edition. Translated by Henri Evans with the collaboration of Jonathan Rée. Bloomington and Indianapolis, IN: Indiana University Press.

Hume, David. 1825. *Essays and Treatises on Several Subjects. Volume First, containing Essays, Moral, Political, and Literary*. Edinburgh: Bell & Bradfute, and W. Blackwood et al.

Husserl, Edmund. 1962. *Phänomenologische Psychologie: Vorlesungen Sommersemester 1925* (Hua IX). The Hague: Martinus Nijhoff.

Husserl, Edmund. 1970. *The Crisis of European Sciences and Transcendental Phenomenology. An Introduction to Phenomenological Philosophy*. Translated by David Carr. Evanston; IL: Northwestern University Press.

Kant, Immanuel. 2011. *Observations on the Feeling of the Beautiful and Sublime and Other Writings*, edited by Patrick Frierson and Paul Guyer. *Observations on the Feeling of the Beautiful and Sublime* is translated by Paul Guyer. Cambridge: Cambridge University Press.

Kunst, Hans Joachim. 1967. *L'Africain dans l'art européen*. Cologne: Dumont Presse.

Lalande, André. 1997. *Vocabulaire technique et critique de la philosophie. Volume 2: N-Z*. Paris: Presses Universitaires de France.

Mahjoubi, Ammar. 2000. "The Roman and post-Roman Period in North Africa. Part I: The Roman Period." In *General History of Africa II: Ancient Civilizations of Africa*, edited by Gamal Mokhtar, 465–99. Paris: UNESCO; London: Heinemann; Berkeley, CA: University of California Press.

Masolo, Dismas A. 1991. "An Archaeology of African Knowledge: A Discussion of V.Y. Mudimbe." *Callaloo* 14, no. 4: 998–1011. https://doi.org/10.2307/2931218.

Mudimbe, V.Y. 1971. *Déchirures*. Kinshasa: Éditions du Mont Noir.

Mudimbe, V.Y. 1973. *Entre les eaux. Dieu, un prêtre, la révolution*. Paris: Présence africaine.

Mudimbe, V.Y. 1973. *Entretailles, précédé de Fulgurances d'une lézarde*. Paris: Saint-Germain-des-Prés.

Mudimbe, V.Y. 1979. *Air, étude sémantique*. Vienna-Föhrenau: E. Stiglmayr.

Mudimbe, V.Y. 1979. *L'écart*. Paris: Présence africaine.

Mudimbe, V.Y. 1982. *L'odeur du père: Essai sur des limites de la science et de la vie en Afrique noire*. Paris: Présence africaine.

Mudimbe, V.Y. 1988. *The Invention of Africa: Gnosis, Philosophy and the Order of Knowledge*. Bloomington and Indianapolis, IN: Indiana University Press; London: James Currey.

Mudimbe, V.Y. 1991a. *Parables and Fables: Exegesis, Textuality and Politics in Central Africa*. Madison, WI: The University of Wisconsin Press.

Mudimbe, V.Y. 1991b. *Between Tides*. Translated by Stephen Becker. New York: Simon and Schuster.

Mudimbe, V.Y. 1993. *The Rift*. Translated by Marjolijn de Jager. Minneapolis, MN: University of Minnesota Press.

Mudimbe, V.Y. 1994. *The Idea of Africa*. Bloomington and Indianapolis, IN: Indiana University Press; London: James Currey.

Mudimbe, V.Y. 1994. *Les Corps glorieux des mots et des êtres: esquisse d'un jardin africain à la bénédictine*. Paris: Présence africaine; Montréal: Humanitas.

Mudimbe V.Y. 1997. *Tales of Faith: Religion as Political Performance in Central Africa*. London and Atlantic Highlands, NJ: The Athlone Press.

Mudimbe, V.Y. 2013. *On African Fault Lines: Meditations on Alterity Politics*. Scottsville, South Africa: University of Kwa-Zulu Natal Press.

Mudimbe, V.Y. 2023. *The Scent of the Father: Essay on the Limits of Life and Science in Sub-Saharan Africa*. Translated by Jonathan Adjemian. Cambridge, United Kingdom, and Hoboken, NJ: Polity Press.

Mudimbe, V.Y., and Kwame Anthony Appiah. 1993. "The Impact of African Studies on Philosophy." In *Africa and the Disciplines: The Contributions of Research in Africa to the Social Sciences and Humanities*, edited by Robert H. Bates, V.Y. Mudimbe and Jean O'Barr, 113–38. Chicago, IL, and London: The University of Chicago Press.

Norwich, Oscar I. 1997. *Norwich's Maps of Africa*. Second edition revised and edited by Jeffrey C. Stone. Norwich, VT: G.B. Manasek, Inc.

Peele, Jordan. 2017. *Get out*. Blumhouse Productions, QC Entertainment, Monkeypaw Productions, Universal Pictures, 1 hr 44min.

Revel, Judith. 2009. *Le vocabulaire de Foucault*. Paris: Ellipses.

Said, Edward. 1978. *Orientalism*. New York City: Pantheon Books.

Sartre, Jean-Paul. 1964–65. "Black Orpheus." Translated by John MacCombie. *The Massachusetts Review* 6, no. 1: 13–52. https://www.massreview.org/sites/default/files/Sartre.pdf [archive].

Sayadi, Abderrazak. 2012. "L'Afrique dans l'imaginaire islamique médiéval." In *L'Afrique indéfinie*, edited by Pierre-Yves Dufeu and Antoine Hatzenberger, 77–94. Louvain-la-Neuve: L'Harmattan/Academia.

Tempels, Placide. 1945. *La philosophie bantoue*. Translated from Dutch to French by A. Rubbens. Elisabethville: Lovania.

Tempels, Placide. 1959. *Bantu Philosophy*. Translated from French and Dutch to English by Colin King. Paris: Présence africaine. https://www.cyrho.com/data/Placide%20Tempels%20Bantu%20Philosophy%201959.pdf [archive].

www.ingramcontent.com/pod-product-compliance
Ingram Content Group UK Ltd.
Pitfield, Milton Keynes, MK11 3LW, UK
UKHW022022190726
13853UKWH00005B/2068